THE
WISDOM OF NAPOLEON HILL

All titles in this series

The Wisdom of James Allen
The Wisdom of Joseph Murphy
The Wisdom of Napoleon Hill
The Wisdom of Robert Collier
The Wisdom of Wallace D. Wattles

THE WISDOM OF NAPOLEON HILL

edited and introduced
by Mitch Horowitz

Published 2020 by Gildan Media LLC
aka G&D Media
www.GandDmedia.com

THE WISDOM OF NAPOLEON HILL. Introduction, Chapter Notes, Timeline and Epilogue, copyright © 2020 by Mitch Horowitz

No part of this book may be used, reproduced or transmitted in any manner whatsoever, by any means (electronic, photocopying, recording, or otherwise), without the prior written permission of the author, except in the case of brief quotations embodied in critical articles and reviews. No liability is assumed with respect to the use of the information contained within. Although every precaution has been taken, the author and publisher assume no liability for errors or omissions. Neither is any liability assumed for damages resulting from the use of the information contained herein.

Front Cover design by David Rheinhardt of Pyrographx

Interior design by Meghan Day Healey of Story Horse, LLC

Library of Congress Cataloging-in-Publication Data is available upon request

ISBN: 978-1-7225-0147-1

10 9 8 7 6 5 4 3 2 1

Contents

The Philosopher of Success
Introduction by Mitch Horowitz
9

I
Possessing a Definite Chief Aim
A Definite Chief Aim, chapter
from *The Law of Success* (1928)
15

II
Reciprocity and the Golden Rule
The Golden Rule, chapter
from *The Law of Success* (1928)
73

III
Faith: Your Key to Courage and Confidence
Applied Faith, from *The Master Key to Riches* (1945)
135

IV
Procrastination and Fear
Outwitting the Six Ghosts of Fear,
from *Think and Grow Rich* (1937)
173

V
Leadership
Initiative and Leadership,
from *The Law of Success* (1928)
225

VI
The Master Mind
The Master Mind, article
from *Napoleon Hill's Magazine* (March 1922)
281

VII
Sex Energy: Your Magic Elixir
The Mystery of Sex Transmutation,
from *Think and Grow Rich* (1937)
289

VIII
Rebounding from Failure
How Success Grows from Failure,
article from *Napoleon Hill's Magazine* (April 1921)
321

IX
How Cosmic Law Helps You
The Law of Cosmic Habitforce,
from *The Master Key to Riches* (1945)
339

X
Taking it All the Way
Condensation of *Think and Grow Rich* (1937)
399

Napoleon Hill's Secret
Epilogue by Mitch Horowitz
435

Napoleon Hill Timeline   438
About the Authors   442

The Philosopher of Success

INTRODUCTION BY MITCH HOROWITZ

Few writers have made as deep an impact on the past century as Napoleon Hill (1883–1970). The Virginia-born journalist virtually defined the field of motivational literature in the first half of the twentieth century. His impact is reflected in the posterity of his work. Although you can find more hallowed books of metaphysics and therapeutic philosophy than *Think and Grow Rich*, *The Law of Success*, and others by Hill, few have attracted such sustained and varied readership. And few, I venture, will do more to improve your personal abilities and sense of purpose. This has been my experience.

With his first book, *The Law of Success* in 1928, Hill accomplished exactly what he set out to do, which was create a methodical "philosophy of success." Over the years critics have complained that Hill's notion of success is too single-minded or outwardly focused. (I challenge that, as Hill's ethics run deeper than detected.) Others point to questionable aspects of his biography. (Like whether he really met and interviewed industrialist Andrew Carnegie, who never mentions Hill in his memoirs. I'm agnostic on this point.). And still others note Hill's tendency to favor the powerful while running down policies of social equity. (I join in this criticism.) But these critiques, while valid to varying degrees, are blunted by the remarkable effectiveness of Hill's program.

In order to understand Napoleon Hill, you must have the experience of really working with his ideas. I've met people who found themselves at a dead end in life only to immerse themselves in *Think and Grow Rich* and discover a new set of practical, actionable possibilities—of transforming fallow prospects into abundant ones by working with Hill's insights. It happened to me.

I write these words in 2020, about seven years from when I returned to Hill's work with real commitment. Until then I had read dozens of self-help books (including Hill's), had worked for years as a publisher in the field, and harbored something of a "been there, done that" attitude toward much of the genre. This kind of outlook is easy to fall into. However, in fall of 2013, feeling that my longtime job as a publishing executive might be in jeopardy, I revisited *Think and Grow Rich* with a new sense of vigor and urgency. For the first time, I did every exercise as though my life depended on it, which I often say is the "magic formula" for unlocking the work's benefits. As I did this, my work as a writer, narrator, and lecturer began to dramatically expand—work that is now my fulltime vocation.

* * *

Starting around 1908, Hill, then a young journalist, reached the conviction that it is possible to codify principles of success, which are found, to greater or lesser measure, in the lives of exceptional people across every field, from industry and consumer products to diplomacy and the arts.

Hill said that steel magnate Andrew Carnegie urged him on in this task, a story that he told with greater drama and vividness as the years passed from the industrialist's death in 1919. Whatever the source of Hill's inspiration, it is evident that the writer spent about twenty years studying the lives of high achievers of all types—inventors, generals, diplomats, artists, statesmen—and catalogued their common traits into a step-by-step program. Hill was certain (as are many of his readers) that he created a model of *what great figures do* when translating an idea from the conceptual to physical stage.

The purpose of this collection is to highlight what I consider Hill's most important and practical insights, reached at varying points in his career. Although this anthology does not substitute for any of Hill's books, *The Wisdom of Napoleon Hill* serves as a clarifier, refresher, instigator, and source of inspiration.

The book elucidates and expands on the most impactful themes of Hill's program, which he never stopping developing—and neither should you:

1. **A Definite Chief Aim.** If you take one just idea from Hill's work, this is it. Nothing does more to positively reorder

your life than possessing one obsessively felt, actionable aim to which all else is subordinated. To reach such an aim requires radical self-honesty and undivided commitment. Power comes from focus.

2. **Reciprocity.** Hill's program is deeply ethical: he emphasizes transparency, plain dealing, non-prejudice, and delivering clear benefits to your end user, client, or employer. He stresses how gossip, trash-talk, and frivolous opining (i.e., blather) degrade you and deter your goals.

3. **Applied Faith.** I once defined faith as persistence; but Hill's work has taught me that faith is persistence combined with mature and sustained confidence that you *will* succeed based on immutable laws of growth, which his program helps you tap into.

4. **Overcoming Procrastination and Fear.** These two traits are the same. Learning to control one controls the other. Begin your effort with overcoming procrastination, which is task-specific and thus easier to work on than fear in general.

5. **Leadership.** Hill defines leadership as initiative—as doing what needs to be done without being told. You cannot claim leadership or have it bestowed on you. It is a form of behavior that stems from accountability, foresight, and know-how. Those traits create the kind of leadership that no one can grant or take away.

6. **The Master Mind.** A Master Mind is a harmonious support group convened at least weekly to support each member's wishes. Hill taught that such a group pools and heightens each participant's insights, intuition, enthusiasm, and acumen. It is vital to his program.

7. **Sex Transmutation.** Hill taught that sexual desire is the force of life seeking expression. When you place the sexual urge at the back of your efforts, you supercharge your efforts and abilities. The formula simple: upon feeling sexual desire mentally shift attention away from physical satisfaction and toward the achievement of a vital task. Do this at times of your own choosing.

8. **Rebounding from Failure.** Obstacles do not impede growth, they facilitate it. Setbacks and failures refine plans, abilities, ideas, and relationships. Without opposition we'd remain mental and emotional children. Every failure carries commensurate seeds of compensation.

9. **Cosmic Habit Force.** Generative habits and natural cycles, like the rotation of the planets, are the medium through which creation maintains itself. When you cultivate the right personal habits, Hill taught, you join with a wave of enormous natural power, which supports and forwards your efforts.

In addition to these nine points, chapter ten provides a thorough digest of *Think and Grow Rich*. This condensation allows you to profitably and quickly review Hill's central text. It is not a substitute for the original but a refresher and primer.

Finally, in the epilogue I reveal what I consider the "secret" of *Think and Grow Rich*, which Hill says appears at least once in every chapter but which he never names. I think you will find this passage a powerful and possibly breakthrough experience.

I have never met anyone dedicated to Hill's ideas who was not changed by them in concrete, measurable ways. Hill's success philosophy is not just for people who desire material wealth or wealth alone. It is for anyone possessed of any wish—whether student, soldier, teacher, artist, entrepreneur, or activist—that he or she hungers to actualize.

After reading Hill and following his steps, you will approach your work (which is often the deepest part of a person's life, whether or not we acknowledge that) more effectively, fully, and successfully. By committing yourself to the ideas in book you will experience positive and remarkable change. Of that I have no doubt.

I
Possessing a Definite Chief Aim

A Definite Chief Aim,
chapter from
The Law of Success
(1928)

Nothing matters more to your success than possessing one absolute aim. If you have a Definite Chief Aim (Hill always capitalized the term) you experience heightened energies, intellectual powers, and resources. We often disperse our energies by harboring a wide variety of aims, some of them contradictory. Or we tell ourselves that we already possess a clear aim when we have nothing of the sort—rather, we have a generalized half-wish for which we are prepared to sacrifice little.

A Definite Chief Aim is something that you want with burning desire, unfettered passion, and upon which you are willing to stake your existence. Per-

former Sammy Davis Jr. wrote this in 1965 in his memoir Yes I Can: "I have to be a star like another man has to breathe." That's what a Definite Chief Aim sounds like. Guitarist Keith Richards said that he knew his life's aim when, as a budding musician in the mid-1950s, he heard the playing style of Elvis Presley's first guitarist, Scotty Moore. "All I wanted to do in the world was to be able to play and sound like that," Richards said. That, too, is what a real aim sounds like, in any field.

A Definite Chief Aim is the closest thing that life grants to a magic elixir. A definite aim clarifies and aligns your efforts; orders and prioritizes your relationships; defines your daily existence; drives to continue when you feel dejected; distinguishes you from the crowd; and engenders sustained passion and enthusiasm. These traits are the best guarantee of getting where you want to go.

Some people object that life places too many demands on us to allow for one exclusive aim. How can a single aim cover all the roles we are required to play, from parent and caregiver to worker and artist? I can say from experience that a single, well-defined aim can cover many different bases. So choose carefully. But I must also admit that your aim may not cover everything. That is part of a tough bargain that life strikes with us.

But—and I ask you to take this with deepest seriousness—without one absolute aim you will not break through to what matters most to you. And with that kind of aim, you will discover possibilities everywhere.

—MH

A DEFINITE CHIEF AIM

"YOU CAN DO IT IF YOU BELIEVE YOU CAN!"

You are at the beginning of a course of philosophy which, for the first time in the history of the world, has been organized from the known factors which have been used and must always be used by successful people.

Literary style has been completely subordinated for the sake of stating the principles and laws included in this course in such a manner that they may be quickly and easily assimilated by people in every walk of life.

Some of the principles described in the course are familiar to all who will read the course. Others are here stated for the first time. It should be kept in mind, from the first lesson to the last, that the value of the philosophy lies entirely in the thought stimuli it will produce in the mind of the student, and not merely in the lessons themselves.

Stated in another way, this course is intended as a mind stimulant that will cause the student to organize and direct to a DEFINITE end the forces of his or her mind, thus harnessing the stupendous power which most people waste in spasmodic, purposeless thought.

Singleness of purpose is essential for success, no matter what may be one's idea of the definition of success. Yet singleness of purpose is a quality which may, and generally does, call for thought on many allied subjects.

This author traveled a long distance to watch Jack Dempsey train for an oncoming battle. It was observed that he did not rely entirely upon one form of exercise, but resorted to many forms. The punching bag helped him develop one set of muscles, and also trained his eye to be quick. The dumbbells trained still another set of muscles. Running developed the muscles of his legs and hips. A well balanced food ration supplied the materials needed for building muscle without fat. Proper sleep, relaxation and rest habits provided still other qualities which he must have in order to win.

The student of this course is, or should be, engaged in the business of training for success in the battle of life. To win there are many factors which must have attention. A well organized, alert and energetic mind is produced by various and sundry stimuli, all of which are plainly described in these lessons.

It should be remembered, however, that the mind requires, for its development, a variety of exercise, just as the physical body, to be properly developed, calls for many forms of systematic exercise.

Horses are trained to certain gaits by trainers who hurdle-jump them over handicaps which cause them to develop the desired steps, through habit and repetition. The human mind must be trained in a similar manner, by a variety of thought-inspiring stimuli.

You will observe, before you have gone very far into this philosophy, that the reading of these lessons will super induce a flow of thoughts covering a wide range of subjects. For this reason the student should read the course with a note-book and pencil at hand, and follow the practice of recording these thoughts or "ideas" as they come into the mind.

By following this suggestion the student will have a collection of ideas, by the time the course has been read two or three times, sufficient to transform his or her entire life-plan.

By following this practice it will be noticed, very soon, that the mind has become like a magnet in that it will attract useful ideas right out of the "thin air," to use the words of a noted scientist who has experimented with this principle for a great number of years.

You will do yourself a great injustice if you undertake this course with even a remote feeling that you do not stand in need of more knowledge than you now possess. In truth, no man knows enough about any worth-while subject to entitle him to feel that he has the last word on that subject.

In the long, hard task of trying to wipe out some of my own ignorance and make way for some of the useful truths of life, I have often seen, in my imagination, the Great Marker who stands at the gateway entrance of life and writes "Poor Fool" on the brow of those who believe they are wise, and "Poor Sinner" on the brow of those who believe they are saints.

Which, translated into workaday language, means that none of us know very much, and by the very nature of our being can never know as much as we need to know in order to live sanely and enjoy life while we live.

Humility is a forerunner of success!

Until we become humble in our own hearts we are not apt to profit greatly by the experiences and thoughts of others.

Sounds like a preachment on morality? Well, what if it does?

Even "preachments," as dry and lacking in interest as they generally are, may be beneficial if they serve to reflect the shadow of our real selves so we may get an approximate idea of our smallness and superficiality.

Success in life is largely predicated upon our knowing men!

The best place to study the man-animal is in your own mind, by taking as accurate an inventory as possible of YOURSELF. When you know yourself thoroughly (if you ever do) you will also know much about others.

To know others, not as they seem to be, but as they really are, study them through:

1. The posture of the body, and the way they walk.
2. The tone of the voice, its quality, pitch, volume.
3. The eyes, whether shifty or direct.
4. The use of words, their trend, nature and quality.

Through these open windows you may literally "walk right into a man's soul" and take a look at the REAL MAN!

Going a step further, if you would know men study them:

When angry
When in love
When money is involved
When eating (alone, and unobserved, as they believe)
When writing
When in trouble
When joyful and triumphant
When downcast and defeated
When facing catastrophe of a hazardous nature
When trying to make a "good impression" on others
When informed of another's misfortune
When informed of another's good fortune
When losing in any sort of a game of sport
When winning at sport
When alone, in a meditative mood.

Before you can know any man, as he really is, you must observe him in all the foregoing moods, and perhaps more, which is practically the equivalent of saying that you have no right to judge others at sight. Appearances count, there can be no doubt of that, but appearances are often deceiving.

This course has been so designed that the student who masters it may take inventory of himself and of others by other than "snap-judgment" methods. The student who masters this philosophy will be able to look through the outer crust of personal adornment, clothes, so-called culture and the like, and down deep into the heart of all about him.

This is a very broad promise!

It would not have been made if the author of this philosophy had not known, from years of experimentation and analysis, that the promise can be met. Some who have examined the manuscripts of this course have asked why it was not called a course in Master Salesmanship. The answer is that the word "salesmanship" is commonly, associated with the marketing of goods or services, and it would, therefore, narrow down and circumscribe the real nature of the course. It is true that this is a course in Master Salesmanship, providing one takes a deeper-than-the-average view of the meaning of salesmanship.

This philosophy is intended to enable those who master it to "sell" their way through life successfully, with the minimum amount of resistance and friction. Such a course, therefore, must help the student organize and make use of much truth which is overlooked by the majority of people who go through life as mediocres.

Not all people are so constituted that they wish to know the truth about all matters vitally affecting life. One of the great surprises the author of this course has met with, in connection with his research activities, is that so few people are willing to hear the truth when it shows up their own weaknesses.

We prefer illusions to realities!

New truths, if accepted at all, are taken with the proverbial grain of salt. Some of us demand more than a mere pinch of salt; we demand enough to pickle new ideas so they become useless.

For these reasons the Introductory Lesson of this course, and this lesson as well, cover subjects intended to pave the way for new ideas so those ideas will not be too severe a shock to the mind of the student.

The thought the author wishes to "get across" has been quite plainly stated by the editor of the American Magazine, in an editorial which appeared in a recent issue, in the following words:

"On a recent rainy night, Carl Lomen, the reindeer king of Alaska, told me a true story. It has stuck in my crop ever since. And now I am going to pass it along.

"'A certain Greenland Eskimo,' said Lomen, 'was taken on one of the American North Polar expeditions a number of years ago. Later, as a reward for faithful service, he was brought to New York City for a short visit. At all the miracles of sight and sound he was filled with a most amazed wonder. When he returned to his native village he told stories of buildings that rose into the very face of the sky; of street cars, which he described as houses that moved along the trail, with people living in them as they moved; of mammoth bridges, artificial lights, and all the other dazzling concomitants of the metropolis.

"'His people looked at him coldly and walked away. And forthwith throughout the whole village he was dubbed "Sagdluk," meaning "the Liar," and this name he carried in shame to his grave. Long before his death his original name was entirely forgotten.

"'When Knud Rasmussen made his trip from Greenland to Alaska he was accompanied by a Greenland Eskimo named Mitek (Eider Duck). Mitek visited Copenhagen and New York, where he saw many things for the first time and was greatly impressed. Later, upon his return to Greenland, he recalled the tragedy of Sagdluk, and decided that it would not be wise to tell the truth. Instead, he would narrate stories that his people could grasp, and thus save his reputation.

"'So he told them how he and Doctor Rasmussen maintained a kayak on the banks of a great river, the Hudson, and how, each morning, they paddled out for their hunting. Ducks, geese and seals were to be had a-plenty, and they enjoyed the visit immensely.

"'Mitek, in the eyes of his countrymen, is a very honest man. His neighbors treat him with rare respect.'

"The road of the truth-teller has always been rocky. Socrates sipping the hemlock, Christ crucified, Stephen stoned, Bruno burned at the stake, Galileo terrified into retraction of his starry truths—forever could one follow that bloodly trail through the pages of history.

"Something in human nature makes us resent the impact of new ideas."

We hate to be disturbed in the beliefs and prejudices that have been handed down with the family furniture. At maturity too many of us go into hibernation, and live off the fat of ancient fetishes. If a new idea invades our, den we rise up snarling from our winter sleep.

The Eskimos, at least, had some excuse. They were unable to visualize the startling pictures drawn by Sagdluk. Their simple lives had been too long circumscribed by the brooding arctic night.

But there is no adequate reason why the average man should ever close his mind to fresh "slants" on life. He does, just the same. Nothing is more tragic—or more common—than mental inertia. For every ten men who are physically lazy there are ten thousand with stagnant minds. And stagnant minds are the breeding places of fear.

An old farmer up in Vermont always used to wind up his prayers with this plea: "Oh, God, give me an open mind!" If more people followed his example they might escape being hamstrung by prejudices. And what a pleasant place to live in the world would be.

Every person should make it his business to gather new ideas from sources other than the environment in which he daily lives and works.

The mind becomes withered, stagnant, narrow and closed unless it searches for new ideas. The farmer should come to the city quite often, and walk among the strange faces and the tall buildings. He will go back to his farm, his mind refreshed, with more courage and greater enthusiasm.

The city man should take a trip to the country every so often and freshen his mind with sights new and different from those associated with his daily labors.

Everyone needs a change of mental environment at regular periods, the same as a change and variety of food are essential. The mind becomes more alert, more elastic and more ready to work with speed and accuracy after it has been bathed in new ideas, outside of one's own field of daily labor.

As a student of this course you will temporarily lay aside the set of ideas with which you perform your daily labors, and enter a field of entirely new (and in some instances, heretofore unheard-of) ideas.

Splendid! You will come out, at the other end of this course, with a new stock of ideas which will make you more efficient, more enthusiastic and more courageous, *no matter in what sort of work you may be engaged*.

Do not be afraid of new ideas! They may mean to you the difference between success and failure.

Some of the ideas introduced in this course will require no further explanation or proof of their soundness because they are familiar to practically everyone. Other ideas here introduced are new, and for that very reason many students of this philosophy may hesitate to accept them as sound.

Every principle described in this course has been thoroughly tested by the author, and the majority of the principles covered have been tested by scores of scientists and others who were quite capable of distinguishing between the merely theoretic and the practical.

For these reasons all principles here covered are known to be workable in the exact manner claimed for them. However, no student of this course is asked to accept any statement made in these lessons without having first satisfied himself or herself, by tests, experiments and analysis, that the statement is sound.

The major evil the student is requested to avoid is that of forming opinions without definite FACTS as the basis, which brings to mind Herbert Spencer's famous admonition, in these words:

"There is a principle which is a bar against all information; which is proof against all argument; and which cannot fail to keep a man in everlasting ignorance. This principle is contempt prior to examination."

It may be well to bear this principle in mind when you come to study the Law of the Master Mind described in these lessons. This law embodies an entirely new principle of mind operation, and, for this reason alone, it will be difficult for many students to accept it as sound until after they have experimented with it.

When the fact is considered, however, that the Law of the Master Mind is believed to be the real basis of most of the achievements of those who are considered geniuses, this Law takes on an aspect which calls for more than "snap-judgment" opinions.

It is believed by many scientific men whose opinions on the subject have been given the author of this philosophy, that the Law of the Master Mind is the basis of practically all of the more important achievements resulting from group or co-operative effort.

The late Dr. Alexander Graham Bell said he believed the Law of the Master Mind, as it has been described in this philosophy, was not only sound, but that all the higher institutions of learning would soon be teaching that Law as a part of their courses in psychology.

Charles P. Steinmetz said he had experimented with the Law and had arrived at the same conclusion as that stated in these lessons, long before he talked to the author of the Law of Success philosophy about the subject.

Luther Burbank and John Burroughs made similar statements.

Edison was never interrogated on the subject, but other statements of his indicate that he would endorse the Law as being a possibility, if not in fact a reality.

Dr. Elmer Gates endorsed the Law, in a conversation with this author more than fifteen years ago. Dr. Gates is a scientist of the highest order, ranking along with Steinmetz, Edison and Bell.

The author of this philosophy has talked to scores of intelligent business men who, while they were not scientists, admitted they believed in the soundness of the Law of the Master Mind. It is hardly excusable, therefore, for men of less ability to judge such matters, to form opinions as to this Law, without serious, systematic investigation.

Let me lay before you a brief outline of what this lesson is and what it is intended to do for *you!*

Having prepared myself for the practice of law I will offer this introduction as a "statement of my case." The evidence with which to back up my case will be presented in the sixteen lessons of which the course is composed.

The facts out of which this course has been prepared have been gathered through more than twenty-five years of business and professional experience, and my only explanation of the rather free use of the personal pronoun throughout the course is that I am writing from *first-hand experience.*

Before this Reading Course on the Law of Success was published the manuscripts were submitted to two prominent universities with the request that they be read by competent professors with the object of eliminating or correcting any statements that appeared to be unsound, from an economic viewpoint.

This request was complied with and the manuscripts were carefully examined, with the result that not a single change was made with the exception of one or two slight changes in wording.

One of the professors who examined the manuscripts expressed himself, in part, as follows: "It is a tragedy that every boy and girl who enters high school is not efficiently drilled on the fifteen major parts of your Reading Course on the Law of Success. It is regrettable that the great university with which I am connected, and every other university, does not include your course as a part of its curriculum."

Inasmuch as this Reading Course is intended as a map or blueprint that will guide you in the attainment of that coveted goal called "Success," may it not be well here to define success?

Success is the development of the power with which to get whatever one wants in life without interfering with the rights of others.

I would lay particular stress upon the word "power" because it is inseparably related to success. We are living in a world and during an age of intense competition, and the law of the survival of the fittest is everywhere in evidence. Because of these facts all who would enjoy enduring success must go about its attainment through the use of power.

And what is *power?*

Power is *organized* energy or effort. This course is properly called the Law of Success for the reason that it teaches how one may organize *facts* and *knowledge* and the faculties, of one's mind into a unit of power.

This course brings you a definite promise, namely:

That through its mastery and application you can get whatever you want, with but two qualifying words—"within reason."

This qualification takes into consideration your education, your wisdom or your lack of it, your physical endurance, your temperament, and all of the other qualities mentioned in the sixteen lessons of this course as being the factors most essential in the attainment of success.

Without a single exception those who have attained unusual success have done so, either consciously or unconsciously, through the aid of all or a portion of the fifteen major factors of which this course is compiled. If you doubt this statement, then master these sixteen lessons so you can go about the analysis with reasonable accuracy and analyze such men as Carnegie, Rockefeller, Hill, Harriman, Ford and others of this type who have accumulated great fortunes of material wealth, and you will see that they understood and applied the principle of *organized effort* which runs, like a golden cord of indisputable evidence, throughout this course.

Nearly twenty years ago I interviewed Mr. Carnegie for the purpose of writing a story about him. During the interview I asked him to what he attributed his *success*. With a merry little twinkle in his eyes he said:

"Young man, before I answer your question will you please define your term 'success'?"

After waiting until he saw that I was somewhat embarrassed by his request he continued: "By success you have reference to my money, have you not?" I assured him that money was the term by which most people measured success, and he then said: "Oh, well—if you wish to know how I got my money—*if that is what you call success*—I will answer your question by saying that we have a master mind here in our business, and that mind is made up of more than a score of men who constitute my personal staff of superintendents and managers and accountants and chemists and other necessary types. No one person in this group is the master mind of which I speak, but the sum total of the minds in the group, co-ordinated, organized and directed to a *definite* end in a spirit of harmonious co-operation is the power that got my money for me. No two minds in the group are exactly alike, but each man in the group does the thing that he is supposed to do and he does it better than any other person in the world could do it."

Then and there the seed out of which this course has been developed was sown in my mind, but that seed did not take root or germinate until later. This interview marked the beginning of years of research which led, finally, to the discovery of the principle of psychology described in the Introductory Lesson as the "Master Mind."

I heard all that Mr. Carnegie said, but it took the knowledge gained from many years of subsequent contact with the business world to enable me to assimilate that which he said and clearly grasp and understand the principle back of it, which was nothing more nor less than the principle of *orga-*

nized effort upon which this course on the Law of Success is founded.

Carnegie's group of men constituted a "Master Mind" and that mind was so well organized, so well co-ordinated, so powerful, that it could have accumulated millions of dollars for Mr. Carnegie in practically any sort of endeavor of a commercial or industrial nature. The steel business in which that mind was engaged was but an incident in connection with the accumulation of the Carnegie wealth. The same wealth could have been accumulated had the "Master Mind" been directed in the coal business or the banking business or the grocery business, for the reason that back of the mind was *power*— that sort of power which *you* may have when you shall have organized the faculties of your own mind and allied yourself with other well organized minds for the attainment of a *definite chief aim* in life.

A careful check-up with several of Mr. Carnegie's former business associates, which was made after this course was begun, proves conclusively not only that there is such a law as that which has been called the "Master Mind," but that this law was the chief source of Mr. Carnegie's success.

Perhaps no man was ever associated with Mr. Carnegie who knew him better than did Mr. C. M. Schwab. In the following words Mr. Schwab has very accurately described that "subtle something" in Mr. Carnegie's personality which enabled him to rise to such stupendous heights.

"I never knew a man with so much imagination, lively intelligence and instinctive comprehension. You sensed that he probed your thoughts and took stock of everything that you had ever done or might do. He seemed to catch at your next word before it was spoken. The play of his mind was dazzling and his habit of close observation gave him a store of knowledge about innumerable matters.

"But his outstanding quality, from so rich an endowment, was the power of inspiring other men. Confidence radiated from him. You might be doubtful about something and discuss the matter with Mr. Carnegie. In a flash he would make you see that it was right and then absolutely believe it; or he might settle your doubts by pointing out its weakness. This quality of attracting others, then spurring them on, arose from his own strength.

"The results of his leadership were remarkable. Never before in the history of industry, I imagine, was there a man who, without understanding his business in its working details, making no pretense of technical knowledge concerning steel or engineering, was yet able to build up such an enterprise.

"Mr. Carnegie's ability to inspire men rested on something deeper than any faculty of judgment."

In the last sentence Mr. Schwab has conveyed a thought which corroborates the theory of the "Master Mind" to which the author of this course has attributed the chief source of Mr. Carnegie's power.

Mr. Schwab has also confirmed the statement that Mr. Carnegie could have succeeded as well in any other business as he did in the steel business. It is obvious that his success was due to his understanding of his own mind and the minds of other men, and not to mere knowledge of the steel business itself.

This thought is most consoling to those who have not yet attained outstanding success, for it shows that success is solely a matter of correctly applying laws and principles which are available to all; and these laws, let us not forget, are fully described in the Sixteen Lessons of this course.

Mr. Carnegie learned how to apply the law of the "Master Mind." This enabled him to organize the faculties of his own mind and the faculties of other men's minds, and co-ordinate the whole behind a DEFINITE CHIEF AIM.

Every strategist, whether in business or war or industry or other callings, understands the value of *organized*, co-ordinated effort. Every military strategist understands the value of sowing seeds of dissension in the ranks of the opposing forces, because this breaks up the power of co-ordination back of the opposition. During the late world war much was heard about the effects of propaganda, and it seems not an exaggeration to say that the disorganizing forces of propaganda were much more destructive than were all the guns and explosives used in the war.

One of the most important turning-points of the world war came when the allied armies were placed under the direction of the French General, Foch. There are well informed military men who claim that this was the move which spelled doom for the opposing armies.

Any modern railroad bridge is an excellent example of the value of *organized effort*, because it demonstrates quite simply and clearly how thousands of tons of weight may be borne by a comparatively small group of steel bars and beams so arranged that the weight is spread over the entire group.

There was a man who had seven sons who were always quarreling among themselves. One day he called them together and informed them that he wished to demonstrate just what their lack of co-operative effort meant. He had prepared a bundle of seven sticks which he had carefully tied together. One by one he asked his sons to take the bundle and break it. Each son tried, but in vain. Then he cut the strings and handed one of the sticks to each of his sons and asked him to break it over his knee. After the sticks had all been broken, with ease, he said:

"When you boys work together in a spirit of harmony you resemble the bundle of sticks, and no one can defeat you; but when you quarrel among yourselves anyone can defeat you one at a time."

There is a worth-while lesson in this story of the man and his seven quarrelsome sons, and it may be applied to the people of a community, the employees and employers in a given place of employment, or to the state and nation in which we live.

Organized effort may be made a power, but it may also be a dangerous power unless guided with intelligence, which is the chief reason why the sixteenth lesson of this course is devoted largely to describing how to direct the power of organized effort so that it will lead to *success;* that sort of success which is founded upon truth and justice and fairness that lead to ultimate *happiness*.

One of the outstanding tragedies of this age of struggle and money-madness is the fact that so few people are engaged in the effort which they like best. One of the objects of this course is to help each student find his or her particular niche in the world's work, where both material prosperity and *happiness* in abundance may be found. For this purpose a Character Analysis Chart accompanies the sixteenth lesson. This chart is designed to help the student take inventory of himself and find out what latent ability and hidden forces lie sleeping within him.

This entire course is intended as a stimulus with which to enable you to see yourself and your hidden forces as they are, and to awaken in you the ambition and the vision and the determination to cause you to go forth and claim that which is rightfully yours.

Less than thirty years ago a man was working in the same shop with Henry Ford, doing practically the same sort of work that he was doing. It has been said that this man was really a more competent workman, in that particular sort of work, than Ford. Today this man is still engaged in the same sort of work, at wages of less than a hundred dollars a week, while Mr. Ford is the world's richest man.

What outstanding difference is there between these two men which has so widely separated them in terms of material wealth? Just this—Ford understood and applied the principle of *organized effort* while the other man did not.

In the little city of Shelby, Ohio, as these lines are being written, for the first time in the history of the world this principle of *organized effort* is being applied for the purpose of bringing about a closer alliance between the churches and the business houses of a community.

The clergymen and business men have formed an alliance, with the result that practically every church in the city is squarely back of every business man, and every business man is squarely back of every church. The effect has been the strengthening of the churches and the business houses to such an extent that it has been said that it would be practically impossible for any individual member of either class to fail in his calling. The others who belong to the alliance will permit no such failures.

Here is an example of what may happen when groups of men form an alliance for the purpose of placing the combined power of the group back of each individual unit. The alliance has brought both material and moral advantages to the city of Shelby such as are enjoyed by but few other cities of its size in America. The plan has worked so effectively and so satisfactorily that a movement is now under way to extend it into other cities throughout America.

That you may gain a still more concrete vision of just how this principle of *organized effort* can be made powerful, stop for a moment and allow your imagination to draw a picture of what would likely be the result if every church and every newspaper and every Rotary Club and every Kiwanis Club and every Advertising Club and every Woman's Club and every other civic organization of a similar nature, in your city, or in any other city in the United States, should form an alliance for the purpose of pooling their power and using it for the benefit of all members of these organizations.

The results which might easily be attained by such an alliance stagger the imagination!

There are three outstanding powers in the world of *organized effort*. They are: The churches, the schools and the newspapers. Think what might easily happen if these three great powers and molders of public opinion should ally themselves together for the purpose of bringing about any needed change in human conduct. They could, in a single generation, so modify the present standard of business ethics, for example, that it would practically be business suicide for anyone to try to transact business under any standard except that of the Golden Rule. Such an alliance could be made to produce sufficient influence to change, in a single generation, the business, social and moral tendencies of the entire civilized world. Such an alliance would have sufficient power to *force* upon the minds of the oncoming generations any ideals desired.

Power is *organized effort,* as has already been stated! Success is based upon power!

That you may have a clear conception of what is meant by the term "organized effort" I have made use of the foregoing illustrations, and for the sake of further emphasis I am going to repeat the statement that the accumulation of great wealth and the attainment of any high station in life such as constitute what we ordinarily call *success,* are based upon the vision to comprehend and the ability to assimilate and apply the major principles of the sixteen lessons of this course.

This course is in complete harmony with the principles of economics and the principles of Applied Psychology. You will observe that those lessons, which depend, for their practical application, upon knowledge of psychology, have been supplemented with sufficient explanation of the psychological principles involved to render the lessons easily understood.

Possessing a Definite Chief Aim

Before the manuscripts for this course went to the publisher they were submitted to some of the foremost bankers and business men of America, that they might be examined, analyzed and criticized by the most practical type of mind. One of the best known bankers in New York City returned the manuscripts with the following comment:

"I hold a master's degree from Yale, but I would willingly exchange all that this degree has brought me in return for what your course on the Law of Success would have brought me had I been afforded the privilege of making it a part of my training while I was studying at Yale.

"My wife and daughter have also read the manuscripts, and my wife has named your course 'the master key-board of life' because she believes that all who understand how to apply it may play a perfect symphony in their respective callings, just as a pianist may play any tune when once the keyboard of the piano and the fundamentals of music have been mastered."

No two people on earth are exactly alike, and for this reason no two people would be expected to attain from this course the same viewpoint. Each student should read the course, understand it and then appropriate from its contents whatever he or she needs to develop a well rounded personality.

Before this appropriation can be properly made it will be necessary for the student to analyze himself, through the use of the questionnaire that comes with the sixteenth lesson of the course, for the purpose of finding out what his deficiencies may be. This questionnaire should not be filled out until the student thoroughly masters the contents of the entire course, for he will then be in position to answer the questions with more accuracy and understanding of himself. Through the aid of this questionnaire an experienced character analyst can take inventory of one's faculties as easily and as accurately as a merchant can inventory the goods on his shelves.

This course has been compiled for the purpose of helping the student find out what are his or her natural talents, and for the purpose of helping organize, coordinate and put into use the knowledge gained from experience. For more than twenty years I have been gathering, classifying and organizing the material that has gone into the course. During the past fourteen years I have analyzed more than 16,000 men and women, and all of the vital facts gathered from these analyses have been carefully organized and woven into this course. These analyses brought out many interesting facts which have helped to make this course practical and usable. For example, it was discovered that ninety-five per cent of all who were analyzed were failures, and but five per cent were successes. (By the term "failure" is meant that they had failed to find happiness and the ordinary necessities of life without struggle that was almost unbearable.) Perhaps this is about the proportion of successes and failures that might be found if all the people of the world were accurately analyzed. The struggle for a mere existence is terrific among people who have not learned how to organize and direct their natural talents, while the attainment of those necessities, as well as the acquiring of many of the luxuries, is comparatively simple among those who have mastered the principle of *organized effort*.

One of the most startling facts brought to light by those 16,000 analyses was the discovery that the ninety-five per cent who were classed as failures were in that class *because they had no definite chief aim in life*, while the five per cent constituting the successful ones not only had purposes that were *definite*, but they had, also, *definite plans* for the attainment of their purposes.

Another important fact disclosed by these analyses was that the ninety-five percent constituting the failures were engaged in work which they did not like, while the five per cent constituting the successful ones were doing that which they liked best. It is doubtful whether a person could be a failure while engaged in work which he liked best. Another vital fact learned from the analyses was that all of the five per cent who were succeeding had formed the habit of systematic saving of money, while the ninety-five per cent who were failures saved nothing. This is worthy of serious thought.

One of the chief objects of this course is to aid the student in performing his or her chosen work in such a manner that it will yield the greatest returns in both money and happiness.

A Definite Chief Aim

The key-note of this entire lesson may be found in the word "definite."

It is most appalling to know that ninety-five per cent of the people of the world are drifting aimlessly through life, without the slightest conception of the work for which they are best fitted, and with no conception whatsoever of even the need of such a thing as a *definite* objective toward which to strive.

There is a psychological as well as an economic reason for the selection of a *definite chief aim* in life. Let us devote our attention to the psychological side of the question first. It is a well established principle of psychology that a person's acts are always in harmony with the dominating thoughts of his or her mind.

Any *definite chief aim* that is deliberately fixed in the mind and held there, with the determination to realize it, finally saturates the entire subconscious mind until it automatically influences the physical action of the body toward the attainment of that purpose.

Your *definite chief aim* in life should be selected with deliberate care, and after it has been selected it should be written out and placed where you will see it at least once a day, the psychological effect of which is to impress this purpose upon your subconscious mind so strongly that it accepts that purpose as a pattern or blueprint that will eventually dominate your activities in life and lead you, step by step, toward the attainment of the object back of that purpose.

The principle of psychology through which you can impress your *definite chief aim* upon your subconscious mind is called Auto-suggestion, or suggestion which you repeatedly make to yourself. It is a degree of self-hypnotism, but do not be afraid of it on that account, for it was this same principle through the aid of which Napoleon lifted himself from the lowly station of poverty-stricken Corsican to the dictatorship of France. It was through the aid of this same principle that

Thomas A. Edison has risen from the lowly beginning of a news butcher to where he is accepted as the leading inventor of the world. It was through the aid of this same principle that Lincoln bridged the mighty chasm between his lowly birth, in a log cabin in the mountains of Kentucky, and the presidency of the greatest nation on earth. It was through the aid of this same principle that Theodore Roosevelt became one of the most aggressive leaders that ever reached the presidency of the United States.

You need have no fear of the principle of Auto-suggestion as long as you are sure that the objective for which you are striving is one that will bring you happiness of an enduring nature. Be sure that your *definite purpose* is constructive; that its attainment will bring hardship and misery to no one; that it will bring you peace and prosperity, then apply, to the limit of your understanding, the principle of self-suggestion for the speedy attainment of this purpose.

On the street corner, just opposite the room in which I am writing, I see a man who stands there all day long and sells peanuts. He is busy every minute. When not actually engaged in making a sale he is roasting and packing the peanuts in little bags. He is one of that great army constituting the ninety-five per cent who have no *definite purpose* in life. He is selling peanuts, not because he likes that work better than anything else he might do, but because he never sat down and thought out a *definite purpose* that would bring him greater returns for his labor. He is selling peanuts because he is a drifter on the sea of life, and one of the tragedies of his work is the fact that the same amount of effort that he puts into it, if directed along other lines, would bring him much greater returns.

Another one of the tragedies of this man's work is the fact that he is unconsciously making use of the principle of self-suggestion, but he is doing it to his own disadvantage. No doubt, if a picture could be made of his thoughts, there would be nothing in that picture except a peanut roaster, some little paper bags and a crowd of people buying peanuts. This man could get out of the peanut business if he had the vision and the ambition first to imagine himself in a more profitable calling, and the perseverance to hold that picture before his mind until it influenced him to take the necessary steps to enter a more profitable calling. He puts sufficient labor into his work to bring him a substantial return if that labor were directed toward the attainment of a *definite purpose* that offered bigger returns.

One of my closest personal friends is one of the best known writers and public speakers of this country. About ten years ago he caught sight of the possibilities of this principle of self-suggestion and began, immediately, to harness it and put it to work. He worked out a plan for its application that proved to be very effective. At that time he was neither a writer nor a speaker.

Each night, just before going to sleep, he would shut his eyes and see, *in his imagination*, a long council table at which he placed (in his imagination) certain well known men whose characteristics he wished to absorb into his own personality. At the end of the table he placed Lincoln, and on either side of the table he placed Napoleon, Washington, Emerson and

Elbert Hubbard. He then proceeded to talk to these imaginary figures that he had seated at his imaginary council table, something after this manner:

Mr. Lincoln: I desire to build in my own character those qualities of patience and fairness toward all mankind and the keen sense of humor which were your outstanding characteristics. I need these qualities and I shall not be contented until I have developed them.

Mr. Washington: I desire to build in my own character those qualities of patriotism and self-sacrifice and leadership which were your outstanding characteristics.

Mr. Emerson: I desire to build in my own character those qualities of vision and the ability to interpret the laws of Nature as written in the rocks of prison walls and growing trees and flowing brooks and growing flowers and the faces of little children, which were your outstanding characteristics.

Napoleon: I desire to build in my own character those qualities of self-reliance and the strategic ability to master obstacles and profit by mistakes and develop strength out of defeat, which were your outstanding characteristics.

Mr. Hubbard: I desire to develop the ability to equal and even to excel the ability that you possessed with which to express yourself in clear, concise and forceful language.

Night after night, for many months, this man saw these men seated around that imaginary council table until finally he had imprinted their outstanding characteristics upon his own subconscious mind so clearly that he began to develop a personality which was a composite of their personalities.

The subconscious mind may be likened to a magnet, and when it has been vitalized and thoroughly saturated with any *definite purpose* it has a decided tendency to attract all that is necessary for the fulfillment of that purpose. Like attracts like, and you may see evidence of this law in every blade of grass and every growing tree. The acorn attracts from the soil and the air the necessary materials out of which to grow an oak tree. It never grows a tree that is part oak and part poplar. Every grain of wheat that is planted in the soil attracts the materials out of which to grow a stalk of wheat.

It never makes a mistake and grows both oats and wheat on the same stalk.

And men are subject, also, to this same Law of Attraction. Go into any cheap boarding house district in any city and there you will find people of the same general trend of mind associated together. On the other hand, go into any prosperous community and there you will find people of the same general tendencies associated together. Men who are successful always seek the company of others who are successful, while men who are on the ragged side of life always seek the company of those who are in similar circumstances. "Misery loves company."

Water seeks its level with no finer certainty than man seeks the company of those who occupy his own general status financially and mentally. A professor of Yale University and an illiterate hobo have nothing in common. They would be miserable if thrown together for any great length of time. Oil and water will mix as readily as will men who have nothing in common.

All of which leads up to this statement:

That you will attract to you people who harmonize with your own philosophy of life, whether you wish it or not. This being true, can you not see the importance of vitalizing your mind with a *definite chief aim* that will attract to you people who will be of help to you and not a hindrance? Suppose your *definite chief aim* is far above your present station in life. What of it? It is your privilege—nay, your DUTY, to aim high in life. You owe it to yourself and to the community in which you live to set a high standard for yourself.

There is much evidence to justify the belief that nothing *within reason* is beyond the possibility of attainment by the man whose *definite chief aim* has been well developed. Some years ago Louis Victor Eytinge was given a life sentence in the Arizona penitentiary. At the time of his imprisonment he was an all-around "bad man," according to his own admissions. In addition to this it was believed that he would die of tuberculosis within a year.

Eytinge had reason to feel discouraged, if anyone ever had. Public feeling against him was intense and he did not have a single friend in the world who came forth and offered him encouragement or help. Then something happened in his own mind that gave him back his health, put the dreaded "white plague" to rout and finally unlocked the prison gates and gave him his freedom.

What was that "something"?

Just this: He made up his mind to whip the white plague and regain his health. That was a very *definite chief aim*. In less than a year from the time the decision was made he had won. Then he extended that *definite chief aim* by making up his mind to gain his freedom. Soon the prison walls melted from around him.

No undesirable environment is strong enough to hold the man or woman who understands how to apply the principle of Auto-suggestion in the creation of a *definite chief aim*. Such a person can throw off the shackles of poverty; destroy the most deadly disease germs; rise from a lowly station in life to power and plenty.

All great leaders base their leadership upon a *definite chief aim*. Followers are willing followers when they know that their leader is a person with a definite chief aim who has the courage to back up that purpose with action. Even a balky horse knows when a driver with a *definite chief aim* takes hold of the reins; and yields to that driver. When a man with a *definite chief aim* starts through a crowd everybody stands aside and makes a way for him, but let a man hesitate and show by his actions that he is not sure which way he wants to go and the crowd will step all over his toes and refuse to budge an inch out of his way.

Nowhere is the lack of a *definite chief aim* more noticeable or more detrimental than it is in the relationship between parent and child. Children sense very quickly the wavering attitude of their parents and take advantage of that attitude quite freely. It is the same all through life—men with a *definite chief aim* command respect and attention at all times.

So much for the psychological viewpoint of a *definite purpose*. Let us now turn to the economic side of the question.

If a steamship lost its rudder, in mid-ocean, and began circling around, it would soon exhaust its fuel supply without reaching shore, despite the fact that it would use up enough energy to carry it to shore and back several times.

The man who labors without a *definite purpose* that is backed up by a definite plan for its attainment, resembles the ship that has lost its rudder. Hard labor and good intentions are not sufficient to carry a man through to success, for how may a man be sure that he has attained success unless he has established in his mind some definite object that he wishes?

Every well built house started in the form of a *definite purpose* plus a definite plan in the nature of a set of blueprints. Imagine what would happen if one tried to build a house by the haphazard method, without plans. Workmen would be in each other's way, building material would be piled all over the lot before the foundation was completed, and everybody on the job would have a different notion as to how the house ought to be built. Result, chaos and misunderstandings and cost that would be prohibitive.

Yet had you ever stopped to think that most people finish school, take up employment or enter a trade or profession without the slightest conception of anything that even remotely resembles a *definite purpose* or a definite plan? In view of the fact that science has provided reasonably accurate ways and means of analyzing character and determining the life-work for which people are best fitted, does it not seem a modern tragedy that ninety-five per cent of the adult population of the world is made up of men and women who are failures because they have not found their proper niches in the world's work?

If *success* depends upon power, and if power is *organized effort*, and if the first step in the direction of organization is a *definite purpose*, then one may easily see why such a purpose is essential.

Until a man selects a *definite purpose* in life he dissipates his energies and spreads his thoughts over so many subjects and in so many different directions that they lead not to power, but to indecision and weakness.

With the aid of a small reading glass you can teach yourself a great lesson on the value of *organized effort*. Through the use of such a glass you can focus the sun-rays on a *definite* spot so strongly that they will burn a hole through a plank. Remove the glass (which represents the *definite purpose*) and the same rays of sun may shine on that same plank for a million years without burning it.

A thousand electric dry batteries, when properly organized and connected together with wires, will produce enough power to run a good sized piece of machinery for several hours, but take those same cells singly, disconnected, and not one of them would exert enough energy to turn the machinery over once. The faculties of your mind might properly be likened to those dry cells. When you organize your faculties, according to the plan laid down in the sixteen lessons of this Reading Course on the Law of Success, and direct them toward the attainment of a *definite purpose* in life, you then take advantage of the co-operative or accumulative principle out of which *power* is developed, which is called Organized Effort.

Andrew Carnegie's advice was this: "Place all your eggs in one basket and then watch the basket to see that no one kicks it over." By that advice he meant, of course, that we should not dissipate any of our energies by engaging in side lines. Carnegie was a sound economist and he knew that most men would do well if they so harnessed and directed their energies that some one thing would be done well.

When the plan back of this Reading Course was first born I remember taking the first manuscript to a professor of the University of Texas, and in a spirit of enthusiasm I suggested to him that I had discovered a principle that would be of aid to me in every public speech I delivered thereafter, because I would be better prepared to organize and marshal my thoughts.

He looked at the outline of the fifteen points for a few minutes, then turned to me and said:

"Yes, your discovery is going to help you make better speeches, but that is not all it will do. It will help you become a more effective writer, for I have noticed in your previous writings a tendency to scatter your thoughts. For instance, if you started to describe a beautiful mountain yonder in the distance you would be apt to sidetrack your description by calling attention to a beautiful bed of wildflowers, or a running brook, or a singing bird, detouring here and there, zig-zag fashion, before finally arriving at the proper point from which to view the mountain. In the future you are going to find it much less difficult to describe an object, whether you are speaking or writing, *because your fifteen points represent the very foundation of organization.*"

A man who had no legs once met a man who was blind. To prove conclusively that the lame man was a *man of vision* he proposed to the blind man that they form an alliance that would be of great benefit to both. "You let me climb upon your back," said he to the blind man, "then I will use your legs and you may use my eyes. Between the two of us we will get along more rapidly."

Out of allied effort comes greater power. This is a point that is worthy of much repetition, *because it forms one of the most important parts of the foundation of this Reading Course.* The great fortunes of the world have been accumulated through the use of this principle of allied effort. That which one man can accomplish single handed, during an entire lifetime, is but meagre at best, no matter how well organized that man may be, but that which one man may accomplish through the principle of alliance with other men is practically without limitation.

That "master mind" to which Carnegie referred during MY interview with him was made up of more than a score of minds. In that group were men of practically every temperament and inclination. Each man was there to play a certain part and he did nothing else. There was perfect understanding and teamwork between these men. It was Carnegie's business to keep harmony among them.

And he did it wonderfully well.

If you are familiar with the game of football you know, of course, that the winning team is the one that best coordinates the efforts of its players. Team-work is the thing that wins. It is the same in the great game of life.

In your struggle for *success* you should keep constantly in mind the necessity of knowing what it is that you want—of knowing precisely what is your *definite purpose*—and the value of the principle of *organized effort* in the attainment of that which constitutes your *definite purpose*.

In a vague sort of way nearly everyone has a definite purpose—namely, the desire for *money!* But this is not a *definite purpose* within the meaning of the term as it is used in this lesson. Before your purpose could be considered *definite*, even though that purpose were the accumulation of money, you would have to reach a decision as to the precise method through which you intend to accumulate that money. It would be insufficient for you to say that you would make money by going into some sort of business. You would have to decide just what line of business. You would also have to decide just where you would locate. You would also have to decide the business policies under which you would conduct your business.

In answering the question, "What Is Your Definite Purpose In Life," that appears in the questionnaire; which I have used for the analysis of more than 16,000 people, many answered about as follows:

"My definite purpose in life is to be of as much service to the world as possible and earn a good living."

That answer is about as *definite* as a frog's conception of the size of the universe is accurate!

The object of this lesson is not to inform you as to what your life-work should be, for indeed this could be done with accuracy only after you had been completely analyzed, but it is intended as a means of impressing upon your mind a clear conception of the value of a *definite purpose* of some nature, and of the value of understanding the principle of *organized effort* as a means of attaining the necessary power with which to materialize your *definite purpose*.

Careful observation of the business philosophy of more than one hundred men and women who have attained outstanding success in their respective callings, disclosed the fact that each was a person of prompt and definite decision.

The habit of working with a *definite chief aim* will breed in you the habit of prompt decision, and this habit will come to your aid in all that you do.

Moreover, the habit of working with a *definite chief aim* will help you to concentrate all your attention on any given task until you have master edit.

Concentration of effort and the habit of working with a *definite chief aim* are two of the essential factors in success which are always found together. One leads to the other.

The best known successful business men were all men of prompt decision who worked always with one main, outstanding purpose as their chief aim.

Some notable examples are as follows:

Woolworth chose, as his *definite chief aim*, the belting of America with a chain of Five and Ten Cent Stores, and concentrated his mind upon this one task until he "made it and it made him."

Wrigley concentrated his mind on the production and sale of a five-cent package of chewing gum and turned this one idea into millions of dollars.

Edison concentrated upon the work of harmonizing natural laws and made his efforts uncover more useful inventions than any other man who ever lived.

Henry L. Doherty concentrated upon the building and operation of public utility plants and made himself a multimillionaire.

Ingersoll concentrated on a dollar watch and girdled the earth with "tickers" and made this one idea yield him a fortune.

Statler concentrated on "homelike hotel-service" and made himself wealthy as well as useful to millions of people who use his service.

Edwin C. Barnes concentrated on the sale of Edison Dictating Machines, and retired, while still a young man, with more money than he needs.

Woodrow Wilson concentrated his mind on the White House for twenty-five years, and became its chief tenant, thanks to his knowledge of the value of sticking to a *definite chief aim*.

Lincoln concentrated his mind on freeing the slaves and became our greatest American President while doing it.

Martin W. Littleton heard a speech which filled him with the desire to become a great lawyer, concentrated his mind on that one aim, and is now said to be the most successful lawyer in America, whose fees for a single case seldom fall below $50,000.

Rockefeller concentrated on oil and became the richest man of his generation.

Ford concentrated on "flivvers" and made himself the richest and most powerful man who ever lived.

Carnegie concentrated on steel and made his efforts build a great fortune and plastered his name on public libraries throughout America.

Gillette concentrated on a safety razor, gave the entire world a "close shave" and made himself a multi-millionaire.

George Eastman concentrated on the kodak and made the idea yield him a fortune while bringing much pleasure to millions of people.

Russell Conwell concentrated on one simple lecture, "Acres of Diamonds," and made the idea yield more than $6,000,000.

Hearst concentrated on sensational newspapers and made the idea worth millions of dollars.

Helen Keller concentrated on learning to speak, and, despite the fact that she was deaf, dumb and blind, realized her definite chief aim.

John H. Patterson concentrated on cash registers and made himself rich and others "careful."

The late Kaiser of Germany concentrated on war and got a big dose of it, let us not forget the fact!

Fleischmann concentrated on the humble little cake of yeast and made things hump themselves all over the world.

Marshall Field concentrated on the world's greatest retail store and lo! it rose before him, a reality.

Philip Armour concentrated on the butchering business and established a great industry, as well as a big fortune.

Millions of people are concentrating, daily, on POVERTY and FAILURE and getting both in overabundance.

Wright Brothers concentrated on the airplane and mastered the air.

Pullman concentrated on the sleeping car and the idea made him rich and millions of people comfortable in travel.

The Anti-Saloon League concentrated on the Prohibition Amendment and (whether for better or worse) made it a reality.

Thus it will be seen that all who succeed work with some definite, outstanding aim as the object of their labors.

There is some one thing that you can do better than anyone else in the world could do it. Search until you find out what this particular line of endeavor is, make it the object of your *definite chief aim* and then organize all of your forces and attack it with the belief that you are going to win. In your search for the work for which you are best fitted, it will be well if you bear in mind the fact that you will most likely attain the greatest success by finding out what work you like best, for it is a well known fact that a man generally best succeeds in the particular line of endeavor into which he can throw his whole heart and soul.

Let us go back, for the sake of clarity and emphasis, to the psychological principles upon which this lesson is founded, because it will mean a loss that you can ill afford if you fail to grasp the real reason for establishing a *definite chief aim* in your mind. These principles are as follows:

First: Every voluntary movement of the human body is caused, controlled and directed by *thought*, through the operation of the mind.

Second: The presence of any thought or idea in your consciousness tends to produce an associated feeling and to urge you to transform that feeling into appropriate muscular action that is in perfect harmony with the nature of the thought.

For example, if you think of winking your eyelid and there are no counter influences or thoughts in your mind at the time to arrest action, the motor nerve will carry your thought from the seat of government, in your brain, and appropriate or corresponding muscular action takes place immediately.

Stating this principle from another angle: You choose, for example, a *definite purpose* as your lifework and make up your mind that you will carry out that purpose. *From the very moment that you make this choice, this purpose becomes the dominating thought in your consciousness, and you are constantly on the alert for facts, information and knowledge with which to achieve that purpose.* From the time that you plant a *definite purpose* in your mind, your mind begins, both consciously and unconsciously, to gather and store away the material with which you are to accomplish that purpose.

Desire is the factor which determines what your *definite purpose* in life shall be. No one can select your dominating *desire* for you, but once you select it yourself it becomes your *definite chief aim* and occupies the spotlight of your mind until it is satisfied by transformation into reality, unless you permit it to be pushed aside by conflicting desires.

To emphasize the principle that I am here trying to make clear, I believe it not unreasonable to suggest that to be sure of successful achievement, one's *definite chief aim* in life should be backed up with a *burning desire* for its achievement. I have noticed that boys and girls who enter college and pay their way through by working seem to get more out of their schooling than do those whose expenses are paid for them. The secret of this may be found in the fact that those who are willing to work their way through are blessed with a *burning desire* for education, and such a desire, if the object of the desire is within reason, is practically sure of realization.

Science has established, beyond the slightest room for doubt, that through the principle of Auto-suggestion any deeply rooted *desire* saturates the entire body and mind with the nature of the desire and literally transforms the mind into a powerful magnet that will attract the object of the desire, if it be within reason. For the enlightenment of those who might not properly interpret the meaning of this statement I will endeavor to state this principle in another way. For example, merely desiring an automobile will not cause that automobile to come rolling in, but, if there is a *burning desire* for an automobile, that desire will lead to the appropriate action through which an automobile may be paid for.

Merely desiring freedom would never release a man who was confined in prison if it were not sufficiently strong to cause him to do something to entitle himself to freedom.

These are the steps leading from *desire* to fulfillment: First the *burning desire*, then the crystallization of that desire into a *definite purpose*, then sufficient appropriate *action* to achieve that purpose. *Remember that these three steps are always necessary to insure success.*

I once knew a very poor girl who had a *burning desire* for a wealthy husband, and she finally got him, but not without having transformed that desire into the development of a very attractive personality which, in turn, attracted the desired husband.

I once had a *burning desire* to be able to analyze character accurately and that desire was so persistent and so deeply seated that it practically drove me into ten years of research and study of men and women.

George S. Parker makes one of the best fountain pens in the world, and despite the fact that his business is conducted from the little city of Janesville, Wisconsin, he has spread his product all the way around the globe and he has his pen on sale in every civilized country in the world. More than twenty years ago, Mr. Parker's *definite purpose* was established in his mind, and that purpose was to produce the best fountain pen that money could buy. He backed that purpose with a *burning desire* for its realization and if you carry a fountain pen the chances are that you have evidence in your own possession that it has brought him abundant success.

You are a contractor and builder, and, like men who build houses out of mere wood and brick and steel, you must draw up a set of plans after which to shape your *success building*. You are living in a wonderful age, when the materials that go into *success* are plentiful and cheap. You have at your disposal, in the archives of the public libraries, the carefully compiled results of two thousand years of research covering practically every possible line of endeavor in which one would wish to engage. If you would become a preacher you have at hand the entire history of what has been learned by men who have preceded you in this field. If you would become a mechanic you have at hand the entire history of the inventions of machines and the discovery and usages of metals and things metallic in nature. If you would become a lawyer you have at your disposal the entire history of law procedure. Through the Department of Agriculture, at Washington, you have at your disposal all that has been learned about farming and agriculture, where you may use it should you wish to find your life-work in this field.

The world was never so resplendent with *opportunity* as it is today. On every hand there is an ever-increasing demand for the services of the man or the woman who makes a better mouse-trap or performs better stenographic service or preaches a better sermon or digs a better ditch or runs a more accommodating bank.

This lesson will not be completed until you shall have made your choice as to what your *definite chief aim* in life is to be and then recorded a description of that purpose in writing and placed it where you may see it every morning when you arise and every night when you retire.

Procrastination is—but why preach about it? You know that *you* are the hewer of your own wood and the drawer of your own water and the shaper of your own *definite chief aim* in life; therefore, why dwell upon that which you already know?

A *definite purpose* is something that you must create for yourself. No one else will create it for you and it will not create itself. What are you going to do about it? and when? and how?

Start now to analyze your desires and find out what it is that you wish, then make up your mind to get it. Lesson Three will point out to you the next step and show you how to proceed. Nothing is left to chance, in this Reading Course. Every step is marked plainly. Your part is to follow the directions until you arrive at your destination, which is represented by your *definite chief aim*. Make that aim clear and back it up with persistence which does not recognize the word "impossible."

When you come to select your *definite chief aim* just keep in mind the fact that you cannot *aim* too high.

Also keep in mind the never-varying truth that you'll get nowhere if you start nowhere. If your aim in life is vague your achievements will also be vague, and it might well be added, very *meager. Know what you want, when you want it, why you want it and HOW you intend to get it.* This is known to teachers and students of psychology as the WWWH formula—"what, when, why and how."

Read this lesson four times, at intervals of one week apart.

You will see much in the lesson the fourth time you read it that you did not see the first time.

Your success in mastering this course and in making it bring you success will depend very largely, if not entirely, upon how well you follow ALL the instructions it contains.

Do not set up your own rules of study. Follow those laid down in the Course, as they are the result of years of thought and experimentation. If you wish to experiment wait until you master this course in the manner suggested by its author. You will then be in position to experiment more safely. For the present content yourself by being the student. You will, let us hope, become the teacher as well as the student after you have followed the Course until you have mastered it.

If you follow the instructions laid down in this Course for the guidance of its students, you can no more fail than water can run uphill above the level of its source.

Instructions for Applying the Principles of this Lesson

Through the Introductory Lesson of this course you became familiar with the principle of psychology known as the "Master Mind."

You are now ready to begin use of this principle as a means of transforming your *definite chief aim* into reality. It must have occurred to you that one might as well have no *definite chief aim* unless one has, also, a very definite and practical plan for making that aim become a reality.

Your first step is to decide what your major aim in life shall be. Your next step is to write out a clear, concise statement of this aim. This should be followed by a statement, in writing, of the plan or plans through which you intend to attain the object of your aim.

Your next and final step will be the forming of an alliance with some person or persons who will cooperate with you in carrying out these plans and transforming your *definite chief aim* into reality.

The purpose of this friendly alliance is to employ the law of the "Master Mind" in support of your plans. The alliance should be made between yourself and those who have your highest and best interests at heart. If you are a married man your wife should be one of the members of this alliance, providing there exists between you a normal state of confidence and sympathy. Other members of this alliance may be your mother, father, brothers or sisters, or some close friend or friends.

If you are a single person your sweetheart, if you have one, should become a member of your alliance. This is no joke—you are now studying one of the most powerful laws of the human mind, and you will serve your own best interests by seriously and earnestly following the rules laid down in this lesson, even though you may not be sure where they will lead you.

Those who join with you in the formation of a friendly alliance for the purpose of aiding you in the creation of a "Master Mind" should sign, with you, your statement of the object of your *definite chief aim*. Every member of your alliance must be fully acquainted with the nature of your object in forming the alliance. Moreover, every member must be in hearty accord with this object, and in full sympathy with you. Each member of your alliance must be supplied with a written copy of your statement of your definite chief aim. With this exception, however, *you are explicitly instructed to keep the object of your chief aim to yourself.* The world is full of "Doubting Thomases" and it will do your cause no good to have these rattle-brained people scoffing at you and your ambitions. Remember, what you need is friendly encouragement and help, not derision and doubt.

If you believe in prayer you are instructed to make your *definite chief aim* the object of your prayer at, least once every twenty-four hours, and more often if convenient. If you believe there is a God who can and will aid those who are earnestly striving to be of constructive service in the world, surely you feel that' you have a right to petition Him for aid in the attainment of what should be the most important thing in life to you.

If those who have been invited to join your friendly alliance believe in prayer, ask them, also, to include the object of this alliance as a part of their daily prayer.

Comes, now, one of the most essential rules which you *must follow.* Arrange with one or all of the members of your friendly alliance to state to you, in the most positive and definite terms at their command, that THEY KNOW YOU CAN AND WILL REALIZE THE OBJECT OF YOUR DEFINITE CHIEF AIM. This affirmation or statement should be made to you at least once a day; more often if possible.

These steps must be followed persistently, with full faith that they will lead you where you wish to go! It will not suffice to carry out these plans for a few days or a few weeks and then discontinue them. YOU MUST FOLLOW THE DESCRIBED PROCEDURE. UNTIL YOU ATTAIN THE OBJECT OF YOUR DEFINITE CHIEF AIM, REGARDLESS OF THE TIME REQUIRED.

From time to time it may become necessary to change the plans you have adopted for the achievement of the object of your *definite chief aim.* Make these changes without hesitation. No human being has sufficient foresight to build plans which need no alteration or change.

If any member of your friendly alliance loses faith in the law known as the "Master Mind," immediately remove that member and replace him or her with some other person.

Andrew Carnegie stated to the author of this course that he had found it necessary to replace some of the members of his "Master Mind." In fact he stated that practically every member of whom his alliance was originally composed had, in time, been removed and replaced with some other person who could adapt himself more loyally and enthusiastically to the spirit and object of the alliance.

You cannot succeed when surrounded by disloyal and unfriendly associates, no matter what may be the object of your *definite chief aim*. Success is built upon loyalty, faith, sincerity, co-operation and the other positive forces with which one must surcharge his environment.

Many of the students of this course will want to form friendly alliances with those with whom they are associated professionally or in business, with the object of achieving success in their business or profession. In such cases the same rules of procedure which have been here described should be followed. The object of your *definite chief aim* may be one that will benefit you individually, or it may be one that will benefit the business or profession with which you are connected. The law of the "Master Mind" will work the same in either case. If you fail, either temporarily or permanently, in the application of this law *it will be for the reason that some member of your alliance did not enter into the spirit of the alliance with faith, loyalty and sincerity of purpose.*

Possessing a Definite Chief Aim

The last sentence is worthy of a second reading!

The object of your *definite chief aim* should become your "hobby." You should ride this "hobby" continuously; you should sleep with it, eat with it, play with it, work with it, live with it and THINK with it.

Whatever you want you may get if you want it with sufficient intensity, and keep on wanting it, providing the object wanted is one within reason, and you ACTUALLY BELIEVE YOU WILL GET IT! There is a difference, however, between merely "wishing" for something and ACTUALLY BELIEVING you will get it. Lack of understanding of this difference has meant failure to millions of people. The "doers" are the "believers" in all walks of life. Those who BELIEVE they can achieve the object of their *definite chief aim* do not recognize the word impossible. Neither do they acknowledge temporary defeat. They KNOW they are going to succeed, and if one plan fails they quickly replace it with another plan.

Every noteworthy achievement met with some sort of temporary setback before success came. Edison made more than ten thousand experiments before he succeeded in making the first talking machine record the words, "Mary had a little lamb."

If there is one word which should stand out in your mind in connection with this lesson, it is the word PERSISTENCE!

You now have within your possession the pass-key to achievement. You have but to unlock the door to the Temple of Knowledge and walk in. But you must go to the Temple; it will not come to you. If these laws are new to you the "going" will not be easy at first. You will stumble many times, but keep moving! Very soon you will come to the brow of the mountain you have been climbing, and you will behold, in the valleys below, the rich estate of KNOWLEDGE which shall be your reward for your faith and efforts.

Everything has a price. There is no such possibility as "something for nothing." In your experiments with the Law of the Master Mind you are jockeying with Nature, in her highest and noblest form. Nature cannot be tricked or cheated. She will give up to you the object of your struggles only after you have paid her price, which is CONTINUOUS, UNYIELDING, PERSISTENT EFFORT!

What more could be said on this subject?

You have been shown *what to do, when to do it, how to do it and why you should do it*. If you will master the next lesson, on Self-confidence, you will then have the faith in yourself to enable you to carry out the instructions laid down for your guidance in this lesson.

> *Master of human destinies am I!*
> *Fame, love, and fortune on my footsteps wait.*
> *Cities and fields I walk; I penetrate*
> *Deserts and seas remote, and passing by*
> *Hovel and mart and palace—soon or late*
> *I knock, unbidden, once at every gate!*
> *If sleeping, wake—if feasting, rise before*
> *I turn away. It is the hour of fate,*
> *And they who follow me reach every state*

Mortals desire, and conquer every foe
Save death; but those who doubt or hesitate,
Condemned to failure, penury, and woe,
Seek me in vain and uselessly implore.
I answer not, and I return no more!

—INGALLS.

II
Reciprocity and the Golden Rule

The Golden Rule,
chapter from
The Law of Success
(1928)

I have decided to place Napoleon Hill's final chapter from The Law of Success *toward the front of this book. Hill's insight on the Golden Rule deserves emphasis and renewed attention.*

When Hill adapted his teachings into the more compact Think and Grow Rich *almost ten years after* The Law of Success *he omitted his chapter on the Golden Rule. He didn't omit the ethics behind it, which are woven into the book. But, still, I regret his choice not to include a chapter on the topic. This 1928 chapter still opens a fresh window on this familiar but underestimated principle.*

Hill argues that the Golden Rule applies not only to what you do to others, but also to what you think about others.

He writes that the process of autosuggestion—which means the suggestions we make to ourselves—is set in motion based not only on what we think about ourselves but what we think about others. Hence, every thought that you accept about self or other forms a part of your essential character, whether intended or not. That makes the Golden Rule a deeper and more urgent principle than we realize.

"We have always been inescapably involved in common destiny," Hill writes. I believe deeply in that statement. Life is reciprocal. I have never personally witnessed happy endings in the lives of people whose successes or victories were attained by stepping on the skulls of others. I've known people who attained wealth or comfort unscrupulously, without attention to ethics or fair play; I have known people who won temporary victories by smearing the reputation or character of others; I have known people who made capable Monday-morning warriors but who lacked honor, dignity, and nobility. In my observation, as the years pass, such

people are almost always skittish, angry, uneasy, suspicious, and, ultimately, alone.

There exists a ledger of payback for one's behavior because, as Hill observed, we enact in ourselves the circumstances that we perceive in the world. And perception is a greater matter of choice than we acknowledge. What's more, we're incapable of recognizing a virtue in another that we do not possess in ourselves. Hence, perspective and character are one whole. You are what you see. Observe life carefully and purposefully. Do not submit to prejudice or rote thinking.

Even though I deal later with the question of procrastination and indecision (both of which express fear), I have included with this chapter Hill's "After-the-Lesson-Visit" on these topics because of their vital importance.

—MH

THE GOLDEN RULE

"YOU CAN DO IT IF YOU BELIEVE YOU CAN!"

With this lesson we approach the apex of the pyramid of this course on the Law of Success.

This lesson is the Guiding Star that will enable you to use profitably and *constructively* the knowledge assembled in the preceding lessons.

There is more power wrapped up in the preceding lessons of this course than most men could trust themselves with; therefore, this lesson is a governor that will, if observed and applied, enable you to steer your ship of knowledge over the rocks and reefs of failure that usually beset the pathway of all who come suddenly into possession of power.

For more than twenty-five years I have been observing the manner in which men behave themselves when in possession of power, and I have been forced to the conclusion that the man who attains it in any other than by the slow, step-by-step process, is constantly in danger of destroying himself and all whom he influences.

It must have become obvious to you, long before this, that this entire course leads to the attainment of *power* of proportions which may be made to perform the seemingly "impossible." Happily, it becomes apparent that this power can only be attained by the observance of many fundamental principles all of which converge in this lesson, which is based upon a law that both equals and transcends in importance every other law outlined in the preceding lessons.

Likewise, it becomes apparent to the thoughtful student that this *power* can endure only by faithful observance of the law upon which this lesson is based, wherein lies the "safety-valve" that protects the careless student from the dangers of his own follies; and protects, also, those whom he might endanger if he tried to circumvent the injunction laid down in this lesson.

To "prank" with the power that may be attained from the knowledge wrapped up in the preceding lessons of this course, without a full understanding and strict observance of the law laid down in this lesson, is the equivalent of "pranking" with a power which may destroy as well as create.

I am speaking, now, not of that which I suspect to be true, but, of that which I KNOW TO BE TRUE! The truth upon which this entire course, and this lesson in particular, is founded, is no invention of mine. I lay no claim to it except that of having observed its unvarying application in the everyday walks of life over a period of more than twenty-five years of struggle; and, of having appropriated as much of it as, in the light of my human frailties and weaknesses, I could make use of.

If you demand *positive* proof of the soundness of the laws upon which this course in general, and this lesson in particular, is founded, I must plead inability to offer it except through one witness, and that is *yourself*.

You may have *positive* proof only by testing and applying these laws for yourself.

If you demand more substantial and authoritative evidence than my own, then I am privileged to refer you to the teachings and philosophy of Christ, Plato, Socrates, Epictetus, Confucius, Emerson and two of the more modern philosophers, James and Münsterberg, from whose works I have appropriated all that constitutes the more important fundamentals of this lesson, with the exception of that which I have gathered from my own limited experience.

For more than four thousand years men have been preaching the Golden Rule as a suitable rule of conduct among men, but unfortunately the world has accepted the letter while totally missing the spirit of this Universal Injunction. We have accepted the Golden Rule philosophy merely as a sound rule of ethical conduct but we have failed to understand the law upon which it is based.

I have heard the Golden Rule quoted scores of times, but I do not recall having ever heard an explanation of the law upon which it is based, and not until recent years did I understand that law, from which I am led to believe that those who quoted it did not understand it.

The Golden Rule means, substantially, to do unto others as you would wish them to do unto you if your positions were reversed.

But why? What is the *real* reason for this kindly consideration of others?

The real reason is this:

There is an eternal law through the operation of which we reap that which we sow. When you select the rule of conduct by which you guide yourself in your transactions with others, you will be fair and just, very likely, if you know that you are setting into motion, by that selection, a *power* that will run its course for weal or woe in the lives of others, returning, finally, to help or to hinder you, according to its nature.

"Whatsoever a man soweth that shall be also reap"!

It is your privilege to deal unjustly with others, but, if you understand the law upon which the Golden Rule is based, you must know that your unjust dealings will "come home to roost."

If you fully understood the principles described in Lesson Eleven, on *accurate thought,* it will be quite easy for you to understand the law upon which the Golden Rule is based. You cannot pervert or change the course of this law, *but you can adapt yourself to its nature and thereby use it as an irresistible power that will carry you to heights of achievement which could not be attained without it said.*

This law does not stop by merely flinging back upon you your acts of injustice and unkindness toward others; it goes further than this—much further—and returns to you the results of every *thought* that you release.

Therefore, not alone is it advisable to "do unto others as you wish them to do unto you," but to avail yourself fully of the benefits of this great Universal Law you must "think of others as you wish them to think of you."

The law upon which the Golden Rule is based begins affecting you, either for good or evil, the moment you release a *thought*. It has amounted almost to a world-wide tragedy that people have not generally understood this law. Despite the simplicity of the law it is practically all there is to be learned that is of enduring value to man, for it is the medium through which we become the masters of our own destiny.

Understand this law and you understand *all* that the Bible has to unfold to you, for the Bible presents one unbroken chain of evidence in support of the fact that man is the maker of his own destiny; and, that his *thoughts* and *acts* are the tools with which he does the *making*.

During ages of less enlightenment and tolerance than that of the present, some of the greatest thinkers the world has ever produced have paid with their lives for daring to uncover this Universal Law so that it might be understood by all. In the light of the past history of the world, it is an encouraging bit of evidence, in support of the fact that men are gradually throwing off the veil of ignorance and intolerance, to note that I stand in no danger of bodily harm for writing that which would have cost me my life a few centuries ago.

While this course deals with the highest laws of the universe, which man is capable of interpreting, the aim, nevertheless, has been to show how these laws may be used in the practical affairs of life. With this object of practical application in mind, let us now proceed to analyze the effect of the Golden Rule through the following incident.

The Power of Prayer

"No," said the lawyer, "I shan't press your claim against that man; you can get someone else to take the case, or you can withdraw it; just as you please."

"Think there isn't any money in it?"

"There probably would be some little money in it, but it would come from the sale of the little house that the man occupies and calls his home! But I don't want to meddle with the matter, anyhow."

"Got frightened out of it, eh?"

"Not at all."

"I suppose likely the fellow begged hard to be let off?"

"Well, yes, he did."

"And you caved in, likely?"

"Yes."

"What in creation did you do?"

"I believe I shed a few tears."

"And the old fellow begged you hard, you say?"

"No, I didn't say so; he didn't speak a word to me."

"Well, may I respectfully inquire whom he did address in your hearing?"

"God Almighty."

"Ah, he took to praying, did he?"

"Not for my benefit, in the least. You see, I found the little house easily enough and knocked on the outer door, which stood ajar; but nobody heard me, so I stepped into the little hall and saw through the crack of a door a cozy sitting-room, and there on the bed, with her silver head high on the pillows, was an old lady who looked for all the world just like my mother did the last time I ever saw her on earth. Well, I was on the point of knocking, when she said: 'Come, father, now begin; I'm all ready.' And down on his knees by her side went an old, white-haired man, still older than his wife, I should judge, and I couldn't have knocked then, for the life of me. Well, he began. First, he reminded God they were still His submissive children, mother and he, and no matter what He saw fit to bring upon them they shouldn't rebel at His will. Of course 'twas going to be very hard for them to go out homeless in their old age, especially with poor mother so sick and helpless, and, oh! how different it all might have been if only one of the boys had been spared. Then his voice kind of broke, and a white hand stole from under the coverlet and moved softly over his snowy hair. Then he went on to repeat that nothing could be so sharp again as the parting with those three sons—unless mother and he should be separated.

"But, at last, he fell to comforting himself with the fact that the dear Lord knew that it was through no fault of his own that mother and he were threatened with the loss of their dear little home, which meant beggary and the almshouse—a place they prayed to be delivered from entering if it should be consistent with God's will. And then he quoted a multitude of promises concerning the safety of those who put their trust in the Lord. In fact, it was the most thrilling plea to which I ever listened. And at last, he prayed for God's blessing on those who were about to demand justice."

The lawyer then continued, more lowly than ever: "And I—believe—I'd rather go to the poor-house myself tonight than to stain my heart and hands with the blood of such a prosecution as that."

"Little afraid to defeat the old man's prayer, eh?"

"Bless your soul, man, you couldn't defeat it!" said the lawyer. "I tell you he left it all subject to the will of God; but he claimed that we were told to make known our desires unto God; but of all the pleadings I ever heard that beat all. You see, I was taught that kind of thing myself in my childhood. Anyway, why was I sent to bear that prayer? I am sure I don't know, but I hand the case over."

"I wish," said the client, twisting uneasily, "you hadn't told me about the old man's prayer."

"Why so?"

"Well, because I want the money the place would bring; but I was taught the Bible straight enough when I was a youngster and I'd hate to run counter to what you tell about. I wish you hadn't heard a word about it, and, another time, I wouldn't listen to petitions not intended for my ears."

The lawyer smiled.

"My dear fellow," he said, "you're wrong again. It was intended for my ears, and yours, too; and God Almighty intended it. My old mother used to sing about God's moving in a mysterious way, as I remember it."

"Well, my mother used to sing it, too," said the claimant, as he twisted the claim-papers in his fingers.

"You can call in the morning, if you like, and tell 'mother' and 'him' the claim has been met."

"In a mysterious way," added the lawyer, smiling.

Neither this lesson nor the course of which it id a part is based upon an appeal to maudlin sentiment, but there can be no escape from the truth that *success*, in its highest and noblest form, brings one, finally, to view all human relationships with a feeling of deep emotion such as that which this lawyer felt when he overheard the old man's prayer.

It may be an old-fashioned idea, but somehow I can't get away from the belief that *no man can attain success in its highest form without the aid of earnest prayer!*

Prayer is the key with which one may open the secret doorway referred to in Lesson Eleven. In this age of mundane affairs, when the uppermost thought of the majority of people id centered upon the accumulation of wealth, or the struggle for a mere existence, it is both easy and natural for us to overlook the power of earnest prayer.

I am not saying that you should resort to prayer as a means of solving your daily problems which press for immediate attention; no, I am not going that far in a course of instruction which will be studied largely by those who are seeking in it the road to *success* that is measured in dollars; but, may I not modestly suggest to *you* that you, at least, give *prayer* a trial after *everything else fails* to bring you a *satisfying success?*

Thirty men, red-eyed and disheveled, lined up before the judge of the San Francisco police court. It was the regular morning company of drunks and disorderlies. Some were old and hardened; others hung their heads in shame. Just as the momentary disorder attending the bringing in of the prisoners quieted down, a strange thing happened. A strong, clear voice from below began singing:

> *"Last night I lay a-sleeping,*
> *There came a dream so fair."*

"Last night!" It had been for them all a nightmare or a drunken stupor. The song was such a contrast to the horrible fact that no one could fail of a sudden shock at the thought the song suggested.

> *"I stood in old Jerusalem,*
> *Beside the Temple there,"*

the song went on. The judge had paused. He made a quiet inquiry. A former member of a famous opera company known all over the country was awaiting trial for forgery. It was he who was singing in his cell.

Meantime the song went on, and every man in the line showed emotion. One or two dropped on their knees; one boy at the end of the line, after a desperate effort at self-control, leaned against the wall, buried his face against his folded arms, and sobbed, "Oh, mother, mother."

The sobs, cutting to the very heart the men who heard, and the song, still welling its way through the courtroom, blended in the hush. At length one man protested. "Judge," said he, "have we got to submit to this? We're here to take our punishment, but this—" He, too, began to sob.

It was impossible to proceed with the business of the court; yet the court gave no order to stop the song. The police sergeant, after an effort to keep the men in line, stepped back and waited with the rest. The song moved on to its climax:

> *"Jerusalem, Jerusalem!*
> *Sing, for the night is o'er!*
> *Hosanna, in the highest!*
> *Hosanna, for evermore!"*

In an ecstasy of melody the last words rang out, and then there was silence. The judge looked into the faces of the men before him. There was not one who was not touched by the song; not one in whom some better impulse was not stirred. He did not call the cases singly—a kind word of advice, and he dismissed them all. No man was fined or sentenced to the work-house that morning. The song had done more good than *punishment* could possibly have accomplished.

You have read the story of a Golden Rule lawyer and a Golden Rule judge. In these two commonplace incidents of every-day life you have observed how the Golden Rule works when *applied*.

A passive attitude toward the Golden Rule will bring no results; it is not enough merely to *believe* in the philosophy, while, at the same time, failing to *apply* it in your relationships with others. If you want results you must take an *active* attitude toward the Golden Rule. A mere passive attitude, represented by belief in its soundness, will avail you nothing.

Nor will it avail you anything to proclaim to the world your belief in the Golden Rule while your actions are not in harmony with your proclamation. Conversely stated, it will avail you nothing to appear to practice the Golden Rule, while, at heart, you are willing and eager to use this universal law of right conduct as a cloak to cover up a covetous and selfish nature. Murder will out. Even the most ignorant person will "sense" you for what you are.

"Human character does evermore publish itself. It will not be concealed. It hates darkness—it rushes into light.... I heard an experienced counselor say that he never feared the effect upon a jury of a lawyer who does not believe in his heart that his client ought to have a verdict. If he does not believe it, his unbelief will appear to the jury, despite all his protestations, and will become their unbelief. This is that law whereby a work of art, of whatever kind, sets us in the same state of mind wherein the artist was when he made it. That which we do not believe we cannot *adequately say*, though we may repeat the words ever so often. It was this conviction which Swedenborg expressed when he described a group of persons in the spiritual world endeavoring in vain to articulate a proposition which they did not believe; but they could not, though they twisted and folded their lips even to indignation.

"A man passes for what he is worth. What he is engraves itself on his face, on his form, on his fortunes, in letters of light which all men may read but himself.... If you would not be known to do anything, never do it. A man may play the fool in the drifts of a desert, but every grain of sand shall seem to see."—Emerson.

It is the law upon which the Golden Rule philosophy is based to which Emerson has reference in the foregoing quotation. It was this same law that he had in mind when he wrote the following:

"Every violation of truth is not only a sort of suicide in the liar, but is a stab at the health of human society. On the most profitable lie the course of events presently lays a destructive tax; whilst frankness proves to be the best tactics, for it invites frankness, puts the parties on a convenient footing and makes their business a friendship. Trust men and they will be true to you; treat them greatly and they will show themselves great, though they make an exception in your favor to all their rules of trade."

The Golden Rule philosophy is based upon a law which no man can circumvent. This law is the same law that is described in Lesson Eleven, on Accurate Thought, through the operation of which one's thoughts are transformed into reality corresponding exactly to the nature of the thoughts.

"Once grant the creative power of our thought and there is an end of struggling for our own way, and an end of gaining it *at some one else's expense;* for, since by the terms of the hypothesis we can create what we like, the simplest way of getting what we want is, not to snatch it from somebody else, but to make it for ourselves; and, since there is no limit to thought there can be no need for straining, and for everyone to have his own way in *this manner,* would be to banish all strife, want, sickness, and sorrow from the earth."

"Now, it is precisely on this assumption of the creative power of our thought that the whole Bible rests. If not, what is the meaning of being saved by Faith? Faith is essentially thought; and, therefore, every call to have faith in God is a call to trust in the power of our own thought about God. 'According to your faith be it unto you,' says the Old Testament. The entire book is nothing but one continuous statement of the creative power of Thought.

"The Law of Man's Individuality is, therefore, the Law of Liberty, and equally it is the Gospel of peace; for when we truly understand the law of our own individuality, we see that the same law finds its expression in everyone else; and, consequently, we shall reverence *the law in others* exactly in proportion as we value it in ourselves. To do this is to follow the Golden Rule of doing to others what we would they should do unto us; and because we know that the Law of Liberty in ourselves must include the free use of our creative power, there is no longer any inducement to infringe the rights of others, for we can satisfy all our desires by the exercise of our knowledge of the law.

"As this comes to be understood, co-operation will take the place of competition, with the result of removing all ground for enmity, whether between individuals, classes, or nations. . . ."

(The foregoing quotation is from Bible Mystery and Bible Meaning by the late Judge T. Troward, published by Robert McBride & Company, New York City. Judge Troward was the author of several interesting volumes, among them The Edinburgh Lectures, which is recommended to all students of this course.)

If you wish to know what happens to a man when he totally disregards the law upon which the Golden Rule philosophy is based, pick out any man in your community whom you know to live for the single dominating purpose of accumulating wealth, and who has no conscientious scruples as to how he accumulates that wealth. Study this man and you will observe that there is no warmth to his soul; there is no kindness to his words; there is no welcome to his face. He has become a slave to the desire for wealth; he is too busy to enjoy life and too selfish to wish to help others enjoy it. He walks, and talks, and breathes, but he is nothing but a human automaton. Yet there are many who envy such a man and wish that they might occupy his position, foolishly believing him to be a *success*.

There can never be *success* without happiness, and no man can be happy without dispensing happiness to others. Moreover, the dispensation must be voluntary and with no other object in view than that of spreading sunshine into the hearts of those whose hearts are heavy-laden with burdens.

George D. Herron had in mind the law upon which the Golden Rule philosophy is based when he said:

"We have talked much of the brotherhood to come; but brotherhood has always been the fact of our life, long before it became a modern and inspired sentiment. Only we have been brothers in slavery and torment, brothers in ignorance and its perdition, brothers in disease, and war, and want, brothers in prostitution and hypocrisy. What happens to one of us sooner or later happens to all; we have always been unescapably involved in common destiny. The world constantly tends to the level of the downmost man in it; and that downmost man is the world's real ruler, hugging it close to his bosom, dragging it down to his death. You do not think so, but it is true, and it ought to be true. For if there were some way by which some of us could get free, apart from others, if there were some way by which some of us could have heaven while others had hell, if there were some way by which part of the world could escape some form of the blight and peril and misery of disinherited labor, then indeed would our world be lost and damned; but since men have never been able to separate themselves from one another's woes and wrongs, since history is fairly stricken with the lesson that we cannot escape brotherhood of some kind, since the whole of life is teaching us that we are hourly choosing between brotherhood in suffering and brotherhood in good, it remains for us to choose the brotherhood of a co-operative world, with all its fruits thereof—the fruits of *love* and *liberty*."

The world war ushered us into an age of cooperative effort in which the law of "live and let live" stands out like a shining star to guide us in our relationships with each other. This great universal call for co-operative effort is taking on many forms, not the least important of which are the Rotary Clubs, the Kiwanis Clubs, the Lions Clubs and the many other luncheon clubs which bring men together in a spirit of friendly intercourse, for these clubs mark the beginning of an age of friendly competition in business. The next step will be a closer alliance of all such clubs in an out-and-out spirit of friendly co-operation.

The attempt by Woodrow Wilson and his contemporaries to establish the League of Nations, followed by the efforts of Warren G. Harding to give footing to the same cause under the name of the World Court, marked the first attempt in the history of the world to make the Golden Rule effective as a common meeting ground for the nations of the world.

There is no escape from the fact that the world has awakened to the truth in George D. Herron's statement that "we are hourly choosing between brotherhood in suffering and brotherhood in good." The world war has taught us—nay, forced upon us—the truth that a part of the world cannot suffer without injury to the whole world. These facts are called to your attention, not in the nature of a preachment on morality, but for the purpose of directing your attention to the underlying law through which these changes are being brought about. For more than four thousand years the world has been thinking about the Golden Rule philosophy, and that *thought* is now becoming transformed into realization of the benefits that accrue to those who apply it.

Still mindful of the fact that the student of this course is interested in a material success that can be measured by bank balances, it seems appropriate to suggest here that all who will may profit by shaping their business philosophy to conform with this sweeping change toward co-operation which is taking place all over the world.

If you can grasp the significance of the tremendous change that has come over the world since the close of the world war, and if you can interpret the meaning of all the luncheon clubs and other similar gatherings which bring men and women together in a spirit of friendly co-operation, surely your imagination will suggest to you the fact that this is an opportune time to profit by adopting this spirit of friendly co-operation as the basis of your own business or professional philosophy.

Stated conversely, it must be obvious to all who make any pretense of thinking accurately, that the time is at hand when failure to adopt the Golden Rule as the foundation of one's business or professional philosophy is the equivalent of economic suicide.

Perhaps you have wondered why the subject of *honesty* has not been mentioned in this course, as a prerequisite to *success*, and, if so, the answer will be found in this lesson. The Golden Rule philosophy, when rightly understood and applied, makes dishonesty impossible. It does more than this—it makes impossible all the other destructive qualities such as selfishness, greed, envy, bigotry, hatred and malice.

When you apply the Golden Rule, you become, at one and the same time, both the judge and the judged—the accused and the accuser. This places one in a position in which *honesty* begins in one's own heart, toward one's self, and extends to all others with equal effect. *Honesty* based upon the Golden Rule is not the brand of honesty which recognizes nothing but the question of expediency.

It is no credit to be honest, when honesty is obviously the most *profitable* policy, lest one lose a good customer or a valuable client or be sent to jail for trickery. But when honesty means either a temporary or a permanent material loss, then it becomes an *honor* of the highest degree to all who practice it. Such honesty has its appropriate reward in the accumulated power of character and reputation enjoyed, by all who deserve it.

Those who understand and apply the Golden Rule philosophy are always scrupulously honest, not alone out of their desire to be just with others, but because: of their desire to be just with themselves. They understand the eternal law upon which the Golden Rule is based, and they know that through the operation of this law *every thought they release and every act in which they indulge has its counterpart in some fact or circumstance with which they will later be confronted.*

Golden Rule philosophers are honest because they understand the truth that honesty adds to their own character that "vital something" which gives it life and power. Those who understand the law through which the Golden Rule operates would poison their own drinking water as quickly as they would indulge in acts of injustice to others, for they know that such injustice starts a chain of causation that will not only bring them physical suffering, but will destroy their characters, stain for ill their reputations and render impossible the attainment of enduring success.

The law through which the Golden Rule philosophy operates is none other than the law through which the principle of Auto-suggestion operates. This statement gives you a suggestion from which you should be able to make a deduction of a far-reaching nature and of inestimable value.

Test your progress in the mastery of this course by analyzing the foregoing statement and determining, before you read on, what suggestion it offers you.

Of what possible benefit could it be to you to know that when you do unto others as if you were the others, which is the sum and substance of the Golden Rule, you are putting into motion a chain of causation through the aid of a law which affects the others according to the nature of your act, *and at the same time planting in your character, through your subconscious mind, the effects of that act?*

This question practically suggests its own answer, but as I am determined to cause you to think this vital subject out for yourself I will put the question in still another form, viz.:

If all your acts toward others, and even your thoughts of others, are registered in your subconscious mind, through the principle of Auto-suggestion, thereby building your own character in exact duplicate of your *thoughts* and *acts*, can you not see how important it is to guard those acts and thoughts?

We are now in the very heart of the real reason for doing unto others as we would have them do unto us, for it is obvious that whatever we do unto others we do unto ourselves.

Stated in another way, every *act* and every *thought* you release modifies your own character in exact conformity with the nature of the act or thought, and your character is a sort of center of magnetic attraction which attracts to you the people and conditions that harmonize with it.

You cannot indulge in an act toward another person without having first created the nature of that act in your own *thought, and you cannot release a thought without planting the sum and substance and nature of it in your own sub-conscious mind, there to become a part and parcel of your own character.*

Grasp this simple principle and you will understand why you cannot afford to hate or envy another person. You will also understand why you cannot afford to strike back, in kind, at those who do you an injustice. Likewise, you will understand the injunction, "Return good for evil."

Understand the law upon which the Golden Rule injunction is based and you will understand, also, the law that eternally binds all mankind in a single bond of fellowship and renders it impossible for you to injure another person, by *thought* or *deed*, without injuring yourself; and, likewise, adds to your own character the results of every kind *thought* and *deed* in which you indulge.

Understand this law and you will then know, beyond room for the slightest doubt, that you are constantly punishing yourself for every wrong you commit and rewarding yourself for every act of constructive conduct in which you indulge.

It seems almost an act of Providence that the greatest wrong and the most severe injustice ever done me by one of my fellow men was done just as I began this lesson. (Some of the students of this course will know what it is to which I refer.)

This injustice has worked a temporary hardship on me, but that is of little consequence compared to the advantage it has given me by providing a timely opportunity for me to test the soundness of the entire premise upon which this lesson is founded.

The injustice to which I refer left two courses of action open to me. I could have claimed relief by "striking back" at my antagonist, through both civil court action and criminal libel proceedings, or I could have stood upon my right to forgive him. One course of action would have brought me a substantial sum—of money and whatever joy and satisfaction there may be in defeating and *punishing* an enemy. The other course of action would have brought me self-respect which is enjoyed by those who have successfully met the test and discovered that they have evolved to the point at which they can repeat the Lord's Prayer and *mean it!*

I chose the latter course. I did so, despite the recommendations of close personal friends to "strike back," and despite the offer of a prominent lawyer to do my "striking" for me *without cost.*

But the lawyer offered to do the impossible, for the reason that no man can "strike back" at another *without cost*. Not always is the cost of a monetary nature, for there are other things with which one may pay that are dearer than money.

It would be as hopeless to try to make one who was not familiar with the law upon which the Golden Rule is based understand why I refused to strike back at this enemy as it would to try to describe the law of gravitation to an ape. If you understand this law you understand, also, why I chose to *forgive* my enemy.

In the Lord's Prayer we are admonished to forgive our enemies, but that admonition will fall on deaf ears except where the listener understands the law upon which it is based. That law is none other than the law upon which the Golden

Rule is based. It is the law that forms the foundation of this entire lesson, and through which we must inevitably reap that which we sow. There is no escape from the operation of this law, nor is there any cause to try to avoid its consequences if we refrain from putting into motion *thoughts* and *acts* that are destructive.

That we may more concretely describe the law upon which this lesson is based, let us embody the law in a code of ethics such as one who wishes to follow literally the injunction of the Golden Rule might appropriately adopt, as follows.

My Code of Ethics

I. I believe in the Golden Rule as the basis of all human conduct; therefore, I will never do to another person that which I would not be willing for that person to do to me if our positions were reversed.

II. I will be honest, even to the slightest detail, in all my transactions with others, not alone because of my desire to be fair with them, but because of my desire to impress the idea of honesty on my own subconscious mind, thereby weaving this essential quality into my own character.

III. I will forgive those who are unjust toward me, with no thought as to whether they deserve it or not, because I understand the law through which forgiveness of others strengthens my own character and wipes out the effects of my own transgressions, in my subconscious mind.

IV. I will be just, generous and fair with others always, even though I know that these acts will go unnoticed and unrecorded, in the ordinary terms of reward, because I understand and intend to apply the law through the aid of which one's own character is but the sum total of one's own *acts* and *deeds*.

V. Whatever time I may have to devote to the discovery and exposure of the weaknesses and faults of others I will devote, more profitably, to the discovery and *correction* of my own.

VI. I will slander no person, no matter how much I may believe another person may deserve it, because I wish to plant no destructive suggestions in my own subconscious mind.

VII. I recognize the power of Thought as being an inlet leading into my brain from the universal ocean of life; therefore, I will set no destructive thoughts afloat upon that ocean lest they pollute the minds of others.

VIII. I will conquer the common human tendency toward hatred, and envy, and selfishness, and jealousy, and malice, and pessimism, and doubt, and fear; for I believe these to be the seed from which the world harvests most of its troubles.

IX. When my mind is not occupied with thoughts that tend toward the attainment of my *definite chief aim* in life, I will voluntarily keep it filled with thoughts of courage, and self-confidence, and goodwill toward others, and faith, and kindness, and loyalty, and love for truth, and justice, for I believe these to be the seed from which the world reaps its harvest of progressive growth.

X. I understand that a mere passive belief in the soundness of the Golden Rule philosophy is of no value whatsoever, either to myself or to others; therefore, I will *actively* put into operation this universal rule for good in all my transactions with others.

XI. I understand the law through the operation of which my own character is developed from my own *acts* and *thoughts*; therefore, I will guard with care all that goes into its development.

XII. Realizing that enduring happiness comes only through helping others find it; that no act of kindness is without its reward, even though it may never be directly repaid, I will do my best to assist others when and where the opportunity appears.

You have noticed frequent reference to Emerson throughout this course. Every student of the course should own a copy of Emerson's Essays, and the essay on Compensation should be read and studied at least every three months. Observe, as you read this essay, that it deals with the same law as that upon which the Golden Rule is based.

There are people who believe that the Golden Rule philosophy is nothing more than a theory, and that it is in no way connected with an immutable law. They have arrived at this conclusion because of personal experience wherein they rendered service to others without enjoying the benefits of direct reciprocation.

How many are there who have not rendered service to others that was neither reciprocated nor appreciated? I am sure that I have had such an experience, not once, but many times, and I am equally sure that I will have similar experiences in the future, nor will I discontinue rendering service to others merely because *they* neither reciprocate nor appreciate my efforts.

And here is the reason:

When I render service to another, or indulge in an act of kindness, I store away in my sub-conscious mind the effect of my efforts, which may be likened to the "charging" of an electric battery. By and by, if I indulge in a sufficient number of such acts I will have developed a positive, dynamic character that will *attract* to me people who harmonize with or resemble my own character.

Those whom I *attract* to me will reciprocate the acts of kindness and the service that I have rendered others, thus the Law of Compensation will have balanced the scales of justice for me, bringing back from one source the results of service that I rendered through an entirely different source.

You have often heard it said that a salesman's first sale should be to himself, which means that unless he first convinces himself of the merits of his wares he will not be able to convince others. Here, again, enters this same Law of Attraction, for it is a well known fact that *enthusiasm* is contagious, and when a salesman shows great *enthusiasm* over his wares he will arouse a corresponding interest in the minds of others.

You can comprehend this law quite easily by regarding yourself as a sort of human magnet that attracts those whose characters harmonize with your own. In thus regarding yourself as a magnet that attracts to you all who harmonize with your dominating characteristics and repels all who do not so harmonize, you should keep in mind, also, the fact that *you are the builder of that magnet;* also, that you may change its nature so that it will correspond to any ideal that you may wish to set up and follow.

And, most important of all, you should keep in mind the fact that this entire process of change takes place through *thought!*

Your character is but the sum total of your *thoughts* and *deeds!* This truth has been stated in many different ways throughout this course.

Because of this great truth it is impossible for you to render any useful service or indulge in any act of kindness toward others without benefiting thereby. Moreover, it is just as impossible for you to indulge in any destructive *act* or *thought* without paying the penalty in the loss of a corresponding amount of your own power.

Positive thought develops a dynamic personality. *Negative thought* develops a personality of an opposite nature. In many of the preceding lessons of this course, and in this one, definite instructions are given: as to the exact method of developing personality through *positive thought*. These instructions are particularly detailed in Lesson Three, on *Self-confidence*. In that lesson you have a very definite formula to follow. All of the formulas provided in this course are for the purpose of helping you *consciously* to direct the power of *thought* in the development of a personality that will attract to you those who will be of help in the attainment of your *definite chief aim*.

You need no proof that your hostile or unkind *acts* toward others bring back the effects of retaliation. Moreover, this retaliation is usually definite and immediate. Likewise, you need no proof that you can accomplish more by dealing with others in such a way that they will want to co-operate with you. If you mastered the eighth lesson, on Self-control, you now understand how to induce others to act toward you as you wish them to act—*through your own attitude toward them*.

The law of "an eye for an eye and a tooth for a tooth" is based upon the selfsame law as that upon which the Golden Rule operates. This is nothing more than the law of retaliation with which all of us are familiar. Even the most selfish person will respond to this law, *because he cannot help it!* If I speak ill of you, even though I tell the truth, you will not think kindly of me. Furthermore, you will most likely retaliate in kind. But, if I speak of your virtues you will think kindly of me, and when the opportunity appears you will reciprocate in kind in the majority of instances.

Through the operation of this law of attraction the uninformed are constantly attracting trouble and grief and hatred and opposition from others by their *unguarded words* and *destructive acts*.

Do unto others as you would have them do unto you!

We have heard that injunction expressed thousands of times, yet how many of us understand the law upon which it is based? To make this injunction somewhat clearer it might be well to state it more in detail, about as follows:

Do unto others as you would have them do unto you, *bearing in mind the fact that human nature has a tendency to retaliate in kind.*

Confucius must have had in mind the law of retaliation when he stated the Golden Rule philosophy in about this way:

Do not unto others that which you would not have them do unto you.

And he might well have added an explanation to the effect that the reason for his injunction was based upon the common tendency of man to retaliate in kind.

Those who do not understand the law upon which the Golden Rule is based are inclined to argue that it will not work, for the reason that men are inclined toward the principle of exacting "an eye for an eye and a tooth for a tooth," which is nothing more nor less than the law of retaliation. If they would go a step further in their reasoning they would understand that they are looking at the *negative* effects of this law, and that the selfsame law is capable of producing *positive* effects as well.

In other words, if you would not have your own eye plucked out, then insure against this misfortune by refraining from plucking out the other fellow's eye. Go a step further and render the other fellow an act of kindly, helpful service, and *through the operation of this same law of retaliation* he will render you a similar service.

And, if he should fail to reciprocate your kindness—what then?

You have profited, nevertheless, because of the effect of your act on *your own subconscious mind!*

Thus by indulging in acts of kindness and applying, always, the Golden Rule philosophy, you are sure of benefit from one source and at the same time you have a pretty fair chance of profiting from another source.

It might happen that you would base all of your acts toward others on the Golden Rule without enjoying any direct reciprocation for a long period of time, and it might so happen that those to whom you rendered those acts of kindness would never reciprocate, but meantime you have been adding vitality to your own character and sooner or later this *positive character* which you have been building will begin to assert itself and you will discover that you have been receiving compound interest on compound interest in return for those acts of kindness which appeared to have been wasted on those who neither appreciated nor reciprocated them.

Remember that your *reputation* is made by others, but your *character* is made by *you!*

You want your reputation to be a favorable one, but you cannot be sure that it will be for the reason that it is something that exists outside of your own control, in the minds of others. It is what others believe you to be. With your character it is different. Your character is that which *you are,* as the results of your *thoughts* and *deeds.* You control it. You can make it weak, good or bad. When you are satisfied and know in your mind that your character is above reproach you need not worry about your reputation, for it is as impossible for your character to be destroyed or damaged by anyone except yourself as it is to destroy matter or energy.

It was this truth that Emerson had in mind when he said: "A political victory, a rise of rents, the recovery of your sick or the return of your absent friend, or some other quite external event raises your spirits, and you think your days are prepared for you. *Do not believe it.* It can never be so. *Nothing can bring you peace but yourself. Nothing can bring you peace but the triumph of principles.*"

One reason for being just toward others is the fact that such action may cause them to reciprocate, in kind, but a better reason is the fact that kindness and justice toward others develop *positive character* in all who indulge in these acts.

You may withhold from me the reward to which I am entitled for rendering you helpful service, but no one can deprive me of the benefit I will derive from the rendering of that service in so far as it adds to my own *character*.

We are living in a great industrial age. Everywhere we see the evolutionary forces working great changes in the method and manner of living, and re-arranging the relationships between men, in the ordinary pursuit of life, liberty and a living.

This is an age of organized effort. On every hand we see evidence that organization is the basis of all financial success, and while other factors than that of organization enter into the attainment of success, this factor is still one of major importance.

This industrial age has created two comparatively new terms. One is called "capital" and the other "labor." Capital and labor constitute the main wheels in the machinery of organized effort. These two great forces enjoy success in exact ratio to the extent that both understand and apply the Golden Rule philosophy. Despite this fact, however, harmony between these two forces does not always prevail, thanks to the destroyers of confidence who make a living by sowing the seed of dissension and stirring up strife between employers and employees.

During the past fifteen years I have devoted considerable time to the study of the causes of disagreement between employers and employees. Also, I have gathered much information on this subject from other men who, likewise, have been studying this problem.

There is but one solution which will, if understood by all concerned, bring harmony out of chaos and establish a perfect working relationship between capital and labor. The remedy is no invention of mine. It is based upon a great universal law of Nature. This remedy bas been well stated by one of the great men of this generation, in the following words:

"The question we propose to consider is exciting deep interest at the present time, but no more than its importance demands. It is one of the hopeful signs of the times that these subjects of vital interest to human happiness are constantly coming up for a bearing, are engaging the attention of the wisest men, and stirring the minds of all classes of people. The wide prevalence of this movement shows that a new life is beating in the heart of humanity, operating upon their faculties like the warm breath of spring upon the frozen ground and the dormant germs of the plant. It will make a great stir, it will break up many frozen and dead forms, it will produce great and, in some cases, it may be, destructive changes, but it announces the blossoming of new hopes, and the coming of new harvests for the supply of human wants and the means of greater happiness. There is great need of wisdom to guide the new forces coming into action. Every man is under the most solemn obligation to do his part in forming a correct public opinion and giving wise direction to popular will.

"The only solution for the problems of labor, of want, of abundance, of suffering and sorrow can only be found by regarding them from a moral and spiritual point of view. They must be seen end examined in a light that is not of themselves. *The true relations of labor and capital can never be discovered by human selfishness.* They must be viewed from a higher purpose than wages or the accumulation of wealth. They must be regarded from their bearing upon the purposes for which men was created. It is from this point of view I propose to consider the subject before us.

"Capital end labor are essential to each other. Their interests are so bound together that they cannot be separated. In civilized and enlightened communities they are mutually dependent. If there is any difference, capital is more dependent upon labor than labor upon capital. Life can be sustained without capital. Animals, with a few exceptions, have no property, and take no anxious thought for the morrow, and our Lord commends them to our notice as examples worthy of imitation. 'Behold the fowls of the air,' He says, 'for they sow not, neither do they reap nor gather into barns, yet your heavenly Father feedeth them.' The savages live without capital. Indeed, the great mass of human beings live by their labor from day to day, from hand to mouth. But no man can live upon his wealth. He cannot eat his gold and silver; he cannot clothe himself with deeds and certificates of stock. Capital can do nothing without labor, *and its only value consists in its power to purchase labor or its results.* It is itself the product of labor. It has no occasion, therefore, to assume en importance that does not belong to it. Absolutely dependent, however, as it is upon labor for its value, it is en essential factor inhuman progress.

"The moment man begins to rise from a savage and comparatively independent state to a civilized and dependent one, capital becomes necessary. Men come into more intimate relations with one another. Instead of each one doing everything, men begin to devote themselves to special employments, and to depend upon others to provide many things for them while they engage in some special occupation. In this way labor becomes diversified. One man works in iron, another in wood; one manufactures cloth, another makes it into garments; some raise food to feed those who build houses and manufacture implements of husbandry. This necessitates a system of exchanges, and to facilitate exchanges roads must be made, and men must be employed to make them. As population increases and necessities multiply, the business of exchange becomes enlarged, until we have immense manufactories, railroads girding the earth with iron bends, steamships plowing every sea, and a multitude of men who cannot raise bread or make a garment, or do anything directly for the supply of their own wants.

"Now, we can see how we become more dependent upon others as our wants are multiplied and civilization advances.

Each one works in his special employment, does better work, because he can devote his whole thought and time to a form of use for which he is specially fitted, and contributes more largely to the public good. While he is working for others, all others are working for him. Every member of the community is working for the whole body, and the whole body for every member. This is the law of perfect life, a law which rules everywhere in the material body. Every man who is engaged in any employment useful to body or mind is a philanthropist, a public benefactor, whether he raises corn on the prairie, cotton in Texas or India, mines coal in the chambers of the earth, or feeds it to engines in the hold of a steamship. If selfishness did not pervert and blast human motives, all men and women would be fulfilling the law of charity while engaged in their daily employment.

"To carry on this vast system of exchanges, to place the forest and the farm, the factory and the mine side by side, and deliver the products of all climes at every door, requires immense capital. One man cannot work his farm or factory, and build a railroad or a line of steamships. As raindrops acting singly cannot drive a mill or supply steam for an engine, but, collected in a vast reservoir, become the resistless power of Niagara, or the force which drives the engine and steamship like mighty shuttles from mountain to seacoast and from shore to shore, so a few dollars in a multitude of pockets are powerless to provide the means for these vast operations, but combined they move the world.

"Capital is a friend of labor and essential to its economical exercise and just reward. It can be, and often is, a terrible enemy, when employed for selfish purposes alone; but the great mass of it is more friendly to human happiness than is generally supposed. It cannot be employed without in some way, either directly or indirectly, helping the laborer. We think of the evils we suffer, but allow the good we enjoy to pass unnoticed. We think of the evils that larger means would relieve and the comforts they would provide, but overlook the blessings we enjoy that would have been impossible without large accumulations of capital. It is the part of wisdom to form a just estimate of the good we receive as well as the evils we suffer.

"It is a common saying at the present time, that the rich are growing richer and the poor poorer; but when all man's possessions are taken into the account there are good reasons for doubting this assertion. It is true that the rich are growing richer. It is also true that the condition of the laborer is constantly improving. *The common laborer has conveniences and comforts which princes could not command a century ago.* He is better clothed, has a greater variety and abundance of food, lives in a more comfortable dwelling, and has many more conveniences for the conduct of domestic affairs and the prosecution of labor than money could purchase but a few years ago. An emperor could not travel with the ease, the comfort, and the swiftness that the common laborer can today. He may think that he stands alone, with no one to help. But, in truth, he has an immense retinue of servants constantly waiting upon him, ready and anxious to do his bidding. It requires a vast army of men and an immense outlay of capital to provide a common dinner, such as every man and woman, with few exceptions, has enjoyed today.

"Think of the vast combination of means and men and forces necessary to provide even a frugal meal. The Chinaman raises your tea, the Brazilian your coffee, the East Indian your spices, the Cuban your sugar, the farmer upon the western prairies your bread and possibly your beef, the gardener your vegetables, the dairyman your butter and milk; the miner has dug from the hills the coal with which your food was cooked and your house was warmed, the cabinet-maker has provided you with chairs and tables, the cutler with knives and forks, the potter with dishes, the Irishman has made your table-cloth, the butcher has dressed your meat, the miller your flour.

"But these various articles of food, and the means of preparing and serving them, were produced at immense distances from you and from one another. Oceans had to be traversed, hills leveled, valleys filled, and mountains tunneled, ships must be built, railways constructed, and a vast army of men instructed and employed in every mechanical art before the materials for your dinner could be prepared and served. There must also be men to collect these materials, to buy and sell and distribute them. Everyone stands in his own place and does his own work, and receives his wages. But he is none the less working for you, and serving you as truly and effectively as he would be if he were in your special employment and received his wages from your hand. In the light of these facts, which everyone must acknowledge, we may be able to see more clearly the truth, that every man and woman who does useful work is a public benefactor, and the thought of it and the purpose of it will ennoble the labor and the laborer. We are all bound together by common ties. The rich and the poor, the learned and the ignorant, the strong and the weak, are woven together in one social and civic web. Harm to one is harm to all; help to one is help to all.

"You see what a vast army of servants it requires to provide your dinner. Do you not see that it demands a corresponding amount of capital to provide and keep this complicated machinery in motion? And do you not see that every man, woman and child is enjoying the benefit of it? How could we get our coal, our meat, our flour, our tea and coffee, sugar and rice? The laborer cannot build ships and sail them and support himself while doing it. *The farmer cannot leave his farm and take his produce to the market. The miner cannot mine and transport his coal.* The farmer in Kansas may be burning corn today to cook his food and warm his dwelling, and the miner may be hungry for the bread which the corn would supply, because they cannot exchange the fruits of their labor. Every acre of land, every forest and mine has been increased in value by railways and steamboats, and the comforts of life and the means of social and intellectual culture have been carried to the most inaccessible places.

"But the benefits of capital are not limited to supplying present wants and comforts. It opens new avenues for labor. It diversifies it and gives a wider field to everyone to do the kind of work for which he is best fitted by natural taste and genius. The number of employments created by railways, steamships, telegraph, and manufactories by machinery can hardly be estimated. Capital is also largely invested in supplying the means of intellectual and spiritual culture.

Books are multiplied at constantly diminishing prices, and the best thought of the world, by means of our great publishing houses, is made accessible to the humblest workman. There is no better example of the benefits the common laborer derives from capital than the daily newspaper. For two or three cents the history of the world for twenty-four hours is brought to every door. The laborer, while riding to or from his work in a comfortable car, can visit all parts of the known world and get a truer idea of the events of the day than he could if he were bodily present. A battle in China or Africa, an earthquake in Spain, a dynamite explosion in London, a debate in Congress, the movements of men in public and private life for the suppression of vice, for enlightening the ignorant, helping the needy, and improving the people generally, are spread before him in a small compass, and bring him into contact and on equality, in regard to the world's history, with kings and queens, with saints and sages, and people in every condition in life. *Do you ever think,* while reading the morning paper, how many men have been running on your errands, collecting intelligence for you from all parts of the earth, and putting it into a form convenient for your use? It required the investment of millions of money and the employment of thousands of men to produce that paper and leave it at your door. And what did all this service cost you? A few cents.

"These are examples of the benefits which everyone derives from capital, benefits which could not be obtained without vast expenditures of money; benefits which come to us without our care and lay their blessings at our feet. Capital cannot be invested in any useful production without blessing a multitude of people. It sets the machinery of life in motion, it multiplies employment; it places the product of all climes at every door, it draws the people of all nations together; brings mind in contact with mind, and gives to every man and woman a large and valuable share of the product. These are facts which it would be well for everyone, however poor he may be, to consider.

"If capital is such a blessing to labor; if it can only be brought into use by labor, and derives all its value from it, how can there be any conflict between them? There could be none if both the capitalist and laborer acted from humane and Christian principles. But they do not. They are governed by inhuman and unchristian principles. Each party seeks to get the largest returns for the least service. Capital desires larger profits, labor higher wages. The interests of the capitalist and the laborer come into direct collision. In this warfare capital has great advantages, and has been prompt to take them. It has demanded and taken the lion's share of the profits. It has despised the servant that enriched it. It has regarded the laborer as a menial, a slave, whose rights and happiness it was not bound to respect. It influences legislators to enact laws in its favor, subsidizes governments and wields its power for its own advantage. Capital has been a lord and labor a servant. While the servant remained docile and obedient, content with such compensation as its lord chose to give, there was no conflict. But labor is rising from a servile, submissive, and hopeless condition. It has acquired strength and intelligence; has gained the idea that it has rights that has rights that ought to be respected, and begins to assert and combine to support them.

"Each party in this warfare regards the subject from its own selfish interests. The capitalist supposes that gain to labor is loss to him, and that he must look to his own interests first; that the cheaper the labor the larger his gains. Consequently it is for his interest to keep the price as low as possible. On the contrary, the laborer thinks that he loses what the capitalist gains, and, consequently, that it is for his interest to get as large wages as possible. From these opposite points of view their interests appear to be directly hostile. What one party gains the other loses; hence the conflict. Both are acting from selfish motives, and, consequently, must be wrong. Both parties see only half of the truth, and, mistaking that for the whole of it, they fall into a mistake ruinous to both. Each one stands on his own ground, and regards the subject wholly from his point of view and in the misleading light of his own selfishness. Passion inflames the mind and blinds the understanding; and when passion is aroused men will sacrifice their own interests to injure others, and both will suffer loss. They will wage continual warfare against each other; they will resort to all devices, and take advantage of every necessity to win a victory. Capital tries to starve the laborer into submission, like a beleaguered city; and hunger and want are most powerful weapons. Labor sullenly resists, and tries to destroy the value of capital by rendering it unproductive. If necessity or interest compels a truce, it is a sullen one, and maintained with the purpose of renewing hostilities as soon as there is any prospect of success. Thus laborers and capitalists confront each other like two armed hosts, ready at any time to renew the conflict. *It will be renewed, without doubt, and continued with varying success until both parties discover that they are mistaken, that their interests are mutual, and can only be secured to the fullest extent by co-operation and giving to each the reward it deserves.* The capitalist and the laborer must clasp hands across the bottomless pit into which so much wealth and work has been cast.

"How this reconciliation is to be effected is a question that is occupying the minds of many wise and good men on both sides at the present time. Wise and impartial legislation will, no doubt, be an important agent in restraining blind passion and protecting all classes from insatiable greed; and it is the duty of every man to use his best endeavors to secure such legislation both in state and national governments. Organizations of laborers for protecting their own rights and securing a better reward for their labor, will have a great influence. That influence will continue to increase as their temper becomes normal and firm, and their demands are based *on justice and humanity.* Violence and threats will effect no good. Dynamite, whether in the form of explosives or the more destructive force of fierce and reckless passion, will heal no wounds nor subdue any hostile feeling. Arbitration is, doubtless, the wisest and most practicable means now available to bring about amicable relations between these hostile parties and secure justice to both. Giving the laborer a share in the profits of the business has worked well in some cases, but it is attended with great practical difficulties which require more wisdom, self-control and genuine regard for the common interests of both parties than often can be found. Many devices may have a partial and temporary effect. But no permanent progress can be made in settling this conflict without restraining and finally removing its cause.

"Its real central cause is an inordinate love of self and the world, and that cause will continue to operate as long as it exists. It may be restrained and moderated, but it will assert itself when occasion offers. Every wise man must, therefore, seek to remove the cause, and as far as he can do it he will control effects. Purify the fountain, and you make the whole stream pure and wholesome.

"There is a principle of universal influence that must underlie and guide every successful effort to bring these two great factors of human good which now confront each other with hostile purpose, into harmony. It is no invention or discovery of mine. It embodies a higher than human wisdom. It is not difficult to understand or apply. The child can comprehend it and act according to it. It is universal in its application, and wholly useful in its effects. It will lighten the burdens of labor and increase its rewards. It will give security to capital and make it more productive. It is simply the Golden Rule, embodied in these words: *'Therefore all things whatsoever ye would that men should do to you, do ye even so to them: for this is the law and the prophets.'*

"Before proceeding to apply this principle to the case in hand, let me call your special attention to it. It is a very remarkable law of human life which seems to have been generally overlooked by statesmen, philosophers and religious teachers. This rule embodies the whole of religion; it comprises all the precepts, commandments, and means of the future triumphs of good over evil, of truth over error, and the peace and happiness of men, foretold in the glorious visions of the prophets. Mark the words. It does not merely say that it is a wise rule; that it accords with the principles of the Divine order revealed in the law and the prophets. *It embodies them all; it 'IS the law and the prophets.'* It comprises love to God. It says we should regard Him as we desire to have Him regard us; that we should do to Him as we wish to have Him do to us. If we desire to have Him love us with all His heart, with all His soul, with all His mind, and with all His strength, we must love Him in the same manner. If we desire to have our neighbor love us as he loves himself, we must love him as we love ourself. Here, then, is the universal and Divine law of human service and fellowship. It is not a precept of human wisdom; it bas its origin in the Divine nature, and its embodiment in human nature. Now, let us apply it to the conflict between labor and capital.

"You are a capitalist. Your money is invested in manufactures, in land, in mines, in merchandise, railways, and ships, or you loan it to others on interest. You employ, directly or indirectly, men to use your capital. You cannot come to a just conclusion concerning your rights and duties and privileges by looking wholly at your own gains. The glitter of the silver and gold will exercise so potent a spell over your mind that it will blind you to everything else. You can see no interest but your own. The laborer is not known or regarded as a man who has any interests you are bound to regard. You see him only as your slave, your tool, your means of adding to your wealth. In this light he is a friend so far as he serves you, an enemy so far as he does not. But change your point of view. Put yourself in his place; put him in your place. How would you like to have him treat you if you were in his place? Perhaps you have been there. In all probability you have, for the capitalist today was the laborer yesterday, and the laborer today will be the employer tomorrow. You know from lively and painful experience how you would like to be treated. Would you like to be regarded as a mere tool? As a means of enriching another? Would you like to have your wages kept down to the bare necessities of life? Would you like to be regarded with indifference and treated with brutality? Would you like to have your blood, your strength, your soul coined into dollars for the benefit of another? These questions are easy to answer. Everyone knows that he would rejoice to be treated kindly, to have his interests regarded, his rights recognized and protected. Everyone knows that such regard awakens a response in his own heart. Kindness begets kindness; respect awakens respect. Put yourself in his place. Imagine that you are dealing with yourself, and you will have no difficulty in deciding whether you should give the screw another turn, that you may wring a penny more from the muscles of the worker, or relax its pressure, and, if possible, add something to his wages, and give him respect for his service. Do to him as you would have him do to you in changed conditions.

"You are a laborer. You receive a certain sum for a day's work. Put yourself in the place of your employer. How would you like to have the men you employed work for you? Would you think it right that they should regard you as their enemy? Would you think it honest in them to slight their work, *to do as little and to get as much as possible?* If you had a large contract which must be completed at a fixed time or you would suffer great loss, would you like to have your workmen take advantage of your necessity to compel an increase of their wages? Would you think it right and wise in them to interfere with you in the management of your business? To dictate whom you should employ, and on what terms you should employ them? Would you not rather have them do honest work in a kind and good spirit? Would you not be much more disposed to look to their interests, to lighten their labor, to increase their wages when you could afford to do so, and look after the welfare of their families, when you found that they regarded yours? I know that it would be so. It is true that men are selfish, and that some men are so mean and contracted in spirit that they cannot see any interest but their own; whose hearts, not made of flesh but of silver and gold, are so hard that they are not touched by any human feeling, and care not how much others suffer if they can make a cent by it. But they are the exception, not the rule. We are influenced by the regard and devotion of others to our interests. The laborer who knows that his employer feels kindly toward him, desires to treat him justly and to regard his good, will do better work and more of it, and will be disposed to look to his employer's interests as well as his own.

"I am well aware that many will think this Divine and humane law of doing to others as we would have them do to us, is impracticable in this selfish and worldly age. If both parties would be governed by it, everyone can see how happy would be the results. But, it will be said, they will not. The laborer will not work unless compelled by want. He will take advantage of every necessity. As soon as he gains a little independence of his employer he becomes proud, arrogant and hostile. The employer will seize upon every means to keep the workmen dependent upon him, and to make as much out of them as possible. Every inch of ground which labor yields capital will occupy and entrench itself in it, and from its vantage bring the laborer into greater dependence and more abject submission. But this is a mistake. The history of the world testifies that when the minds of men are not embittered by intense hostility and their feelings outraged by cruel wrongs, they are ready to listen to calm, disinterested and judicious counsel. A man who employed a large number of laborers in mining coal told me that he had never known an instance to fail of a calm and candid response when he had appealed to honorable motives, as a man to man, both of whom acknowledged a common humanity. There is a recent and most notable instance in this city of the happy effect of calm, disinterested and judicious counsel in settling difficulties between employers and workmen that were disastrous to both.

"When the mind is inflamed by passion men will not listen to reason. They become blind to their own interests and regardless of the interests of others. *Difficulties are never settled while passion rages. They are never settled by conflict. One party maybe subdued by power; but the sense of wrong will remain; the fire of passion will slumber ready to break out again on the first occasion.* But let the laborer or the capitalist feel assured that the other party has no wish to take any advantage, that there is a sincere desire and determination on both sides to be just and pay due regard to their common interests, and all the conflict between them would cease, as the wild waves of the ocean sink to calm when the winds are at rest. The laborer and the capitalist have a mutual and common interest. Neither can permanently prosper without the prosperity of the other. They are parts of one body. If labor is the arm, capital is the blood. Devitalize or waste the blood, and the arm loses its power. Destroy the arm, and the blood is useless. Let each care for the other, and both are benefited. *Let each take the Golden Rule as a guide,* and all cause of hostility will be removed, all conflict will cease, and they will go hand in hand to do their work and reap their just reward."

If you have mastered the fundamentals upon which this lesson is based, you understand why it is that no public speaker can move his audience or convince men of his argument unless he, himself, believes that which he is saying.

You also understand why no salesman can convince his prospective purchaser unless he has first convinced himself of the merits of his goods.

Throughout this entire course one particular principle has been emphasized for the purpose of illustrating the truth that every personality is the sum total of the individual's *thoughts* and *acts*—that we come to resemble the nature of our dominating *thoughts*.

Thought is the only power that can systematically organize, accumulate and assemble facts and materials according

Reciprocity and the Golden Rule

to a definite plan. A flowing river can assemble dirt and build land, and a storm can gather and assemble sticks into a shapeless mass of debris, but neither storms nor river can *think*; therefore, the materials which they assemble are not assembled in organized, definite form.

Man, alone, has the power to transform his *thoughts* into physical reality; man, alone, can dream and make his dreams come true.

Man has the power to create ideals and rise to their attainment.

How did it happen that man is the only creature on earth that knows how to use the power of *thought?* It "happened" because man is the apex of the pyramid of evolution, the product of millions of years of struggle during which man has risen above the other creatures of the earth *as the result of his own thoughts and their effects upon himself.*

Just when, where and how the first rays of *thought* began to flow into man's brain no one knows, but we all know that thought is the power which distinguishes man from all other creatures; likewise, we all know that *thought* is the power that has enabled man to lift himself above all other creatures.

No one knows the limitations of the power of *thought,* or whether or not it has any limitations. Whatever man *believes* he can do he eventually does. But a few generations back the more imaginative writers dared to write of the "horseless carriage," and lo! it became a reality and is now a common vehicle. Through the evolutionary power of *thought* the hopes and ambitious of one generation become a reality in the next.

The power of *thought* has been given the dominating position throughout this course, for the reason that it belongs in that position. Man's dominating position in the world is the direct result of *thought*, and it must be this power that you, as an individual, will use in the attainment of *success*, no matter what may be your idea of what represents *success*.

You have now arrived at the point at which you should take inventory of yourself for the purpose of ascertaining what qualities you need to give you a well balanced and rounded out personality.

Fifteen major factors entered into the building of this course. Analyze yourself carefully, with the assistance of one or more other persons if you feel that you need it, for the purpose of ascertaining in which of the fifteen factors of this course you are the weakest, and then concentrate your efforts upon those particular lessons until you have fully developed those factors which they represent.

Personal Analysis Service

As a student of this course you are entitled to a continuation of the author's services for the purpose of making a complete Personal Analysis that will indicate your general efficiency and your understanding of the Fifteen Laws of Success.

To avail yourself of this service you must fill out the Personal Analysis Questionnaire, which accompanies the course, and mail it to the author, at the address shown on the Questionnaire.

You will, in due time, receive a graphic chart diagram which will show you, at a glance, the percentage to which you are entitled in connection with each of the Fifteen Laws. It will be both interesting and instructive to compare this analysis with the one which you, yourself, have made, through the aid of the chart shown in Lesson One.

The Questionnaire should not be filled out until after you have read all the lessons of this course at least once. Answer the questions correctly, and frankly, as near as you can. The data contained in your answers will be strictly confidential, and will be seen by no one except the author of this philosophy.

Your analysis will be in the nature of a signed report, which may be used to great advantage in the marketing of your personal services, if you wish so to use it. This analysis will be the same, in every respect, as those for which the author made a charge of $25 during the years he was engaged in research in connection with the organization of this course, and it may, under some circumstances, be worth many times this amount to you, as similar analyses have been to scores of people whom the author has served.

No charge is made for this analysis, as it is a part of the service to which each student of this course is entitled upon completion of the sixteen lessons and the payment of the nominal tuition fee charged for the course.

INDECISION

An After-the-Lesson Visit with the Author

TIME!

Procrastination robs you of opportunity. It is a significant fact that no great leader was ever known to procrastinate. You are fortunate if AMBITION drives you into action, never permitting you to falter or turn back, once you have rendered a DECISION to go forward. Second by second, as the clock ticks off the distance TIME is running a race with YOU. Delay means defeat, because no man may ever makeup a second of lost TIME. TIME is a master worker which heals the wounds of failure and disappointment and rights all wrongs and turns all mistakes into capital, but, it favors only those who kill off procrastination and remain in ACTION when decisions are to made. Life is a great checkerboard. The player opposite you is TIME.

Reciprocity and the Golden Rule

If you hesitate you will be wiped off the board. If you keep moving you may win. The only real capital is TIME, but it is capital only when used.

You may be shocked if you keep accurate account of the TIME you waste in a single day. Take a look at the picture above if you wish to know the fate of all who play carelessly with TIME.

THE picture at top of previous page tells a true story of one of the chief causes of FAILURE!

One of the players is "TIME" and the other is Mr. Average Man; let us call him YOU.

Move by move Time has wiped off Mr. Average Man's men until he is finally cornered, where Time will get him, no matter which way he moves. INDECISION has driven him into the corner.

Ask any well informed salesman and he will tell you that indecision is the outstanding weakness of the majority of people. Every salesman is familiar with that time-worn alibi, "I will think it over," which is the last trench-line of defense of those who have not the courage to say either yes or no. Like the player in the picture above, they cannot decide which way to move. Meanwhile, Time forces them into a corner where they can't move.

The great leaders of the world were men and women of quick decision.

General Grant had but little to commend him as an able General except the quality of firm decision, but this was sufficient to offset all of his weaknesses. The whole story of his military success may be gathered from his reply to his critics when he said "We will fight it out along these lines if it takes all summer."

When Napoleon reached a decision to move his armies in a given direction, he permitted nothing to cause him to change that decision. If his line of march brought his soldiers to a ditch, dug by his opponents to stop him, be would give the order to charge the ditch until it had been filled with dead men and horses sufficient to bridge it.

The suspense of indecision drives millions of people to failure. A condemned man once said that the thought of his approaching execution was not so terrifying, once he had reached the decision in his own mind to accept the inevitable.

Lack of decision is the chief stumbling block of all revival meeting workers. Their entire work is to get men and women to reach a decision in their own minds to accept a given religious tenet. Billy Sunday once said, "Indecision is the devil's favorite tool."

Andrew Carnegie visualized a great steel industry, but that industry would not be what it is today had he not reached a decision in his own mind to transform his vision into reality.

James J. Hill saw, in his mind's eye, a great transcontinental railway system, but that railroad never would have become a reality had he not reached a decision to start the project.

Imagination, alone, is not enough to insure success.

Millions of people have imagination and build plans that would easily bring them both fame and fortune, but those plans never reach the DECISION stage.

Samuel Instil was an ordinary stenographer, in the employ of Thomas A. Edison. Through the aid of his imagination he saw the great commercial possibilities of electricity. But, he did more than see the possibilities—he reached a decision to transform the mere possibilities into realities, and today he is a multimillionaire electric light plant operator.

Demosthenes was a poor Greek lad who had a strong desire to be a great public speaker. Nothing unusual about that; others have "desired" this and similar ability without living to see their desires realized. But, Demosthenes added DECISION to DESIRE, and, despite the fact that he was a stammerer he mastered this handicap and made himself one of the great orators of the world.

Martin W. Littleton was a poor lad who never saw the inside of a school house until he was past twelve years of age. His father took him to hear a great lawyer defend a murderer, in one of the southern cities. The speech made such a profound impression on the lad's mind that he grabbed his father by the hand and said, "Father, one of these days I am going to become the ablest lawyer in America."

That was a DEFINITE DECISION!

Today Martin W. Littleton accepts no fee under $50,000, and it is said that he is kept busy all the time. He became an able lawyer because he reached a DECISION to do so.

Edwin C. Barnes reached a DECISION in his own mind to become the partner of Thomas A. Edison. Handicapped by lack of schooling, without money to pay his railroad fare, and with no influential friends to introduce him to Mr. Edison, young Barnes made his way to East Orange on a freight car and so thoroughly sold himself to Mr. Edison that he got his opportunity which led to a partnership. Today, just twenty years since that decision was reached, Mr. Barnes lives at Bradenton, Florida, retired, with all the money he needs.

Men of decision usually get all that they go after!

Well within the memory of this writer a little group of men met at Westerville, Ohio, and organized what they called the Anti-Saloon League. Saloon men treated them as a joke. People, generally, made fun of them. But, they had reached a decision.

That decision was so pronounced that it finally drove the powerful saloon men into the corner.

William Wrigley, Jr., reached a decision to devote his entire business career to the manufacture and sale of a five-cent package of chewing gum. He has made that decision bring him financial returns running into millions of dollars a year.

Henry Ford reached a decision to manufacture and sell a popular priced automobile that would be within the means of all who wished to own it. That decision has made Ford the most powerful man on earth and brought travel opportunity to millions of people.

All these men had two outstanding qualities: A DEFINITE PURPOSE and a firm DECISION to transform that purpose into reality.

The man of DECISION gets that which he goes after, no matter how long it takes, or how difficult the task. An able salesman wanted to meet a Cleveland banker. The banker would not see him. One morning this salesman waited near the banker's house until he saw him get into his automobile and start downtown.

Watching his opportunity, the salesman drove his own automobile into the banker's, causing slight damage to the automobile. Alighting from his own car, he handed the banker his card, expressed regret on account of the damage done, but promised the banker a new car exactly like the one that had been damaged. That afternoon a new car was delivered to the banker, and out of that transaction grew a friendship that terminated, finally, in a business partnership which still exists.

The man of DECISION cannot be stopped!

The man of INDECISION cannot be started! Take your own choice.

> "Behind him lay the gray Azores,
> Behind the Gates of Hercules;
> Before him not the ghosts of shores;
> Before him only shoreless seas.
> The good mate said: 'Now must we pray,
> For lo! the very stars are gone.
> Brave Adm'r'l, speak; what shall I say?'
> 'Why, say: "Sail on and on!"'"

When Columbus began his famous voyage he made one of the most far-reaching DECISIONS in the history of mankind. Had he not remained firm on that decision the freedom of America, as we know it today, would never have been known.

Take notice of those about you and observe this significant fact—THAT THE SUCCESSFUL MEN AND WOMEN ARE THOSE WHO REACH DECISIONS QUICKLY AND THEN STAND FIRMLY BY THOSE DECISIONS AFTER THEY ARE MADE.

If you are one of those who make up their minds today and change them again tomorrow you are doomed to failure. If you are not sure which way to move it is better to shut your eyes and move in the dark than to remain still and make no move at all.

The world will forgive you if you make mistakes, but it will never forgive you if you make no DECISIONS, because it will never hear of you outside of the community in which you live.

No matter who you are or what may be your lifework, you are playing checkers with TIME! It is always your next move. Move with quick DECISION and Time will favor you. Stand still and Time will wipe you off the board.

You cannot always make the right move, but, if you make enough moves you may take advantage of the law of averages and pile up a creditable score before the great game of LIFE is ended.

> ### III
> ### Faith: Your Key to Courage and Confidence
>
> *Applied Faith,*
> from
> *The Master Key to Riches*
> (1945)

Faith means believing that powerful and productive forces support your needs and wishes. Faith is a combination of both confidence in self and in the existence of beneficent natural laws, each growing from the other. By natural laws, I mean forces that permit the world to operate along lines of expansion, growth, and renewal. Understand this, and you also realize that the forces of creation abet your integral efforts.

If you are functioning in a manner that is generative—such as providing a service that bestows authentic benefit on another and assists in that individual's sustenance, growth, and expansion—you are functioning within the stream of natural law. This brings you tremendous benefit; it makes you part of the overall scheme of creation. Hence, you have good reason to feel faith.

If you study the ten points of faith that Hill outlines in this chapter (he letters them A to J), you'll see that they are, in effect, an encapsulation of his entire success philosophy. This gives you a great hint as to the "secret" that Hill says appears within each chapter of Think and Grow Rich, *which we'll explore at the end of this book.*

—MH

APPLIED FAITH

Faith is a royal visitor which enters only the mind that has been properly prepared for it; the mind that has been set in order through *self-discipline*.

In the fashion of all royalty, Faith commands the best room; nay, the finest suite, in the mental dwelling place.

It will not be shunted into servant's quarters, and it will not associate with envy, greed, superstition, hatred, revenge, vanity, doubt, worry or fear.

Get the full significance of this truth and you will be on the way to an understanding of that mysterious power which has baffled the scientists down through the ages.

Then you will recognize the necessity for *conditioning your mind*, through self discipline, before expecting Faith to become your permanent guest.

Recalling the words of the sage of Concord, Ralph Waldo Emerson, who said, "In every man there is something wherein I may learn of him, and in that I am his pupil," I shall now introduce a man who has been a great benefactor of mankind, so that you may observe how one goes about the conditioning of his mind for the expression of Faith.

Let him tell his own story:

"During the business depression which began in 1929 I took a postgraduate course in the University of Hard Knocks, the greatest of all schools.

"It was then I discovered a hidden fortune which I possessed, but had not been using.

"I made the discovery one morning when a notice came that my bank had closed its doors, possibly never to be reopened again, for it was then that I began to take inventory of my intangible, unused assets.

"Come with me while I describe what the inventory revealed. Let us begin with the most important item on the list, unused *Faith!*

"When I searched deeply into my own heart I discovered, despite my financial losses, I had an abundance of Faith left in Infinite Intelligence and Faith in my fellow men.

"With this discovery came another of still greater importance; the discovery that *Faith can accomplish that which not all the money of the world can achieve.*

"When I possessed all the money I needed I made the grievous error of believing money to be a permanent source of power. Now came the astonishing revelation that money, without Faith, is nothing but so much inert matter, *of itself possessed of no power whatsoever.*

"Recognizing, perhaps for the first time in my life, the stupendous power of enduring Faith. I analyzed myself carefully to determine just how much of this form of riches I possessed. The analysis was both surprising and gratifying.

"I began the analysis by taking a walk into the woods. I wished to get away from the crowd, away from the noise of the city, away from the disturbances of civilization and the fears of men, that I might meditate in silence.

"Ah! what gratification there is in that word 'silence'.

"On my journey I picked up an acorn and held it in the palm of my hand. I found it near the roots of the giant oak tree from which it had fallen. I judged the age of the tree to have been so great that it must have been a fair-sized tree when George Washington was but a small boy.

"As I stood there looking at the great tree, and its small embryonic offspring which I held in my hand, I realized that the tree had grown from a small acorn. I also realized that all the men living could not have built such a tree.

"I was conscious of the fact that some form of intangible Intelligence created the acorn from which the tree grew, and caused the acorn to germinate and begin its climb up from the soil of the earth.

"Then I realized that the greatest powers are the intangible powers, and not those which consist in bank balances or material things.

"I picked up a handful of black soil and covered the acorn with it. I held in my hand the *visible portion* of the substance out of which that magnificent tree had grown.

"At the root of the giant oak I plucked a fern. Its leaves were beautifully designed—yes, *designed*—and I realized as I examined the fern that it, too, was created by the same Intelligence which had produced the oak tree.

"I continued my walk in the woods until I came to a running brook of clear, sparkling water. By this time I was tired, so I sat near the brook to rest and listen to its rhythmic music, as it danced on its way back to the sea.

"The experience brought back memories of my youth. I remembered playing by a similar brook. As I sat there listening to the music of the water I became conscious of an unseen being—an Intelligence—which spoke to me from within and told me the enchanting story of the water, and this is the story it told:

"'Water! Pure sparkling water. The same has been rendering service ever since this planet cooled off and became the home of man, beast and vegetation.

"'Water! Ah, what a story you could tell if you spoke man's language. You have quenched the thirst of endless millions of earthly wayfarers; fed the flowers; expanded into steam and turned the wheels of man-made machinery, condensing and going back again to your original form. You have cleaned the sewers, washed the pavements, rendered countless services to man and beast, returning always to your source in the seas, there to become purified and start your journey of service once again.

"'When you move you travel in one direction only; toward the seas from whence you came. You are forever going and coming, but you always seem to be happy at your labor.

"'Water! Clean, pure, sparkling substance. No matter how much dirty work you perform, you cleanse yourself at the end of your labor.

"'You cannot be created, nor can you be destroyed. You are akin to all life. Without your beneficence no form of life on this earth would exist!'

"And the water of the brook went rippling, laughing, on its way back to the sea.

"The story of water ended, but I had heard a great sermon; I had been close to the greatest of all forms of Intelligence. I felt evidence of that same Intelligence which had created the great oak tree from a tiny acorn; the Intelligence which had fashioned the leaves of the fern with mechanical and esthetic skill such as no man could duplicate.

"The shadows of the trees were becoming longer; the day was coming to a close.

"As the sun slowly descended beyond the western horizon I realized that it, too, had played a part in that marvelous sermon which I had heard.

"Without the beneficent aid of the sun there could have been no conversion of the acorn into an oak tree. Without the sun's help the sparkling water of the flowing brook would have remained eternally imprisoned in the oceans, and life on this earth could never have existed.

"These thoughts gave a beautiful climax to the sermon I had heard; thoughts of the romantic affinity existing between the sun and the water and all life on this earth, beside which all other forms of romance seemed incomparable and unimportant.

"I picked up a small white pebble which had been neatly polished by the waters of the running brook. As I held it in my hand I received, from within, a still more impressive sermon. The Intelligence which conveyed that sermon to my mind seemed to say:

"'Behold, mortal, a miracle which you hold in your hand.

"'I am only a tiny pebble of stone, yet I am, in reality, a small universe in which there is everything that may be found in the more expanded portion of the universe which you see out there among the stars.

"I appear to be dead and motionless, but the appearance is deceiving. I am made of molecules. Inside my molecules are myriads of atoms, each a small universe unto itself. Inside the atoms are countless numbers of electrons which move at an inconceivable rate of speed.

"'I am not a dead mass of stone, but an organized group of units of ceaseless energy.

"'I appear to be a solid mass, but the appearance is an illusion, for my electrons are separated one from another by a distance greater than their mass.

"'Study me carefully, O humble earthly wayfarer, and remember that the great powers of the universe are the intangibles; that the values of life are those which cannot be added by bank balances.'

"The thought conveyed by that climax was so illuminating that it held me spellbound, for I recognized that I held in my hand an infinitesimal portion of the energy which keeps the sun, the stars and the earth, on which we live for a brief period, in their respective places in relation to one another.

"Meditation revealed to me the beautiful reality that there is law and order, even in the small confines of a tiny pebble of stone. I recognized that within the mass of that tiny pebble the romance and the reality of nature were combined. I recognized that within that small pebble fact transcended fancy.

"Never before had I felt so keenly the significance of the evidence of natural law and order and purpose which reveal themselves in everything the human mind can perceive. Never before had I felt myself so near the source of my Faith in Infinite Intelligence.

"It was a beautiful experience, out there in the midst of Mother Nature's family of trees and running brooks, where the very calmness of the surroundings bade my weary soul be quiet and rest awhile, so that I might look, fed and listen while Infinite Intelligence unfolded to me the story of its reality.

"Never in all my life, had I previously been so overwhelmingly conscious of the real evidence of Infinite Intelligence, or of die source of my Faith.

"I lingered in this newly found paradise until the Evening Star began to twinkle; then reluctantly I retraced my footsteps back to the city, there to mingle once again with those who are driven, like galley slaves, by the inexorable rules of civilization, in a mad scramble to gather up material things they do not need.

"I am now back in my study, with my books and my typewriter, on which I am recording the story of my experience. But I am swept by a feeling of loneliness and a longing to be out there by the side of that friendly brook where, only a few hours ago, I had bathed my soul in the satisfying realities of Infinite Intelligence.

"I know that my Faith in Infinite Intelligence is real and enduring. It is not a blind Faith; it is one based on close examination of the handiwork of Infinite Intelligence, and as such has been expressed in the orderliness of the universe.

"I had been looking in the wrong direction for the source of my Faith. I had been seeking it in the deeds of men, in human relationships, in bank balances and material things.

"I found it in a tiny acorn, a giant oak tree, a small pebble or stone, the leaves of a simple fern and the soil of the earth; in the friendly sun which warms the earth and gives motion to the waters; in the Evening Star; in the silence and calm of the great outdoors.

"And I am moved to suggest that Infinite Intelligence reveals itself through silence more readily than through the boisterousness of men's struggles, in their mad rush to accumulate material things.

"My bank account vanished, my bank collapsed, but I was richer than most millionaires, because I had discovered a direct approach to Faith. With this power behind me I can accumulate other bank balances sufficient for my needs.

"Nay, I am richer than are most millionaires, because I depend upon a source of inspired power which reveals itself to me from within, while many of the more wealthy find it necessary to turn to bank balances and the stock ticker for stimulation and power.

"*My source of power is as free as the air I breathe*, and as *limitless!* To avail myself of it I have only to turn on *my* Faith, and this I have in abundance.

"Thus, once again I learned the truth that every adversity carries with it the seed of an equivalent benefit. My adversity cost me my bank balance. It paid off through the revelation of the means to all riches!"

Stated in his own words, you have the story of a man who has discovered how to condition his mind for the expression of Faith.

And what a dramatic story it is! *Dramatic because of its* simplicity.

Here is a man who found a sound basis for an enduring Faith; not in bank balances or material riches, but in the seed of an oak tree, the leaves of a fern, a small pebble, and a running brook; things which everyone may observe and appreciate.

But his observation of these simple things led him to recognize that the greatest powers are intangible powers which are revealed through the simple things around us.

I have related this man's story as I wished to emphasize the manner in which one may clear his mind, even in the midst of chaos and insurmountable difficulties, and prepare it for the expression of Faith.

The most important fact which this story reveals is this:

When the mind has been cleared of a *negative mental attitude* the power of Faith moves in and begins to take possession!

Surely no student of this philosophy will be unfortunate enough to miss this important observation.

Let us turn now to an analysis of Faith, although we must approach the subject with full recognition that Faith is a power which has defied analysis by the entire scientific world.

Faith has been given fourth place in this philosophy because it comes near to representing the "fourth dimension," although it is presented here for its relationship to personal achievement.

Faith is a state of mind which might properly be called the "mainspring of the soul" through which one's aims, desires and purposes may be translated into their physical or financial equivalent.

Previously we observed that great power may be attained by the application of (1) the habit of GOING THE EXTRA MILE, (2) Definiteness of Purpose, and (3) the Master Mind But that power is feeble in comparison with that which is available through the combined application of these principles with the state of mind known as Faith.

We have already observed that *capacity for faith* is one of the Twelve Riches. Let us now recognize the means by which this "capacity" may be filled with that strange power which has been the main bulwark of civilization, the chief cause of all human progress, the guiding spirit of all constructive human endeavor.

Let us remember, at the outset of this analysis, that Faith is a state of mind which may be enjoyed only by those who have learned the art of taking *full and complete control* of their minds! This is the one and only prerogative right over which an individual has been given complete control.

Faith: Your Key to Courage and Confidence

Faith expresses its powers only through the mind that has been prepared for it. But the way of preparation is known and may be attained by all who desire to find it.

The fundamentals of Faith are these:

a. Definiteness of Purpose supported by personal initiative or *action*.
b. The habit of GOING THE EXTRA MILE in all human relationships.
c. A Master Mind alliance with one or more people who radiate courage based on Faith, and who are suited spiritually and mentally to one's needs in carrying out a given purpose.
d. A positive mind, free from all negatives, such as fear, envy, greed, hatred, jealousy and superstition. (A positive mental attitude is the first and the most important of the Twelve Riches.)
e. Recognition of the truth that every adversity carries with it the seed of an equivalent benefit; that *temporary defeat is not failure* until it has been accepted as such.
f. The habit of affirming one's Definite Major Purpose in life, in a ceremony of meditation, at least once daily.
g. Recognition of the existence of Infinite Intelligence which gives orderliness to the universe; that all individuals are minute expressions of this Intelligence, and as such the individual mind has no limitations except those which are accepted and set up by the individual in his own mind.

h. A careful inventory (in retrospect) of one's past defeats and adversities, which will reveal the truth that all such experiences carry the seed of an equivalent benefit.
i. Self-respect expressed through harmony with one's own conscience.
j. Recognition of the oneness of all mankind.

These are the fundamentals of major importance which prepare the mind for the expression of Faith. Their application calls for no degree of superiority, but application does call for intelligence and *a keen thirst for truth and justice.*

Faith fraternizes only with the mind that is positive!

It is the *"elan vital"* that gives power, inspiration and action to a positive mind. It is the power that causes a positive mind to act as an "electro-magnet," attracting to it the exact physical counterpart of the thought it expresses.

Faith gives resourcefulness to the mind, enabling the mind to make "grist of all that comes to its mill." It recognizes favorable opportunities, in every circumstance of one's life, whereby one may attain the object of Faith, *going so far as to provide the means by which failure and defeat may be converted into success of equivalent dimensions.*

Faith enables man to penetrate deeply into the secrets of Nature and to understand Nature's language as it is expressed in all natural laws.

From this sort of revelation have come all the great inventions that serve mankind, and a better understanding of the way to human freedom through harmony in human relationships, such as was provided by the Constitution of the United States.

Faith Your Key to Courage and Confidence

Faith makes it possible to achieve that which man can *conceive* and *believe!*

Thomas A. Edison *believed* he could perfect a practical incandescent electric lamp, and despite the fact that he failed more than 10,000 times that Faith carried him to the discovery of the secret for which he was searching.

Signor Marconi *believed* the energy of the ether could be made to carry the vibrations of sound without the use of wires. His Faith carried him through endless failures until at long last he was rewarded by triumph.

Christopher Columbus *believed* the earth was round; that he would find land in an uncharted ocean if he sailed on. Despite the rebellious protests of his *unbelieving* sailors he sailed on and on until he was rewarded for his Faith.

Helen Keller *believed* she would learn to speak, although she had lost the power of speech, her hearing, and her eyesight as well. Her Faith restored her speech and provided her with the equivalent of hearing, through the sense of touch, thus proving that Faith can and will find a way to the realization of human desires.

If you would have Faith, keep your mind on that which you desire. And remember that there is no such reality as a "blanket" faith, for faith is the outward demonstration of definiteness of purpose.

Faith is guidance from within! The guiding force is Infinite Intelligence directed to definite ends. It will not bring that which one desires, but it will guide one to the attainment of the object of desire.

How to Demonstrate the Power of Faith

a. Know what you want and determine what you have to give in return for it.

b. When you affirm the objects of your desires, through prayer, inspire your imagination to see yourself already in possession of them, and act precisely as if you were in the physical possession thereof. (Remember, the possession of anything first takes place mentally, in the mind.)

c. Keep the mind open at all times for *guidance from within*, and when you are inspired by "hunches" to modify your plans or to move on a new plan, move without hesitancy or doubt.

d. When overtaken by temporary defeat, as you may be overtaken many times, remember that man's Faith is tested in many ways, and your defeat may be only one of your "testing periods." Therefore, accept defeat as an inspiration to greater effort and carry on with *belief* that you will succeed.

e. Any negative state of mind will destroy the capacity for Faith and result in a negative climax of any affirmation you may express. Your state of mind is everything; therefore take possession of your mind and dear it completely of all unwanted interlopers that are unfriendly to Faith, and keep it cleared, no matter what may be the cost in effort.

f. Learn to give expression to your power of Faith by writing out a dear description of your Definite Major

Faith: Your Key to Courage and Confidence

Purpose in life and using it as the basis of your daily meditation.

g. Associate with your Definite Major Purpose as many as possible of the nine basic motives, described previously.

h. Write out a list of all the benefits and advantages you expect to derive from the attainment of the object of your Definite Major Purpose and call these into your mind many times daily, thereby making your mind "success conscious" (This is commonly called autosuggestion.)

i. Associate yourself, as far as possible, with people who are in sympathy with your Definite Major Purpose; people who are in harmony with you, and inspire them to encourage you in every way possible.

j. Let not a single day pass without making at least one definite move toward the attainment of your Definite Major Purpose. Remember, 'Faith without works is dead."

k. Choose some prosperous person of self-reliance and courage as your "pace-maker," and make up your mind not only to keep up with that person, but to excel him. Do this silently, without mentioning your plan to anyone. (Boastfulness will be fatal to your success, as Faith has nothing in common with vanity or self-love.)

l. Surround yourself with books, pictures, wall mottoes and other suggestive reminders of self-reliance founded upon Faith as it has been demonstrated by other people, thus building around yourself an atmosphere of prosperity and achievement This habit will be fruitful of stupendous results.

m. Adopt a policy of never evading or running away from unpleasant circumstances, but recognize such circumstances and build a counter-fire against them right where they overtake you. You will discover that recognition of such circumstances, without fear of their consequence, is nine-tenths of the battle in mastering them.

n. Recognize the truth that everything worth having has a definite price. The price of Faith, among other things, is eternal vigilance in carrying out these simple instructions. Your watchword must be PERSISTENCE!

These are the steps that lead to the development and the maintenance of a *positive mental attitude*, the only one in which Faith will abide. They are steps that lead to riches of both mind and spirit as well as riches of the purse. Fill your mind with this kind of mental food.

These are the steps by which the mind may be prepared for the highest expressions of the soul.

Feed your mind on such mental food and it will be easy for you to adopt the habit of GOING THE EXTRA MILE.

It will be easy for you to keep your mind attuned to that which you desire, with assurance that it shall become yours.

"The key to every man," said Emerson, "is his thought."

That is true. Every man today is the result of his thoughts of yesterday!

Faith: Your Key to Courage and Confidence

It would be difficult for one to imagine Henry Ford fearing anything, for his life work and his achievements are the handi-work of Faith.

And it would be difficult to imagine Henry Ford accepting as impossible any end he might desire to attain.

He gave the whole world notice of his Faith some years ago, when he desired to have the Ford automobile engine blocks cast in one piece. He instructed his engineers to draw up a model for the casting.

"Impossible," they cried!

"You use that word carelessly," exclaimed Ford. "Go ahead and try!"

They went ahead, but proceeded without Ford's Faith!

In a little while they *reported* back to Mr. Ford that they had tried without success.

"Try again," Mr. Ford requested, "and keep on trying until you succeed."

They tried again, again, and again, until eventually they found the method they were seeking. Ford's Faith had won again.

Thomas A. Edison desired to create a machine that would record and reproduce the sound of the human voice. No one had ever seen such a machine, and no one but Edison *believed it* could be produced. His *belief* was more than a desire, for he backed it with Faith, and Faith put in action becomes Wisdom. He went to work on the machine, and lo! his first model justified his Faith, for it worked.

James J. Hill sat with his hand on a telegraph key, waiting for an "open line." But he was not idle. His imagination was at work, building a great Transcontinental Railway System through which he hoped to tap the vast resources of the undeveloped western portion of the United States.

He had no money. He had no influential friends. He had no record of great achievement to give him prestige. But he did have Faith, that irresistible power that recognizes no such reality as "impossible."

He reduced his Definite Major Purpose to writing, omitting no detail.

On a map of the United States he sketched the course of his proposed railroad.

He slept with that map under his pillow. He carried it with him wherever he went. He fed his mind on his desire for the fulfillment of his "dream" until he made that dream a reality.

The morning after the great Chicago fire had laid waste the business portion of the city, Marshall Field came down to the site where, the day before, his retail store stood.

All around him were groups of other merchants whose stores had also been destroyed. He listened in on their conversations and learned that they had given up hope and many of them had already decided to move on further West and start over again.

Calling the nearest groups to him Mr. Field said:

"Gentlemen, you may do as you please, but as for me I intend to stay right here. Over there where you see the smoking remains of what was once my store I shall build the worlds greatest retail store."

The store that Mr. Field built on Faith still stands on that spot, in Chicago. It is recognized the world over as the greatest retail store on earth.

These men and others like them have been the pioneers who produced our great American way of life.

They gave us the American System of Free Enterprise that inspires every worker of industry to express his personal initiative backed by Faith.

They gave us our system of railroads and our system of communications. They gave us the talking pictures; the talking machines; the airplanes; the skyscrapers skeletoned with steel; the automobile; the improved highways; the household electrical appliances; the electric power installations; the x-ray; the banking and investment institutions; the great life insurance companies; the strongest Navy in the world; yes, and more important than all these, they prepared the way, through their Faith, for the freedom each and every one of us enjoys as an American citizen.

Human progress is no matter of accident or luck!

But it is the result of *applied faith*, expressed by men who have conditioned their minds, through the seventeen principles of this philosophy, for the expression of Faith.

Verily, the United States is a nation founded on Faith and maintained by Faith. Moreover, it provides all the essentials that inspire Faith, so that the humblest citizen may attain the highest ambitions of his heart and soul.

Therefore, our nation is justly known as a "land of opportunity"; the richest and the freest nation of the world!

And all freedom and riches have their roots in an abiding Faith.

The space that every man occupies in the world is measured by the Faith he expresses in connection with his aims and purposes.

Let us remember this, we who aspire to enjoy freedom and riches.

Let us remember, too, that Faith fixes no limitations of freedom or riches, but it guides every man to the realization of his desires whether they be great or small, according to his expression of it.

And though Faith is the one power which defies the scientists to analyze it, the procedure by which it may be applied is simple and within the understanding of the humblest, thus it is the common property of all mankind.

All that is known of this procedure has been simply stated in this chapter, and not a single step of it is beyond the reach of the humblest person.

Faith begins with *definiteness of purpose* functioning in a mind that has been prepared for it by the development of a *positive mental attitude*. It attains its greatest scope of power by *physical action* directed toward the attainment of a definite purpose.

All voluntary physical action is inspired by one or more of the nine basic motives. It is not difficult for one to develop Faith in connection with the pursuit of one's desires.

Let a man be motivated by LOVE and see how quickly this emotion is given wings for action through Faith. And action in pursuit of the objective of that love quickly follows. The action becomes a labor of love, which is one of the Twelve Riches.

Let a man set his heart upon the accumulation of material riches and see how quickly his every effort becomes a labor of love. The hours of the day are not long enough for his needs, and though he labors long he finds that fatigue is softened by the joy of *self-expression*, which is another of the Twelve Riches.

Thus, one by one the resistances of life fade into nothingness for the man who has prepared his mind for self-expression through faith. Success becomes inevitable. Joy crowns his every effort. He has no time or inclination for hatred. *Harmony in human relationships* comes naturally to him. His *hope of achievement* is high and continuous, for he sees himself already in possession of the object of his definite purpose. Intolerance has been supplanted by an *open mind*.

And *self-discipline* becomes as natural as the eating of food. He *understands people* because he loves them, and because of this love he is willing to *share his blessings*. *Of fear he knows nothing*, for all his fears have been driven away by his Faith. The Twelve Riches have become his own!

Faith is an expression of gratitude for man's relationship to his Creator. Fear is an acknowledgment of the influences of evil and it connotes a lack of *belief* in the Creator.

The greatest of life's riches consist in the understanding of the four principles which I have mentioned. These principles are known as the "Big Four" of this philosophy, because they are the warp and the woof and the major foundation-stones of the Master-Key to the power of thought and the inner secrets of the soul.

Use this Master-Key wisely and you shall be free!

Some to Whom the Master-Key Has Been Revealed

In a one-room log cabin, in Kentucky, a small boy was lying on the hearth, learning to write, using the back of a wooden shovel as a slate, and a piece of charcoal as a pencil.

A kindly woman stood over him, encouraging him to keep on trying. The woman was his mother! The boy grew into manhood without having shown any promise of greatness.

He took up the study of law and tried to make a living at that profession, but his success was meager.

He tried store-keeping, but the sheriff soon caught up with him.

He entered the army, but he made no noteworthy record there. Everything to which he turned his hand seemed to wither and disappear into nothingness.

Then a great love came into his life. It ended with the death of the one and only woman he ever loved, but the sorrow over that death reached deeply into the man's soul and there it made contact with the *secret power* that comes from within.

He seized that power and began to put it to work. It made him President of the United States. It wiped out the curse of slavery in America. And it saved the Union from dissolution in the time of a great national emergency.

The great Emancipator is now a citizen of the universe, but the spirit of his great soul—a spirit that was set free by the secret power from within his own mind—goes marching on. That spirit has helped to make the United States the freest country of the world.

So, this power that comes to men from within knows no social caste! It is as available to the poor and the humble as it is to the rich and the powerful. It need not be passed on from one person to another. It is possessed by all who think. It cannot be put into effect for you by any one except yourself. It must be acquired from within, and it is free to all who will appropriate it.

What strange fear is it that gets into the minds of men and short-circuits their approach to this secret power from within, and when it is recognized and used lifts men to great heights of achievement? How and why do the vast majority of the people of the world become the victims of a hypnotic rhythm which destroys their capacity to use the secret power of their own minds? How can this rhythm be broken?

The approach to the source of all genius has been charted. It is the self-same path that was followed by Thomas A. Edison, Henry Ford, Andrew Carnegie, Dr. Alexander Graham Bell, and the other great leaders who have contributed, from their rich experiences, to the establishment of the American way of life.

"How may one tap that secret power that comes from within?" some will wish to ask! Let us see how others have drawn upon it.

A young clergyman by the name of Frank Gunsaulus had long desired to build a new type of college. He knew exactly what he wanted, but the hitch came in the fact that it required a million dollars in cash.

He made up his mind to get the million dollars! Definiteness of decision, based upon definiteness of purpose, constituted the first step of his plan.

Then he wrote a sermon entitled "WHAT I WOULD DO WITH A MILLION DOLLARS!" and announced in the newspapers that he would preach on that subject the following Sunday morning.

At the end of the sermon a strange man whom the young preacher had never seen before, arose, walked down to the pulpit, extended his hand and said, "I like your sermon, and you may come down to my office tomorrow morning and I will give you the million dollars you desire."

The man was Philip D. Armour, the packing-house founder of Armour & Company. His gift was the beginning of the Armour School of Technology, one of the great schools of the country.

This is the sum and the substance of what happened. What went on in the mind of the young preacher, that enabled him to contact the secret power that is available through the mind of man, is something with which we can only conjecture, but the modus operandi by which that power was stimulated was *applied Faith!*

Shortly after birth Helen Keller was stricken by a physical affliction which deprived her of sight, hearing and speech. With two of the more important of the five physical senses stilled forever she faced life under difficulties such as most people never know throughout their lives.

With the aid of a kindly woman who recognized the existence of that secret power which comes from within, Helen Keller began to contact that power and use it. In her own words, she gives a definite clue as to one of the conditions under which the power may be revealed.

"Faith," said Miss Keller, "rightly understood, is *active* not *passive!* Passive faith is no more a force than sight is in an eye that does not look or search out. Active faith knows no fear. It denies that God has betrayed His creatures and given the world over to darkness. It denies despair. Reinforced with faith, the weakest mortal is mightier than disaster."

Faith, *backed by action,* was the instrument with which Miss Keller bridged her affliction so that she was restored to a useful life.

Through applied faith she learned to speak.

Through her faith she substituted the sense of touch to do the work of the sense of hearing and the sense of sight, thus proving that no matter how great may be one's physical handicaps, there always is a means by which they may be eliminated or bridged.

The way may be found through that secret power from within one's mind, the approach to which must be discovered by the individual himself.

Go back through the pages of history and you will observe that the story of civilization's unfoldment leads inevitably to the works of men and women who opened the door to that secret power from within, with *applied faith* as the master-key! Observe, too, that great achievements always are born of hardship and struggle and barriers which seem insurmountable; obstacles which yield to nothing but *an indomitable will backed by an abiding faith!*

And here, in one short phrase—*indomitable will backed by an abiding faith*—you have the approach of major importance that leads to the discovery of the door of the mind, behind which the secret power from within is hidden!

Men who penetrate that secret power and apply it in the solution of personal problems sometimes are called "dreamers!" But, observe that they back their dreams with action, thus proving the soundness of Helen Keller's statement that *"Faith, rightly understood, is active, not passive."*

One of the strange features of "faith, rightly understood," is that it generally appears because of some emergency which forces men to look beyond the power of ordinary thought for the solution of their problems.

It is during these emergencies that we draw upon that secret power from within which knows no resistance strong enough to defeat it. Such emergencies, for example, as that faced by the fifty-six men who gave birth to this nation when they signed their names to the most profound document of all times—the Declaration of Independence.

That was "active faith, rightly understood!" for each man who signed that document knew that it might become his own death-warrant! Fortunately it became a license to liberty for all mankind claiming its protection, and it may well prove yet to be a license to liberty for the entire world.

Faith: Your Key to Courage and Confidence

The benefits of the document were proportionate to the risk assumed by those who signed it. The signers pledged their lives, their fortunes and their rights to liberty, the greatest privileges of a civilized people, and they made the pledge without mental reservations.

Here, then, is the suggestion of a test by which men may measure their capacity for *active faith!* To be effective it must be based on a willingness to risk whatever the circumstances demand; liberty, material fortune, and life itself. Faith without risk is a passive faith which, as Helen Keller stated, "is no more a force than sight is in an eye that does not look or search out."

And let us examine the records of some of the great leaders who came after the signers of the Declaration of Independence, for theirs was also an active faith. The men who gave us the American way of life and the American standard of living, the highest the world has ever known.

They, too, discovered that secret power that comes from within, drew upon it, applied it and converted a vast wilderness into the "cradle of democracy," which is now the envy of the rest of the world.

Such men as James J. Hill, who pushed back the frontiers of the West and brought the Atlantic and Pacific Oceans into easy access of the people, through a great transcontinental railroad system.

And Andrew Carnegie, who perfected the manufacture and distribution of steel products until that metal served to advance American industry in a thousand ways which had been prohibited, because of high costs.

And Henry Ford, who supplanted the horse and buggy mode of travel with a more rapid means of transportation that is within the means of the humblest person. As a result this country was covered with a network of improved highways that added immeasurable wealth to the sections through which they pass.

And Lee De Forest, who perfected the mechanical means by which the boundless force of the ether has been harnessed and made to serve as a means of instantaneous communication between the peoples of the world, through the radio.

And Thomas A. Edison, who pushed civilization ahead by thousands of years, with the perfection of the incandescent electric lamp, the talking machine, the moving picture and scores of other useful inventions which lighten the burdens of mankind and add to his pleasure and education.

These, and others of their type, were men of *active faith!* We sometimes call them "geniuses," but they disclaimed the right to the honor because they recognized that their achievements came as the result of that secret power from within which is available to everyone who will embrace it and use it.

We all know of the achievements of these great leaders; we know the rules of their leadership; we recognize the nature and the scope of the blessings their labors have conferred upon the people of this nation, and, thanks to the vision of Andrew Carnegie, we have preserved for the people the philosophy of individual achievement through which these men helped to make this the world's richest and freest country.

But, unfortunately, not all of us recognize the handicaps under which they worked, the obstacles they had to overcome, and the spirit of *active faith* in which they carried on their work.

Of this we may be sure, however: *Their achievements were in exact proportion to the emergencies they had to overcome!*

They met with opposition from those who were destined to benefit most by their struggles; people who, because of the lack of *active faith*, always view with skepticism and doubt that which is new and unfamiliar.

The emergencies of life often bring men to the crossroads, where they are forced to choose their direction, one road being marked Faith and another Fear!

What is it that causes the vast majority to take the Fear road? The choice hinges upon one's *mental attitude!*

The man who takes the Faith road is the man who has conditioned his mind to believe; conditioned it little at a time, by prompt and courageous decisions in the details of his daily experiences. The man who takes the Fear road does so because he has neglected to condition his mind to be positive.

In Washington, a man sits in a wheel chair with a tin cup and a bunch of pencils in his hands, gaining a meager living by begging. The *excuse* for his begging is that he lost the use of his legs, through Infantile Paralysis. His brain has not been affected. He is otherwise strong and healthy. But, his choice led him to accept the Fear road when the dreaded disease overtook him, and his mind atrophies through disuse.

In another part of the same city was another man who was afflicted with the same handicap. He, too, had lost the use of his legs, but his reaction to his loss was far different.

When he came to the cross-roads at which he was forced to make a choice he took the Faith road, and it led straight to the White House and the highest position within the gift of the American people.

That which he lost through incapacity of his limbs, he gained in the use of his brain and his will, and it is a matter of record that his physical affliction did in no way hinder him from being one of the most active men who ever occupied the position of President.

The difference in the stations of these two men was very great! But, let no one be deceived as to the cause of this difference, for it is entirely a difference of *mental attitudes*. One man chose Fear as his guide. The other chose Faith.

And, when you come right down to the circumstances which lift some men to high stations in life and condemn others to penury and want, the likelihood is that their widely separated positions reflect their respective mental attitudes. The high man chooses the high road of Faith, the low man chooses the low road of Fear, and education, experience, and personal skill are matters of secondary importance.

When Thomas A. Edison's teacher sent him home from school, at the end of the first three months, with a note to his parents saying he had an "addled" mind and could not be taught, he had the best of excuses for becoming an outcast, a do-nothing, a nobody, and that is precisely what he proceeded to become for a time. He did odd jobs, sold newspapers, tinkered with gadgets and chemicals until he became what is commonly known as a "jack of all trades" and not very good at any.

Faith: Your Key to Courage and Confidence

Then something took place in the mind of Thomas A. Edison that was destined to make his name immortal. Through some strange process which he never fully disclosed to the world, he discovered that secret power from within, took possession of it, organized it and lo! instead of being a man with an "addled" brain he became the outstanding genius of invention of all time.

And now, wherever we see an electric light, or hear a phonograph, or see a moving picture we should be reminded that we are observing the product of that secret power from within which is as available to us as it was to the great Edison. Moreover, we should feel sorely ashamed if, by neglect or indifference, we are making no appropriate use of this great power.

One of the strange features of this secret power from within is that it aids men in procuring whatever they set their hearts upon, which is but another way of saying it translates into reality one's dominating thoughts.

In the little town of Tyler, Texas, more than a quarter of a century ago, a boy still in his 'teens walked into a grocery store where some loafers were sitting by a stove. One of the men looked at the youth, grinned broadly and said, "Say, Sonny, what are you going to be when you are a man?"

"I'll tell you what I'm going to be," the boy shouted! "I'm going to be the best lawyer in the world—that's what I'm going to be if you wish to know."

The loafers yelled with laughter! The boy picked up his groceries and quietly walked out of the store.

Later, when the loafers laughed, it was in a different vein, for that boy had become a recognized authority in the legal world and his skill at law was so great that he was earning more than the President of the United States.

His name is Martin W. Littleton. He, too, discovered the secret power within his own mind and that power enabled him to set his own price on his services and get it.

As far as knowledge of the law is concerned there are thousands of lawyers who perhaps are as skilled at law as Martin W. Littleton, but few of them are making more than a living from their profession because they have not discovered there s something that brings success in the legal profession which not taught in law schools.

The illustration might be extended to cover every profession and all human endeavor. In every calling there are a few who rise to the top while all around them are others who never get beyond mediocrity.

Those who succeed usually are called "lucky." To be sure they are lucky! But, learn the facts and you will discover that "luck" consists of that secret power from within, which they have applied through a *positive mental attitude*; a determination to follow the road of Faith instead of the road of Fear and self-limitation.

The power that comes from within recognizes no such reality as permanent barriers.

It converts defeat into a challenge to greater effort

It removes self-imposed limitations such as fear and doubt.

And, above all else let us remember that it makes no black marks against any man's record which he cannot erase.

If approached through the power from within, every day brings forth a newly-born opportunity for individual achievement which needs not in any way whatsoever be burdened by the failures of yesterday.

It favors no race or creed, and it is bound by no sort of arbitrary consistency compelling man to remain in poverty because he was born in poverty.

The power from within is the one medium through which the effects of Cosmic Habitforce may be changed from a negative to a positive application, instantaneously.

It recognizes no precedent, follows no hard and fast rules, and makes royal kings of the humblest of men at will— THEIR WILL!

It offers the one and only grand highway to personal freedom and liberty.

It restores health where all else fails, in open defiance of all the rules of modern medical science.

It heals the wounds of sorrow and disappointment regardless of their cause.

It transcends all human experience, all education, all knowledge available to mankind.

And its only fixed price is that of an unyielding faith!— an active applied faith!

It was the inspiration of the poet who wrote:

> "Isn't it strange that princes and kings
> And clowns that caper in saw-dust rings;
> And common folks, like you and me,
> All are builders for eternity.

> "To each is given a book of rules,
> A block of stone and a bag of tools;
> And each must shape ere time has flown,
> A stumbling block or a stepping stone."

Search until you find the point of approach to that secret power from within, and when you find it you will have discovered your true self—that "other self" which makes use of every experience of life.

Then, whether you build a better mouse trap, or write a better book, or preach a better sermon, the world will make a beaten path to your door, recognize you and adequately reward you, no matter who you are or what may have been the nature and scope of your failures of the past.

What if you have failed in the past?

So did Edison, Henry Ford, the Wright Brothers, Andrew Carnegie, and all the other great American leaders who have helped to establish the American way of life. They all met with failure in one way or another, but they didn't call it by that name; they called it *"temporary defeat."*

With the aid of the light that shines from within, these and all truly great men have recognized temporary defeat for exactly what it is—*a challenge to greater effort backed by greater faith!*

Anyone can quit when the going is hard!

Anyone can feel sorry for himself when temporary defeat overtakes him, but self-coddling was no part of the character of the men whom the world has recognized as great.

The approach to that power from within cannot be made by self-pity. It cannot be made through fear and timidity. It cannot be made through envy and hatred. It cannot be made through avarice and greed.

No; your "other self" pays no heed to any of these negatives! It manifests itself only through the mind that has been swept clean of all negative mental attitudes. *It thrives in the mind that is guided by faith!*

It is not a new philosophy of achievement that the world needs!

But it is a re-dedication of the old and tried principles which led unerringly to the discovery of that power from within which "moves mountains."

The power that has brought forth great leaders in every walk of life and in every generation is still available. Men of vision and faith, who have pushed back the frontiers of ignorance and superstition and fear, have given the world all that we know as civilization.

The power is clothed in no mystery and It performs no miracles, but it works through the daily deeds of men, and reflects itself in every form of service rendered for the benefit of mankind.

It is called by myriad names, but its nature never changes, no matter by what name it is known.

It works through but one medium, and that is the mind.

It expresses itself in thoughts, ideas, plans and purposes of men, and the grandest thing to be said about it is that *it is as free as the air we breathe and as abundant as the scope and space of the universe.*

IV
Procrastination and Fear

Outwitting the Six Ghosts of Fear,
from
Think and Grow Rich
(1937)

Procrastination and fear are the same. This is one of the reasons why it's essential to choose a Definite Chief Aim for which you feel passion. During periods of dejection, failure, fear of failure, or setback—and these will come, no matter your progress—the emotional depth of your aim will push you forward.

We cannot talk ourselves out of fear. To do so means pitting thought against emotion. But emotion is stronger than thought. Pitting thought against emotion is like pitting steam power against nuclear power—the latter wins every time. But we can pit emotion against emotion. The passion that you feel for your aim can outweigh fear of failure, provided you've chosen rightly.

Personal excellence also helps overcome fear. A good friend of mine is actor Yul Vazquez who you'd recognize from many screen performances including HBO's The Outsider *in 2020. Yul pointed out to me that every actor's audition is hit or miss—the performer may or may not be right for the part. But what is vitally important, and what helps the artist stand on his or her feet time after time, is accurate knowledge of his own abilities as a performer. Yul puts it this way:*

> *It's not up to anybody else to determine if someone is good at what they do. The person reaches a certain point—for the artist it doesn't come early, it comes later—where they realize that they are good at what they do; and they may or may not be right for a part but the verdict of whether they are good is already in.*

Your earned sense of personal excellence protects you. If you can reach this point in your outlook, whatever the nature of your work, you have gone a long way toward overcoming the debilitating effects of fear.

In this chapter, Hill writes about the destructiveness of fear—and of how fear itself is more detracting from your quality of life than nearly anything that could actually befall you. "Kill the habit of worry," Hill writes, "by reaching a general, blanket decision that nothing which has to offer is worth the price of worry."

Remember those words. They capture one of the key principles of successful living.

—MH

HOW TO OUTWIT THE SIX GHOSTS OF FEAR

*Take Inventory of Yourself,
As You Read This Closing Chapter,
and Find out How Many of the "Ghosts"
Are Standing in Your Way.*

BEFORE you can put any portion of this philosophy into successful use, your mind must be prepared to receive it. The preparation is not difficult. It begins with study, analysis, and understanding of three enemies which you shall have to clear out. These are INDECISION, DOUBT, and FEAR!

The Sixth Sense will never function while these three negatives, or any of them remain in your mind. The members of this unholy trio are closely related; where one is found, the other two are close at hand.

INDECISION is the seedling of FEAR! Remember this, as you read. Indecision crystalizes into DOUBT, the two blend and become FEAR! The "blending" process often is slow. This is one reason why these three enemies are so dangerous. They germinate and grow *without their presence being observed*.

The remainder of this chapter describes an end which must be attained before the philosophy, as a whole, can be put into practical use. It also analyzes a condition which has, but lately, reduced huge numbers of people to poverty, and it states a truth which must be understood by all who accumulate riches, whether measured in terms of money or a state of mind of far greater value than money.

The purpose of this chapter is to turn the spotlight of attention upon the cause and the cure of the six basic fears. Before we can master an enemy, we must know its name, its habits, and its place of abode. As you read, analyze yourself carefully, and determine which, if any, of the six common fears have attached themselves to you.

Do not be deceived by the habits of these subtle enemies. Sometimes they remain hidden in the subconscious mind, where they are difficult to locate, and still more difficult to eliminate.

The Six Basic Fears

There are six basic fears, with some combination of which every human suffers at one time or another. Most people are fortunate if they do not suffer from the entire six. Named in the order of their most common appearance, they are:

The fear of POVERTY ⎫ At the bottom
The fear of CRITICISM ⎬ of most
The fear of ILL HEALTH ⎭ of one's worries
The fear of LOSS OF LOVE OF SOMEONE
The fear of OLD AGE
The fear of DEATH

All other fears are of minor importance, they can be grouped under these six headings.

The prevalence of these fears, as a curse to the world, runs in cycles. For almost six years, while the depression was on, we floundered in the cycle of FEAR OF POVERTY. During the world-war, we were in the cycle of FEAR OF DEATH. Just following the war, we were in the cycle of FEAR OF ILL HEALTH, as evidenced by the epidemic of disease which spread itself all over the world.

Fears are nothing more than states of mind. One's state of mind is subject to control and direction. Physicians, as everyone knows, are less subject to attack by disease than ordinary laymen, for the reason that physicians DO NOT FEAR DISEASE. Physicians, without fear or hesitation, have been known to physically contact hundreds of people, daily, who were suffering from such contagious diseases as small-pox, without becoming infected. Their immunity against the disease consisted, largely, if not solely, in their absolute lack of FEAR.

Man can create nothing which he does not first conceive in the form of an impulse of thought. Following this statement, comes another of still greater importance, namely, MAN'S THOUGHT IMPULSES BEGIN IMMEDIATELY TO TRANSLATE THEMSELVES INTO THEIR PHYSICAL EQUIVALENT, WHETHER THOSE THOUGHTS ARE VOLUNTARY OR INVOLUNTARY. Thought impulses which are picked up through the ether, by mere chance (thoughts which have been released by other minds) may determine one's financial, business, professional, or social destiny just as surely as do the thought impulses which one creates by intent and design.

We are here laying the foundation for the presentation of a fact of great importance to the person who does not understand why some people appear to be "lucky" while others of equal or greater ability, training, experience, and brain capacity, seem destined to ride with misfortune. This fact may be explained by the statement that *every human being has the ability to completely control his own mind*, and with this control, obviously, every person may open his mind to the tramp thought impulses which are being released by other brains, or close the doors tightly and admit only thought impulses of his own choice.

Nature has endowed man with absolute control over but one thing, and that is THOUGHT. This fact, coupled with the additional fact that everything which man creates, begins in the form of a thought, leads one very near to the principle by which FEAR may be mastered.

If it is true that ALL THOUGHT HAS A TENDENCY TO CLOTHE ITSELF IN ITS PHYSICAL EQUIVALENT (and this is true, beyond any reasonable room for doubt), it is equally true that thought impulses of fear and poverty cannot be translated into terms of courage and financial gain.

The people of America began to think of poverty, following the Wall Street crash of 1929. Slowly, but surely that mass thought was crystalized into its physical equivalent, which was known as a "depression." This had to happen, it is in conformity with the laws of Nature.

The Fear of Poverty

There can be no compromise between POVERTY and RICHES! The two roads that lead to poverty and riches travel in opposite directions. If you want riches, you must refuse to accept any circumstance that leads toward poverty. (The word "riches" is here used in its broadest sense, meaning financial, spiritual, mental and material estates). The starting point of the path that leads to riches is DESIRE. In chapter one, you received full instructions for the proper use of DESIRE. In this chapter, on FEAR, you have complete instructions for preparing your mind to make practical use of DESIRE.

Here, then, is the place to give yourself a challenge which will definitely determine how much of this philosophy you have absorbed. Here is the point at which you can turn prophet and foretell, accurately, what the future holds in store for you. If, after reading this chapter, you are willing to accept poverty, you may as well make up your mind to receive poverty. This is one decision you cannot avoid.

If you demand riches, determine what form, and how much will be required to satisfy you. You know the road that leads to riches. You have been given a road map which, if followed, will keep you on that road. If you neglect to make the start, or stop before you arrive, no one will be to blame, but YOU. This responsibility is yours. No alibi will save you from accepting the responsibility if you now fail or refuse to demand riches of Life, because the acceptance calls for but one thing—incidentally, the only thing you can control—and that is a STATE OF MIND. A state of mind is something that one assumes. It cannot be purchased, it must be created.

Fear of poverty is a state of mind, nothing else! But it is sufficient to destroy one's chances of achievement in any undertaking, a truth which became painfully evident during the depression.

This fear paralyzes the faculty of reason, destroys the faculty of imagination, kills off self-reliance, undermines enthusiasm, discourages initiative, leads to uncertainty of purpose, encourages procrastination, wipes out enthusiasm and makes self-control an impossibility. It takes the charm from one's personality, destroys the possibility of accurate thinking, diverts concentration of effort, it masters persistence, turns the will-power into nothingness, destroys ambition, beclouds the memory and invites failure in every conceivable form; it kills love and assassinates the finer emotions of the heart, discourages friendship and invites disaster in a hundred forms, leads to sleeplessness, misery and unhappiness—and all this despite the obvious truth that we live in a world of overabundance of everything the heart could desire, with nothing standing between us and our desires, excepting lack of a definite purpose.

The Fear of Poverty is, without doubt, the most destructive of the six basic fears. It has been placed at the head of the list, because it is the most difficult to master. Considerable courage is required to state the truth about the origin of this fear, and still greater courage to accept the truth after it has been stated. The fear of poverty grew out of man's inherited tendency to PREY UPON HIS FELLOW-MAN ECONOMICALLY. Nearly all animals lower than man are motivated by instinct, but their capacity to "think" is limited, therefore, they prey upon one another physically. Man, with his superior sense of intuition, with the capacity to think and to reason, does not eat his fellowman bodily, he gets more satisfaction out of "eating" him FINANCIALLY. Man is so avaricious that every conceivable law has been passed to safeguard him from his fellowman.

Of all the ages of the world, of which we know anything, the age in which we live seems to be one that is outstanding because of man's money-madness. A man is considered less than the dust of the earth, unless he can display a fat bank account; but if he has money—NEVER MIND HOW HE ACQUIRED IT—he is a "king" or a "big shot"; he is above the law, he rules in politics, he dominates in business, and the whole world about him bows in respect when he passes.

Nothing brings man so much suffering and humility as POVERTY! Only those who have experienced poverty understand the full meaning of this.

It is no wonder that man *fears* poverty. Through a long line of inherited experiences man has learned, for sure, that some men cannot be trusted, where matters of money and earthly possessions are concerned. This is a rather stinging indictment, the worst part of it being that it is TRUE.

The majority of marriages are motivated by the wealth possessed by one, or both of the contracting parties. It is no wonder, therefore, that the divorce courts are busy.

So eager is man to possess wealth that he will acquire it in whatever manner he can—through legal methods if possible—through other methods if necessary or expedient.

Self-analysis may disclose weaknesses which one does not like to acknowledge. This form of examination is essential to all who demand of Life more than mediocrity and poverty. Remember, as you check yourself point by point, that you are both the court and the jury, the prosecuting attorney and the attorney for the defense, and that you are the plaintiff and the defendant, also, that you are on trial. Face the facts squarely. Ask yourself definite questions and demand direct replies. When the examination is over, you will know more about yourself. If you do not feel that you can be an impartial judge in this self-examination, call upon someone who knows you well to serve as judge while you cross-examine yourself. You are after the truth. *Get it, no matter at what cost even, though it may temporarily embarrass you!*

The majority of people, if asked what they fear most, would reply, "I fear nothing." The reply would be inaccurate, because few people realize that they are bound, handicapped, whipped spiritually and physically through some form of fear. So subtle and deeply seated is the emotion of fear that one may go through life burdened with it, never recognizing its presence. Only a courageous analysis will disclose the presence of this universal enemy. When you begin such an analysis, search deeply into your character. Here is a list of the symptoms for which you should look:

Symptoms of The Fear of Poverty

INDIFFERENCE. Commonly expressed through lack of ambition; willingness to tolerate poverty; acceptance of whatever compensation life may offer without protest; mental and physical laziness; lack of initiative, imagination, enthusiasm and self-control

INDECISION. The habit of permitting others to do one's thinking. Staying "on the fence."

DOUBT. Generally expressed through alibis and excuses designed to cover up, explain away, or apologize for one's failures, sometimes expressed in the form of envy of those who are successful, or by criticizing them.

WORRY. Usually expressed by finding fault with others, a tendency to spend beyond one's income, neglect of personal appearance, scowling and frowning; intemperance in the use of alcoholic drink, sometimes through the use of narcotics; nervousness, lack of poise, self-consciousness and lack of self-reliance.

OVER-CAUTION. The habit of looking for the negative side of every circumstance, thinking and talking of possible failure instead of concentrating upon the means of succeeding. Knowing all the roads to disaster, but never searching for the plans to avoid failure. Waiting for "the right time" to begin putting ideas and plans into action, until the waiting becomes a permanent habit. Remembering those who have failed, and forgetting those who have succeeded. Seeing the hole in the doughnut, but overlooking the doughnut. Pessimism, leading to indigestion, poor elimination, auto-intoxication, bad breath and bad disposition.

PROCRASTINATION. The habit of putting off until tomorrow that which should have been done last year. Spending enough time in creating alibis and excuses to have done the job. This symptom is closely related to over-caution, doubt and worry. Refusal to accept responsibility when it can be avoided. Willingness to compromise rather than put up a stiff fight. Compromising with difficulties instead of harnessing and using them as stepping stones to advancement. Bargaining with Life for a penny, instead of demanding prosperity, opulence, riches, contentment and happiness. Planning what to do IF AND WHEN OVERTAKEN BY FAILURE, INSTEAD OF BURNING ALL BRIDGES AND MAKING RETREAT IMPOSSIBLE. Weakness of, and often total lack of self-confidence, definiteness of purpose, self-control, initiative, enthusiasm, ambition, thrift and sound reasoning ability. EXPECTING POVERTY INSTEAD OF DEMANDING RICHES. Association with those who accept poverty instead of seeking the company of those who demand and receive riches.

Money Talks!

Some will ask, "Why did you write a book about money? Why measure riches in dollars, alone?" Some will believe, and rightly so, that there are other forms of riches more desirable than money. Yes, there are riches which cannot be measured in terms of dollars, but there are millions of people who will say, "Give me all the money I need, and I will find everything else I want."

The major reason why I wrote this book on how to get money is the fact that the world has but lately passed through an experience that left millions of men and women paralyzed with the FEAR OF POVERTY. What this sort of fear does to one was well described by Westbrook Pegler, in the New York World-Telegram, viz:

Money is only clam shells or metal discs or scraps of paper, and there are treasures of the heart and soul which money cannot buy, but most people, being broke, are unable to keep this in mind and sustain their spirits. When a man is down and out and on the street, unable to get any job at all, something happens to his spirit which can be observed in the droop of his shoulders, the set of his hat, his walk and his gaze. He cannot escape a feeling of inferiority among people with regular employment, even though he knows they are definitely not his equals in character, intelligence or ability.

These people—even his friends—feel, on the other hand, a sense of superiority and regard him, perhaps unconsciously, as a casualty. He may borrow for a time, but not enough to carry on in his accustomed way, and he cannot continue to borrow very long. But borrowing in itself, when a man is borrowing merely to live, is a depressing experience, and the money lacks the power of earned money to revive his spirits. Of course, none of this applies to bums or habitual ne'er-do-wells, but only to men of normal ambitions and self-respect.

WOMEN CONCEAL DESPAIR

Women in the same predicament must be different. We somehow do not think of women at all in considering the down-and-outers. They are scarce in the breadlines, they rarely are seen begging on the streets, and they are not recognizable in crowds by the same plain signs which identify busted men. Of course, I do not mean the shuffling hags of the city streets who are the opposite number of the confirmed male bums. I mean reasonably young, decent and intelligent women. There must be many of them, but their despair is not apparent. Maybe they kill themselves.

When a man is down and out he has time on his hands for brooding. He may travel miles to see a man about a job and discover that the job is filled or that it is one of those jobs with no base pay but only a commission on the sale of some useless knickknack which nobody would buy, except out of pity. Turning that down, he finds himself back on the street with nowhere to go but just anywhere. So he walks and walks. He gazes into store windows at luxuries which are not for him, and feels inferior and gives way to people who stop to look with an active interest. He wanders into the railroad station or puts himself down in the library to ease his legs and soak up a little heat, but that isn't looking for a job, so he gets going again. He may not know it, but his aimlessness would give him away even if the very lines of his figure did not. He may be well dressed in the clothes left over from the days when he had a steady job, but the clothes cannot disguise the droop.

MONEY MAKES DIFFERENCE

He sees thousands of other people, bookkeepers or clerks or chemists or wagon hands, busy at their work and envies them from the bottom of his soul. They have their independence, their self-respect and manhood, and he simply cannot convince himself that he is a good man, too, though he argue it out and arrive at a favorable verdict hour after hour.

It is just money which makes this difference in him. With a little money he would be himself again.

Some employers take the most shocking advantage of people who are down and out. The agencies hang out little colored cards offering miserable wages to busted men—$12 a week, $15 a week. An $18 a week job is a plum, and anyone with $25 a week to offer does not hang the job in front of an agency or a colored card. I have a want ad clipped from a local paper demanding a clerk, a good, clean penman, to take telephone orders for a sandwich shop from 11 A.M. to 2 P.M. for $8 a month—not $8 a week but $8 a month. The ad says also, "State religion." Can you imagine the brutal effrontery of anyone who demands a good, clean penman for 11 cents an hour inquiring into the victim's religion? But that is what busted people are offered.

The Fear Of Criticism

Just how man originally came by this fear, no one can state definitely, but one thing is certain—he has it in a highly developed form. Some believe that this fear made its appearance about the time that politics became a "profession." Others believe it can be traced to the age when women first began to concern themselves with "styles" in wearing apparel.

This author, being neither a humorist nor a prophet, is inclined to attribute the basic fear of criticism to that part of man's inherited nature which prompts him not only to take away his fellowman's goods and wares, but to justify his action by CRITICISM of his fellowman's character. It is a well known fact that a thief will criticize the man from whom he steals—that politicians seek office, not by displaying their own virtues and qualifications, but by attempting to besmirch their opponents.

The fear of criticism takes on many forms, the majority of which are petty and trivial. Baldheaded men, for example, are bald for no other reason than their fear of criticism. Heads become bald because of the tight fitting bands of hats which cut off the circulation from the roots of the hair. Men wear hats, not because they actually need them, but mainly because "everyone is doing it." The individual falls into line and does likewise, lest some other individual CRITICIZE him. Women seldom have bald heads, or even thin hair, because they wear hats which fit their heads loosely, the only purpose of the hats being adornment.

But, it must not be supposed that women are free from the fear of criticism. If any woman claims to be superior to man with reference to this fear, ask her to walk down the street wearing a hat of the vintage of 1890.

The astute manufacturers of clothing have not been slow to capitalize this basic fear of criticism, with which all mankind has been cursed. Every season the styles in many articles of wearing apparel change. Who establishes the styles? Certainly not the purchaser of clothing, but the manufacturer. Why does he change the styles so often? The answer is obvious. He changes the styles so he can sell more clothes.

For the same reason the manufacturers of automobiles (with a few rare and very sensible exceptions) change styles of models every season. No man wants to drive an automobile which is not of the latest style, although the older model may actually be the better car.

We have been describing the manner in which people behave under the influence of fear of criticism as applied to the small and petty things of life. Let us now examine human behavior when this fear affects people in connection with the more important events of human relationship. Take for example practically any person who has reached the age of "mental maturity" (from 35 to 40 years of age, as a general average), and if you could read the secret thoughts of his mind, you would find a very decided disbelief in most of the fables taught by the majority of the dogmatists and theologians a few decades back.

Not often, however, will you find a person who has the courage to openly state his belief on this subject. Most people will, if pressed far enough, tell a lie rather than admit that they do not believe the stories associated with that form of religion which held people in bondage prior to the age of scientific discovery and education.

Why does the average person, even in this day of enlightenment, shy away from denying his belief in the fables which were the basis of most of the religions a few decades ago? The answer is, "because of the fear of criticism." Men and women have been burned at the stake for daring to express disbelief in ghosts. It is no wonder we have inherited a consciousness which makes us fear criticism. The time was, and not so far in the past, when criticism carried severe punishments—it still does in some countries.

The fear of criticism robs man of his initiative, destroys his power of imagination, limits his individuality, takes away his self-reliance, and does him damage in a hundred other ways. Parents often do their children irreparable injury by criticizing them. The mother of one of my boyhood chums used to punish him with a switch almost daily, always completing the job with the statement, "You'll land in the penitentiary before you are twenty." He was sent to a Reformatory at the age of seventeen.

Criticism is the one form of service, of which everyone has too much. Everyone has a stock of it which is handed out, gratis, whether called for or not. One's nearest relatives often are the worst offenders. It should be recognized as a crime (in reality it is a crime of the worst nature), for any parent to build inferiority complexes in the mind of a child, through unnecessary criticism. Employers who understand human nature, get the best there is in men, not by criticism, but by constructive suggestion. Parents may accomplish the same results with their children. Criticism will plant FEAR in the human heart, or resentment, but it will not build love or affection.

Symptoms of the Fear of Criticism

This fear is almost as universal as the fear of poverty, and its effects are just as fatal to personal achievement, mainly because this fear destroys initiative, and discourages the use of imagination. The major symptoms of the fear are:

SELF-CONSCIOUSNESS. Generally expressed through nervousness, timidity in conversation and in meeting strangers, awkward movement of the hands and limbs, shifting of the eyes.

LACK OF POISE. Expressed through lack of voice control, nervousness in the presence of others, poor posture of body, poor memory.

PERSONALITY. Lacking in firmness of decision, personal charm, and ability to express opinions definitely. The habit of side-stepping issues instead of meeting them squarely. Agreeing with others without careful examination of their opinions.

INFERIORITY COMPLEX. The habit of expressing self-approval by word of mouth and by actions, as a means of covering up a feeling of inferiority. Using "big words" to impress others, (often without knowing the real meaning of the words). Imitating others in dress, speech and manners. Boasting of imaginary achievements. This sometimes gives a surface appearance of a feeling of superiority.

EXTRAVAGANCE. The habit of trying to "keep up with the Joneses," spending beyond one's income.

LACK OF INITIATIVE. Failure to embrace opportunities for self-advancement, fear to express opinions, lack of confidence in one's own ideas, giving evasive answers to questions asked by superiors, hesitancy of manner and speech, deceit in both words and deeds.

LACK OF AMBITION. Mental and physical laziness, lack of self-assertion, slowness in reaching decisions, easily influenced by others, the habit of criticizing others behind their backs and flattering them to their faces, the habit of accepting defeat without protest, quitting an undertaking when opposed by others, suspicious of other people without cause, lacking in tactfulness of manner and speech, unwillingness to accept the blame for mistakes.

The Fear of Ill Health

This fear may be traced to both physical and social heredity. It is closely associated, as to its origin, with the causes of fear of Old Age and the fear of Death, because it leads one closely to the border of "terrible worlds" of which man knows not, but concerning which he has been taught some discomforting stories. The opinion is somewhat general, also, that certain unethical people engaged in the business of "selling health" have had not a little to do with keeping alive the fear of ill health.

In the main, man fears ill health because of the terrible pictures which have been planted in his mind of what may happen if death should overtake him. He also fears it because of the economic toll which it may claim.

A reputable physician estimated that 75% of all people who visit physicians for professional service are suffering with hypochondria (imaginary illness). It has been shown most convincingly that the fear of disease, even where there is not the slightest cause for fear, often produces the physical symptoms of the disease feared.

Powerful and mighty is the human mind! It builds or it destroys.

Playing upon this common weakness of fear of ill health, dispensers of patent medicines have reaped fortunes. This form of imposition upon credulous humanity became so prevalent some twenty years ago that Colliers' Weekly Magazine conducted a bitter campaign against some of the worst offenders in the patent medicine business.

During the "flu" epidemic which broke out during the world war, the mayor of New York City took drastic steps to check the damage which people were doing themselves through their inherent fear of ill health. He called in the newspaper men and said to them, "Gentlemen, I feel it necessary to ask you not to publish any *scare headlines* concerning the 'flu' epidemic. Unless you cooperate with me, we will have a situation which we cannot control." The newspapers quit publishing stories about the "flu," and within one month the epidemic had been successfully checked.

Through a series of experiments conducted some years ago, it was proved that people may be made ill by suggestion. We conducted this experiment by causing three acquaintances to visit the "victims," each of whom asked the question, "What ails you? You look terribly ill." The first questioner usually provoked a grin, and a nonchalant "Oh, nothing, I'm alright," from the victim. The second questioner usually was answered with the statement, "I don't know exactly, but I do feel badly." The third questioner was usually met with the frank admission that the victim was actually feeling ill.

Try this on an acquaintance if you doubt that it will make him uncomfortable, but do not carry the experiment too far. There is a certain religious sect whose members take vengeance upon their enemies by the "hexing" method. They call it "placing a spell" on the victim.

There is overwhelming evidence that disease sometimes begins in the form of negative thought impulse. Such an impulse may be passed from one mind to another, by suggestion, or created by an individual in his own mind.

A man who was blessed with more wisdom than this incident might indicate, once said "When anyone asks me how I feel, I always want to answer by knocking him down."

Doctors send patients into new climates for their health, because a change of "mental attitude" is necessary. The seed of fear of ill health lives in every human mind. Worry, fear, discouragement, disappointment in love and business affairs, cause this seed to germinate and grow. The recent business depression kept the doctors on the run, because every form of negative thinking may cause ill health.

Disappointments in business and in love stand at the head of the list of causes of fear of ill health. A young man suffered a disappointment in love which sent him to a hospital. For months he hovered between life and death. A specialist in suggestive therapeutics was called in. The specialist changed nurses, placing him in charge of a very *charming young woman* who began (by pre-arrangement with the doctor) to make love to him the first day of her arrival on the job. Within three weeks the patient was discharged from the hospital, still suffering, but with an entirely different malady. HE WAS IN LOVE AGAIN. The remedy was a hoax, but the patient and the nurse were later married. Both are in good health at the time of this writing.

Symptoms of The Fear of Ill Health

The symptoms of this almost universal fear are:

AUTO-SUGGESTION. The habit of negative use of self-suggestion by looking for, and expecting to find the symptoms of all kinds of disease. "Enjoying" imaginary illness and speaking of it as being real. The habit of trying all "fads" and "isms" recommended by others as having therapeutic value. Talking to others of operations, accidents and other forms of illness. Experimenting with diets, physical exercises, reducing systems, without professional guidance. Trying home remedies, patent medicines and "quack" remedies.

HYPOCHONDRIA. The habit of talking of illness, concentrating the mind upon disease, and expecting its appearance until a nervous break occurs. Nothing that comes in bottles can cure this condition. It is brought on by negative thinking and nothing but positive thought can affect a cure. Hypochondria, (a medical term for imaginary disease) is said to do as much damage on occasion, as the disease one fears might do. Most so-called cases of "nerves" come from imaginary illness.

EXERCISE. Fear of ill health often interferes with proper physical exercise, and results in over-weight, by causing one to avoid outdoor life.

SUSCEPTIBILITY. Fear of ill health breaks down Nature's body resistance, and creates a favorable condition for any form of disease one may contact.

The fear of ill health often is related to the fear of Poverty, especially in the case of the hypochondriac, who constantly worries about the possibility of having to pay doctor's bills, hospital bills, etc. This type of person spends much time preparing for sickness, talking about death, saving money for cemetery lots, and burial expenses, etc.

SELF-CODDLING. The habit of making a bid for sympathy, using imaginary illness as the lure. (People often resort to this trick to avoid work). The habit of feigning illness to cover plain laziness, or to serve as an alibi for lack of ambition.

INTEMPERANCE. The habit of using alcohol or narcotics to destroy pains such as headaches, neuralgia, etc., instead of eliminating the cause.

The habit of reading about illness and worrying over the possibility of being stricken by it. The habit of reading patent medicine advertisements.

The Fear of Loss of Love

The original source of this inherent fear needs but little description, because it obviously grew out of man's polygamous habit of stealing his fellow man's mate, and his habit of taking liberties with her whenever he could.

Jealousy, and other similar forms of dementia praecox grow out of man's inherited fear of the loss of love of someone. This fear is the most painful of all the six basic fears. It probably plays more havoc with the body and mind than any of the other basic fears, as it often leads to permanent insanity.

The fear of the loss of love probably dates back to the stone age, when men stole women by brute force. They continue to steal females, but their technique has changed. Instead of force, they now use persuasion, the promise of pretty clothes, motor cars, and other "bait" much more effective than physical force. Man's habits are the same as they were at the dawn of civilization, but he expresses them differently.

Careful analysis has shown that women are more susceptible to this fear than men. This fact is easily explained. Women have learned, from experience, that men are polygamous by nature, that they are not to be trusted in the hands of rivals.

Symptoms of The Fear of Loss of Love

The distinguishing symptoms of this fear are:

JEALOUSY. The habit of being suspicious of friends and loved ones without any reasonable evidence of sufficient grounds. (Jealousy is a form of dementia praecox which sometimes becomes violent without the slightest cause). The habit of accusing wife or husband of infidelity without grounds. General suspicion of everyone, absolute faith in no one.

FAULT FINDING. The habit of finding fault with friends, relatives, business associates and loved ones upon the slightest provocation, or without any cause whatsoever.

GAMBLING. The habit of gambling, stealing, cheating, and otherwise taking hazardous chances to provide money for loved ones, with the belief that love can be bought. The habit of spending beyond one's means, or incurring debts, to provide gifts for loved ones, with the object of making a favorable showing. Insomnia, nervousness, lack of persistence, weakness of will, lack of self-control, lack of self-reliance, and bad temper.

The Fear of Old Age

In the main, this fear grows out of two sources. First, the thought that old age may bring with it POVERTY. Secondly, and by far the most common source of origin, from false and cruel teachings of the past which have been too well mixed with "fire and brimstone," and other bogies cunningly designed to enslave man through fear.

In the basic fear of old age, man has two very sound reasons for his apprehension—one growing out of his distrust of his fellowman, who may seize whatever worldly goods he may possess, and the other arising from the terrible pictures of the world beyond, which were planted in his mind, through social heredity before he came into full possession of his mind.

The possibility of ill health, which is more common as people grow older, is also a contributing cause of this common fear of old age. Eroticism also enters into the cause of the fear of old age, as no man cherishes the thought of diminishing sex attraction.

The most common cause of fear of old age is associated with the possibility of poverty. "Poorhouse" is not a pretty word. It throws a chill into the mind of every person who faces the possibility of having to spend his declining years on a poor farm.

Another contributing cause of the fear of old age, is the possibility of loss of freedom and independence, as old age may bring with it the loss of both physical and economic freedom.

Symptoms of The Fear of Old Age

The commonest symptoms of this fear are:

> The tendency to slow down and develop an inferiority complex at the age of mental maturity, around the age of forty, falsely believing one's self to be "slipping" because of age. (The truth is that man's most useful years, mentally and spiritually, are those between forty and sixty).
>
> The habit of speaking apologetically of one's self as "being old" merely because one has reached the age of forty, or fifty, instead of reversing the rule and expressing gratitude for having reached the age of wisdom and understanding.
>
> The habit of killing off initiative, imagination, and self-reliance by falsely believing one's self too old to exercise these qualities. The habit of the man or woman of forty dressing with the aim of trying to appear much younger, and affecting mannerisms of youth; thereby inspiring ridicule by both friends and strangers.

The Fear of Death

To some this is the cruelest of all the basic fears. The reason is obvious. The terrible pangs of fear associated with the thought of death, in the majority of cases, may be charged directly to religious fanaticism. So-called "heathen" are less afraid of death than the more "civilized." For hundreds of millions of years man has been asking the still unanswered questions, "whence" and "whither." Where did I come from, and where am I going?

During the darker ages of the past, the more cunning and crafty were not slow to offer the answer to these questions, FOR A PRICE. Witness, now, the major source of origin of the FEAR OF DEATH.

"Come into my tent, embrace my faith, accept my dogmas, and I will give you a ticket that will admit you straightaway into heaven when you die," cries a leader of sectarianism. "Remain out of my tent," says the same leader, "and may the devil take you and burn you throughout eternity."

ETERNITY is a long time. FIRE is a terrible thing. The thought of eternal punishment, with fire, not only causes man to fear death, it often causes him to lose his reason. It destroys interest in life and makes happiness impossible.

During my research, I reviewed a book entitled "A Catalogue of the Gods," in which were listed the *30,000 gods* which man has worshiped. Think of it! Thirty thousand of them, represented by everything from a crawfish to a man. It is little wonder that men have become frightened at the approach of death.

While the religious leader may not be able to provide safe conduct into heaven, nor, by lack of such provision, allow the unfortunate to descend into hell, the possibility of the latter seems so terrible that the very thought of it lays hold of the imagination in such a realistic way that it paralyzes reason, and sets up the fear of death.

In truth, NO MAN KNOWS, and no man has ever known, what heaven or hell is like, nor does any man know if either place actually exists. This very lack of positive knowledge opens the door of the human mind to the charlatan so he may enter and control that mind with his stock of legerdemain and various brands of pious fraud and trickery.

The fear of DEATH is not as common now as it was during the age when there were no great colleges and universities. Men of science have turned the spotlight of truth upon the world, and this truth is rapidly freeing men and women from this terrible fear of DEATH. The young men and young women who attend the colleges and universities are not easily impressed by "fire" and "brimstone." Through the aid of biology, astronomy, geology, and other related sciences, the fears of the dark ages which gripped the minds of men and destroyed their reason have been dispelled.

Insane asylums are filled with men and women who have gone mad, because of the FEAR OF DEATH.

This fear is useless. Death will come, no matter what anyone may think about it. Accept it as a necessity, and pass the thought out of your mind. It must be a necessity, or it would not come to all. Perhaps it is not as bad as it has been pictured.

The entire world is made up of only two things, ENERGY and MATTER. In elementary physics we learn that neither matter nor energy (the only two realities known to man) can be created nor destroyed. Both matter and energy can be transformed, but neither can be destroyed.

Life is energy, if it is anything. If neither energy nor matter can be destroyed, of course life cannot be destroyed. Life, like other forms of energy, may be passed through various processes of transition, or change, but it cannot be destroyed. Death is mere transition.

If death is not mere change, or transition, then nothing comes after death except a long, eternal, peaceful sleep, and sleep is nothing to be feared. Thus you may wipe out, forever, the fear of Death.

Symptoms of the Fear of Death

The general symptoms of this fear are:

> The habit of THINKING about dying instead of making the most of LIFE, due, generally, to lack of purpose, or lack of a suitable occupation. This fear is more prevalent among the aged, but sometimes the more youthful are victims of it. The greatest of all remedies for the fear of death is a BURNING DESIRE FOR ACHIEVEMENT, backed by useful service to others. A busy person seldom has time to think about dying. He finds life too thrilling to worry about death. Sometimes the fear of death is closely associated with the Fear of Poverty, where one's death would leave

loved ones poverty-stricken. In other cases, the fear of death is caused by illness and the consequent breaking down of physical body resistance. The commonest causes of the fear of death are: ill-health, poverty, lack of appropriate occupation, disappointment over love, insanity, religious fanaticism.

Old Man Worry

Worry is a state of mind based upon fear. It works slowly, but persistently. It is insidious and subtle. Step by step it "digs itself in" until it paralyzes one's reasoning faculty, destroys self-confidence and initiative. Worry is a form of sustained fear caused by indecision therefore it is a state of mind which can be controlled.

An unsettled mind is helpless. Indecision makes an unsettled mind. Most individuals lack the willpower to reach decisions promptly, and to stand by them after they have been made, even during normal business conditions. During periods of economic unrest (such as the world recently experienced), the individual is handicapped, not alone by his inherent nature to be slow at reaching decisions, but he is influenced by the indecision of others around him who have created a state of "mass indecision."

During the depression the whole atmosphere, all over the world, was filled with "Fearenza" and "Worryitis," the two mental disease germs which began to spread themselves after the Wall Street frenzy in 1929. There is only one known antidote for these germs; it is the habit of prompt and firm

DECISION. Moreover, it is an antidote which every individual must apply for himself.

We do not worry over conditions, once we have reached a decision to follow a definite line of action. I once interviewed a man who was to be electrocuted two hours later. The condemned man was the calmest of some eight men who were in the death-cell with him. His calmness prompted me to ask him how it felt to know that he was going into eternity in a short while. With a smile of confidence on his face, he said, "It feels fine. Just think, brother, my troubles will soon be over. I have had nothing but trouble all my life. It has been a hardship to get food and clothing. Soon I will not need these things. I have felt fine ever since I learned FOR CERTAIN that I must die. I made up my mind then, to accept my fate in good spirit."

As he spoke he devoured a dinner of proportions sufficient for three men, eating every mouthful of the food brought to him, and apparently enjoying it as much as if no disaster awaited him. DECISION gave this man resignation to his fate! Decision can also prevent one's acceptance of undesired circumstances.

The six basic fears become translated into a state of worry, through indecision. Relieve yourself, forever of the fear of death, by reaching a decision to accept death as an inescapable event. Whip the fear of poverty by reaching a decision to get along with whatever wealth you can accumulate WITHOUT WORRY. Put your foot upon the neck of the fear of criticism by reaching a decision NOT TO WORRY about what other people think, do, or say. Eliminate the fear of old age by reaching a decision to accept it, not as a handicap, but as a great blessing which carries with it wisdom, self-control, and understanding not known to youth. Acquit yourself of the fear of ill health by the decision to forget symptoms. Master the fear of loss of love by reaching a decision to get along without love, if that is necessary.

Kill the habit of worry, in all its forms, by reaching a general, blanket decision that nothing which life has to offer is worth the price of worry. With this decision will come poise, peace of mind, and calmness of thought which will bring happiness.

A man whose mind is filled with fear not only destroys his own chances of intelligent action, but, he transmits these destructive vibrations to the minds of all who come into contact with him, and destroys, also their chances.

Even a dog or a horse knows when its master lacks courage; moreover, a dog or a horse will pick up the vibrations of fear thrown off by its master, and behave accordingly. Lower down the line of intelligence in the animal kingdom, one finds this same capacity to pick up the vibrations of fear. A honey-bee immediately senses fear in the mind of a person— for reasons unknown, a bee will sting the person whose mind is releasing vibrations of fear, much more readily than it will molest the person whose mind registers no fear.

The vibrations of fear pass from one mind to another just as quickly and as surely as the sound of the human voice passes from the broadcasting station to the receiving set of a radio—and BY THE SELF-SAME MEDIUM.

Mental telepathy is a reality. Thoughts pass from one mind to another, voluntarily, whether or not this fact is recognized by either the person releasing the thoughts, or the persons who pick up those thoughts.

The person who gives expression, by word of mouth, to negative or destructive thoughts is practically certain to experience the results of those words in the form of a destructive "kick-back." The release of destructive thought impulses, alone, without the aid of words, produces also a "kickback" in more ways than one. First of all, and perhaps most important to be remembered, the person who releases thoughts of a destructive nature, must suffer damage through the breaking down of the faculty of creative imagination. Secondly, the presence in the mind of any destructive emotion develops a negative personality which repels people, and often converts them into antagonists. The third source of damage to the person who entertains or releases negative thoughts, lies in this significant fact—these thought-impulses are not only damaging to others, but they IMBED THEMSELVES IN THE SUBCONSCIOUS MIND OF THE PERSON RELEASING THEM, and there become a part of his character.

One is never through with a thought, merely by releasing it. When a thought is released, it spreads in every direction, through the medium of the ether, but it also plants itself *permanently* in the subconscious mind of *the person releasing it*.

Your business in life is, presumably to achieve success. To be successful, you must find peace of mind, acquire the material needs of life, and above all, attain HAPPINESS. All of these evidences of success begin in the form of thought impulses.

You may control your own mind, you have the power to feed it whatever thought impulses you choose. With this privilege goes also the responsibility of using it constructively. You are the master of your own earthly destiny just as surely as you have the power to control your own thoughts. You may influence, direct, and eventually control your own environment, making your life what you want it to be—or, you may neglect to exercise the privilege which is yours, to make your life to order, thus casting yourself upon the broad sea of "Circumstance" where you will be tossed hither and yon, like a chip on the waves of the ocean.

The Devil's Workshop
THE SEVENTH BASIC EVIL

In addition to the Six Basic Fears, there is another evil by which people suffer. It constitutes a rich soil in which the seeds of failure grow abundantly. It is so subtle that its presence often is not detected. This affliction cannot properly be classed as a fear. IT IS MORE DEEPLY SEATED AND MORE OFTEN FATAL THAN ALL OF THE SIX FEARS. For want of a better name, let us call this evil SUSCEPTIBILITY TO NEGATIVE INFLUENCES.

Men who accumulate great riches always protect themselves against this evil! The poverty stricken never do! Those who succeed in any calling must prepare their minds to resist the evil. If you are reading this philosophy for the purpose of accumulating riches, you should examine yourself very carefully, to determine whether you are susceptible to negative influences. If you neglect this self-analysis, you will forfeit your right to attain the object of your desires.

Make the analysis searching. After you read the questions prepared for this self-analysis, hold yourself to a strict accounting in your answers. Go at the task as carefully as you would search for any other enemy you knew to be awaiting you in ambush and deal with your own faults as you would with a more tangible enemy.

You can easily protect yourself against highway robbers, because the law provides organized cooperation for your benefit, but the "seventh basic evil" is more difficult to master, because it strikes when you are not aware of its presence, when you are asleep, and while you are awake. Moreover, its weapon is intangible, because it consists of merely—a STATE OF MIND. This evil is also dangerous because it strikes in as many different forms as there are human experiences. Sometimes it enters the mind through the well-meant words of one's own relatives. At other times, it bores from within, through one's own mental attitude. Always it is as deadly as poison, even though it may not kill as quickly.

How To Protect Yourself Against Negative Influences

To protect yourself against negative influences, whether of your own making, or the result of the activities of negative people around you, recognize that you have a WILL-POWER, and put it into constant use, until it builds a wall of immunity against negative influences in your own mind.

Recognize the fact that you, and every other human being, are, by nature, lazy, indifferent, and susceptible to all suggestions which harmonize with your weaknesses.

Recognize that you are, by nature, susceptible to all the six basic fears, and set up habits for the purpose of counteracting all these fears.

Recognize that negative influences often work on you through your subconscious mind, therefore they are difficult to detect, and keep your mind closed against all people who depress or discourage you in any way.

Clean out your medicine chest, throw away all pill bottles, and stop pandering to colds, aches, pains and imaginary illness.

Deliberately seek the company of people who influence you to THINK AND ACT FOR YOURSELF.

Do not EXPECT troubles as they have a tendency not to disappoint.

Without doubt, the most common weakness of all human beings is the habit of leaving their minds open to the negative influence of other people. This weakness is all the more damaging, because most people do not recognize that they are cursed by it, and many who acknowledge it, neglect or refuse to correct the evil until it becomes an uncontrollable part of their daily habits.

To aid those who wish to see themselves as they really are, the following list of questions has been prepared. Read the questions and state your answers aloud, so you can hear your own voice. This will make it easier for you to be truthful with yourself.

Self-Analysis Test Questions

- Do you complain often of "feeling bad," and if so, what is the cause?
- Do you find fault with other people at the slightest provocation?
- Do you frequently make mistakes in your work, and if so, why?
- Are you sarcastic and offensive in your conversation?
- Do you deliberately avoid the association of anyone, and if so, why?
- Do you suffer frequently with indigestion? If so, what is the cause?
- Does life seem futile and the future hopeless to you? If so, why?
- Do you like your occupation? If not, why? Do you often feel self-pity, and if so why? Are you envious of those who excel you?
- To which do you devote most time, thinking of SUCCESS, or of FAILURE?
- Are you gaining or losing self-confidence as you grow older?
- Do you learn something of value from all mistakes? Are you permitting some relative or acquaintance to worry you? If so, why?
- Are you sometimes "in the clouds" and at other times in the depths of despondency?
- Who has the most inspiring influence upon you? What is the cause?

- Do you tolerate negative or discouraging influences which you can avoid?
- Are you careless of your personal appearance? If so, when and why?
- Have you learned how to "drown your troubles" by being too busy to be annoyed by them?
- Would you call yourself a "spineless weakling" if you permitted others to do your thinking for you?
- Do you neglect internal bathing until auto-intoxication makes you ill-tempered and irritable?
- How many preventable disturbances annoy you, and why do you tolerate them?
- Do you resort to liquor, narcotics, or cigarettes to "quiet your nerves"? If so, why do you not try will-power instead?
- Does anyone "nag" you, and if so, for what reason? Do you have a DEFINITE MAJOR PURPOSE, and if so, what is it, and what plan have you for achieving it?
- Do you suffer from any of the Six Basic Fears? If so, which ones?
- Have you a method by which you can shield yourself against the negative influence of others? Do you make deliberate use of auto-suggestion to make your mind positive?
- Which do you value most, your material possessions, or your privilege of controlling your own thoughts?
- Are you easily influenced by others, against your own judgment?
- Has today added anything of value to your stock of knowledge or state of mind?

Procrastination and Fear

- Do you face squarely the circumstances which make you unhappy, or sidestep the responsibility?
- Do you analyze all mistakes and failures and try to profit by them, or, do you take the attitude that this is not your duty?
- Can you name three of your most damaging weaknesses? What are you doing to correct them? Do you encourage other people to bring their worries to you for sympathy?
- Do you choose, from your daily experiences, lessons or influences which aid in your personal advancement?
- Does your presence have a negative influence on other people as a rule?
- What habits of other people annoy you most?
- Do you form your own opinions or permit yourself to be influenced by other people?
- Have you learned how to create a mental state of mind with which you can shield yourself against all discouraging influences?
- Does your occupation inspire you with faith and hope?
- Are you conscious of possessing spiritual forces of sufficient power to enable you to keep your mind free from all forms of FEAR?
- Does your religion help you to keep your own mind positive?
- Do you feel it your duty to share other people's worries? If so, why?
- If you believe that "birds of a feather flock together" what have you learned about yourself by studying the friends whom you attract?

- What connection, if any, do you see between the people with whom you associate most closely, and any unhappiness you may experience?
- Could it be possible that some person whom you consider to be a friend is, in reality, your worst enemy, because of his negative influence on your mind?
- By what rules do you judge who is helpful and who is damaging to you?
- Are your intimate associates mentally superior or inferior to you?
- How much time out of every 24 hours do you devote to:
    a. your occupation
    b. sleep
    c. play and relaxation
    d. acquiring useful knowledge
    e. plain waste
- Who among your acquaintances,
    a. encourages you most
    b. cautions you most
    c. discourages you most
    d. helps you most in other ways
- What is your greatest worry? Why do you tolerate it?
- When others offer you free, unsolicited advice, do you accept it without question, or analyze their motive?
- What, above all else, do you most DESIRE? Do you intend to acquire it? Are you willing to subordinate all other desires for this one? How much time daily do you devote to acquiring it?
- Do you change your mind often? If so, why?

Procrastination and Fear

- Do you usually finish everything you begin?
- Are you easily impressed by other people's business or professional titles, college degrees, or wealth? Are you easily influenced by what other people think or say of you?
- Do you cater to people because of their social or financial status?
- Whom do you believe to be the greatest person living? In what respect is this person superior to yourself?
- How much time have you devoted to studying and answering these questions? (At least one day is necessary for the analysis and the answering of the entire list.)

If you have answered all these questions truthfully, you know more about yourself than the majority of people. Study the questions carefully, come back to them once each week for several months, and be astounded at the amount of additional knowledge of great value to yourself, you will have gained by the simple method of answering the questions truthfully. If you are not certain concerning the answers to some of the questions, seek the counsel of those who know you well, especially those who have no motive in flattering you, and see yourself through their eyes. The experience will be astonishing.

You have ABSOLUTE CONTROL over but one thing, and that is your thoughts. This is the most significant and inspiring of all facts known to man! It reflects man's Divine nature. This Divine prerogative is the sole means by which you may control your own destiny. If you fail to control your own mind, you may be sure you will control nothing else.

If you must be careless with your possessions, let it be in connection with material things. *Your mind is your spiritual estate!* Protect and use it with the care to which Divine Royalty is entitled. You were given a WILL-POWER for this purpose.

Unfortunately, there is no legal protection against those who, either by design or ignorance, poison the minds of others by negative suggestion. This form of destruction should be punishable by heavy legal penalties, because it may and often does destroy one's chances of acquiring material things which are protected by law.

Men with negative minds tried to convince Thomas A. Edison that he could not build a machine that would record and reproduce the human voice, "because" they said, "no one else had ever produced such a machine." Edison did not believe them. He knew that the mind could produce ANYTHING THE MIND COULD CONCEIVE AND BELIEVE, and that knowledge was the thing that lifted the great Edison above the common herd.

Men with negative minds told F. W. Woolworth, he would go "broke" trying to run a store on five and ten cent sales. He did not believe them. He knew that he could do anything, within reason, if he backed his plans with faith. Exercising his right to keep other men's negative suggestions out of his mind, he piled up a fortune of more than a hundred million dollars.

Men with negative minds told George Washington he could not hope to win against the vastly superior forces of the British, but he exercised his Divine right to BELIEVE, therefore this book was published under the protection of the Stars and Stripes, while the name of Lord Cornwallis has been all but forgotten.

Doubting Thomases scoffed scornfully when Henry Ford tried out his first crudely built automobile on the streets of Detroit. Some said the thing never would become practical. Others said no one would pay money for such a contraption. FORD SAID, "I'LL BELT THE EARTH WITH DEPENDABLE MOTOR CARS," AND HE DID! His decision to trust his own judgment has already piled up a fortune far greater than the next five generations of his descendants can squander. For the benefit of those seeking vast riches, let it be remembered that practically the sole difference between Henry Ford and a majority of the more than one hundred thousand men who work for him, is this—FORD HAS A MIND AND CONTROLS IT, THE OTHERS HAVE MINDS WHICH THEY DO NOT TRY TO CONTROL.

Henry Ford has been repeatedly mentioned, because he is an astounding example of what a man with a mind of his own, and a will to control it, can accomplish. His record knocks the foundation from under that time-worn alibi, "I never had a chance." Ford never had a chance, either, but he CREATED AN OPPORTUNITY AND BACKED IT WITH PERSISTENCE UNTIL IT MADE HIM RICHER THAN CROESUS.

Mind control is the result of self-discipline and habit. You either control your mind or it controls you. There is no half-way compromise. The most practical of all methods for controlling the mind is the habit of keeping it busy with a definite purpose, backed by a definite plan. Study the record of any man who achieves noteworthy success, and you will observe that he has control over his own mind, moreover, that he exercises that control and directs it toward the attainment of definite objectives. Without this control, success is not possible.

"Fifty-Seven" Famous Alibis by Old Man IF

People who do not succeed have one distinguishing trait in common. They know *all the reasons for failure*, and have what they believe to be air-tight alibis to explain away their own lack of achievement.

Some of these alibis are clever, and a few of them are justifiable by the facts. But alibis cannot be used for money. The world wants to know only one thing—HAVE YOU ACHIEVED SUCCESS?

A character analyst compiled a list of the most commonly used alibis. As you read the list, examine yourself carefully, and determine how many of these alibis, if any, are your own property. Remember, too, the philosophy presented in this book makes every one of these alibis obsolete.

IF I didn't have a wife and family . . .
IF I had enough "pull" . . .
IF I had money . . .
IF I had a good education . . .
IF I could get a job . . .
IF I had good health . . .
IF I only had time . . .

IF times were better . . .
IF other people understood me . . .
IF conditions around me were only different . . .
IF I could live my life over again . . .
IF I did not fear what "THEY" would say . . .
IF I had been given a chance . . .
IF I now had a chance . . .
IF other people didn't "have it in for me" . . .
IF nothing happens to stop me . . .
IF I were only younger . . .
IF I could only do what I want . . .
IF I had been born rich . . .
IF I could meet "the right people" . . .
IF I had the talent that some people have . . .
IF I dared assert myself . . .
IF I only had embraced past opportunities . . .
IF people didn't get on my nerves . . .
IF I didn't have to keep house and look after the children . . .
IF I could save some money . . .
IF the boss only appreciated me . . .
IF I only had somebody to help me . . .
IF my family understood me . . .
IF I lived in a big city . . .
IF I could just get started . . .
IF I were only free . . .
IF I had the personality of some people . . .
IF I were not so fat . . .
IF my talents were known . . .
IF I could just get a "break" . . .

IF I could only get out of debt . . .
IF I hadn't failed . . .
IF I only knew how . . .
IF everybody didn't oppose me . . .
IF I didn't have so many worries . . .
IF I could marry the right person . . .
IF people weren't so dumb . . .
IF my family were not so extravagant . . .
IF I were sure of myself . . .
IF luck were not against me . . .
IF I had not been born under the wrong star . . .
IF it were not true that "what is to be will be" . . .
IF I did not have to work so hard . . .
IF I hadn't lost my money . . .
IF I lived in a different neighborhood . . .
IF I didn't have a "past" . . .
IF I only had a business of my own . . .
IF other people would only listen to me . . .
IF * * * and this is the greatest of them all * * * I had the courage to see myself as I really am, I would *find out what is wrong with me, and correct it*, then I might have a chance to profit by my mistakes and learn something from the experience of others, for I know that there is something WRONG with me, or I would now be where *I WOULD HAVE BEEN IF* I had spent more time analyzing my weaknesses, and less time building alibis to cover them.

Building alibis with which to explain away failure is a national pastime. The habit is as old as the human race, and is *fatal to*

Procrastination and Fear

success! Why do people cling to their pet alibis? The answer is obvious. They defend their alibis because THEY CREATE them! A man's alibi is the child of his own imagination. It is human nature to defend one's own brain-child.

Building alibis is a deeply rooted habit. Habits are difficult to break, especially when they provide justification for something we do. Plato had this truth in mind when he said, "The first and best victory is to conquer self. To be conquered by self is, of all things, the most shameful and vile."

Another philosopher had the same thought in mind when he said, "It was a great surprise to me when I discovered that most of the ugliness I saw in others, was but a reflection of my own nature."

"It has always been a mystery to me," said Elbert Hubbard, "why people spend so much time deliberately fooling themselves by creating alibis to cover their weaknesses. If used differently, this same time would be sufficient to cure the weakness, then no alibis would be needed."

In parting, I would remind you that "Life is a checkerboard, and the player opposite you is TIME. If you hesitate before moving, or neglect to move promptly, your men will be wiped off the board by TIME. You are playing against a partner who will not tolerate INDECISION!"

Previously you may have had a logical excuse for not having forced Life to come through with whatever you asked, but that alibi is now obsolete, because you are in possession of the Master Key that unlocks the door to Life's bountiful riches.

The Master Key is intangible, but it is powerful! It is the privilege of creating, *in your own mind*, a BURNING

DESIRE for a definite form of riches. There is no penalty for the use of the Key, but there is a price you must pay if you do not use it. The price is FAILURE. There is a reward of stupendous proportions if you put the Key to use. It is the satisfaction that comes to all who *conquer self and force Life to pay whatever is asked.*

The reward is worthy of your effort. Will you make the start and be convinced?

"If we are related," said the immortal Emerson, "we shall meet." In closing, may I borrow his thought, and say, "If we are related, we have, through these pages, met."

V
Leadership

Initiative and Leadership,
from
The Law of Success
(1928)

One of the interesting things about this chapter is how little it actually says about leadership as a position, rank, or office. Rather, Hill focuses on the processes that naturally make someone a leader.

To begin with, Hill defines leadership and initiative as essentially the same. Initiative means doing what is necessary without be told, cajoled, or even rewarded. Any manager, director, editor, officer, or supervisor who is feckless or apathetic—who will not go the extra distance to improve a service, product, or outcome—is not a leader, and never will be. Leadership is not a title but an act.

A leader is by definition the best-informed and most capable person in any operation, whatever his or her title. Although I do not view Napoleon Bonaparte as a model of statesmanship, I've always been touched by the passage that Ralph Waldo Emerson attributed to the French conqueror in his 1860 essay "Success":

> *"There is nothing in war," said Napoleon, "which I cannot do by my own hands. If there is nobody to make gunpowder, I can manufacture it. The gun-carriages I know how to construct. If it is necessary to make cannons at the forge, I can make them. The details of working them in battle, if it is necessary to teach, I shall teach them. In administration, it is I alone who have arranged the finances, as you know."*

A real leader never asks subordinates to do something that he is unwilling to do. A leader is not above cleaning up a mess, broadly defined—whether his own or another's. A leader does not find ways to be out of the room or unavailable at a time of reckoning for a mistake or mishap.

A leader also acts decisively. In one of my favorite passages in this chapter Hill writes, "Any reasonable order in an emergency is better than no order." Life favors action. To dither, in matters large or small, is to virtually guarantee defeat. To act decisively may risk defeat—but the better part of such a risk is deliverance.

A leader also must know those who work for him. There is no one-size-fits-all approach to motivation, reward, or correction. I once knew a supervisor who sought to avoid conflict by delivering blanket orders—willfully ignoring differences in people's reliability, output, and work style, and thus sidestepping the question of who was or wasn't contributing, and what support, recognition, or correction each person needed. That is the avoidance of leadership.

In short, there is no such thing as leadership in itself. Rather, leadership is a label that we apply to responsibility and reliability—whether or not it comes with a title.

—MH

INITIATIVE AND LEADERSHIP

Initiative and Leadership are associated terms in this lesson for the reason that *Leadership* is essential for the attainment of *Success,* and *Initiative* is the very foundation upon which this necessary quality of *Leadership* is built. *Initiative* is as essential to success as a hub is essential to a wagon wheel.

And what is *Initiative?*

It is that exceedingly rare quality that prompts—nay, impels—a person to do that which ought to be done *without being told to do it.* Elbert Hubbard expressed himself on the subject of *Initiative* in the words:

"The world bestows its big prizes, both in money and honors, for one thing, and that is *Initiative.*

"What is initiative? I'll tell you: It is doing the right thing without being told.

"But next to doing the right thing without being told is to do it when you are told once. That is say, 'Carry the message to Garcia.' Those who can carry a message get high honors, but their pay is not always in proportion.

"Next, there are those who do the right thing when necessity kicks them from behind, and these 'get indifference instead of honors, and a pittance for pay.

"This kind spend most of the time polishing a bench with a hard luck story.

"Then, still lower down in the scale than this we have the fellow who will not do the right thing even when someone goes along to show him how and stays to see that he does it; he is always out of a job, a receives the contempt he deserves, unless he has a rich pa, in which case destiny patiently waits around the comer with a stuffed club.

"To which class do *you* belong?"

Inasmuch as you will be expected to take inventory of yourself and determine which of the fifteen factors of this course you need most, after you have completed the sixteenth lesson, it may be well if you begin to get ready for this analysis by answering the question that Elbert Hubbard has asked

To which class do you belong?

One of the peculiarities of *Leadership* is the fact that it is never found in those who have not acquired the *habit* of taking the initiative. *Leadership* is something that you must invite yourself into; it will never thrust itself upon you. If you will carefully analyze all leaders whom you know you will see that they not only exercised *Initiative*, but they went about their work with a *definite purpose* in mind. You will also see that they possessed that quality described in the third lesson of this course, *Self-confidence*.

Leadership

These facts are mentioned in this lesson for the reason that it will profit you to observe that successful people make use of all the factors covered by the sixteen lessons of the course; and, for the more important reason that it will profit you to understand thoroughly the principle of *organized effort* which this Reading Course is intended to establish in your mind.

This seems an appropriate place to state that this course is not intended as a *short-cut* to success, nor is it intended as a mechanical formula that you may use in noteworthy achievement without effort on your part. The *real* value of the course lies in the *use* that you will make of it, and not in the course itself. The chief purpose of the course is to help you develop in yourself the fifteen qualities covered by the sixteen lessons of the course, and one of the most important of these qualities is *Initiative*, the subject of this lesson.

We will now proceed to apply the principle upon which this lesson is founded by describing, in detail, just how it served successfully to complete a business transaction which most people would call difficult.

In 1916 I needed $25,000 with which to create an educational institution, but I had neither this sum nor sufficient collateral with which to borrow it through the usual banking sources. Did I bemoan my fate or think of what I might accomplish if some rich relative or Good Samaritan would come to my rescue by loaning me the necessary capital?

I did nothing of the sort!

I did just what you will be advised, throughout this course, to do. First of all, I made the securing of this capital my *defi-*

nite chief aim. Second, I laid out a complete *plan* through which to transform this aim into reality. Backed by sufficient Self-confidence and spurred on by *Initiative*, I proceeded to put my plan into action. But, before the "action" stage of the plan had been reached, more than six weeks of constant, persistent study and effort and thought were embodied in it. If a plan is to be sound it must be built of carefully chosen material.

You will here observe the application of the principle of *organized effort,* through the operation of which it is possible for one to ally or associate several interests in such a way that *each of these interests* is greatly strengthened and each supports all the others, just as one link in a chain supports all the other links.

I wanted this $25,000 in capital for the purpose of creating a school of Advertising and Salesmanship. Two things were necessary for the organization of such a school. One was the $25,000 capital, which I did not have, and the other was the proper course of instruction, which *I did have.* My problem was to *ally myself* with some group of men who needed that which I had, and who would supply the $25,000. This alliance had to be made through a plan that would benefit all concerned.

After my plan had been completed, and I was satisfied that it was equitable and sound, I laid it before the owner of a well known and reputable business college which just then was finding competition quite keen and was badly in need of a plan for meeting this competition.

My plan was presented in about these words:

Whereas, you have one of the most reputable business colleges in the city; and,

Whereas, you need some plan with which to meet the stiff competition in your field; and,

Whereas, your good reputation has provided you with all the credit you need; and,

Whereas, I have the plan that will help you meet this competition successfully.

Be it resolved, that we ally ourselves through a plan that will give you that which you need and at the same time supply me with something which I need.

Then I proceeded to unfold my plan, further, in these words:

I have written a very practical course on Advertising and Salesmanship. Having built this course out of my actual experience in training and directing salesmen and my experience in planning and Directing many successful advertising campaigns, I have back of it plenty of evidence of its soundness.

If you will use your credit in helping market this course I will place it in your business college, as one of the regular departments of your curriculum and take entire charge of this newly created department. No other business college in the city will be able to meet your competition, for the reason that no other college has such a course as this. The advertising that you do in marketing this course will serve, also, to stimulate the demand for your regular business course. You may charge the entire amount that you spend for this advertising, to my department, and the advertising bill will be paid out of that department, leaving you the accumulative advantage that will accrue to your other departments without cost to you.

Now, I suppose you will want to know where I profit by this transaction, and I will tell you. I want you to enter into a contract with me in which it will be agreed that when the cash receipts from my department equal the amount that you have paid out or contracted to pay out for advertising, my department and my course in Advertising and Salesmanship become my own and I may have the privilege of separating this department from your school and running it under my own name.

The plan was agreeable and the contract was closed.

(Please keep in mind that my *definite purpose* was to secure the use of $25,000 for which I had no security to offer.)

In a little less than a year the Business College had paid out slightly more than $25,000 for advertising and marketing my course and the other expenses incidental to the operation of this newly organized department, while the department had collected and, turned back to the College, in tuition fees, a sum equaling the amount the College had spent, and I took the department over, as a going and self-sustaining business, according to the terms of my contract.

As a matter of fact this newly created department not only served to attract students for the other departments of the College, but at the same time the tuition fees collected through this new department were sufficient to place it on a self-sustaining basis before the end of the first year.

Now you can see that while the College did not loan me one penny of actual capital, it nevertheless supplied me with credit which served exactly the same purpose.

I said that my plan was founded upon equity; that it contemplated a benefit to all parties concerned. The benefit accruing to me was the use of the $25,000, which resulted in an established and self-sustaining business by the end of the first year. The benefit accruing to the college was the students secured for its regular commercial and business course as a result of the money spent in advertising my department, all advertising having been done under the name of the College.

Today that business college is one of the most successful schools of its kind, and it stands as a monument of sound evidence with which to demonstrate the value of *allied effort*.

This incident has been related, not alone because it shows the value of *initiative* and *leadership*, but for the reason that it leads up to the subject covered by the next lesson of this Reading Course on the Law of Success, which is *imagination*.

There are generally many plans through the operation of which a desired object may be achieved, and it often happens to be true that the obvious and usual methods employed are not the best. The usual method of procedure, in the case related, would have been that of borrowing from a bank. You can see that this method was impractical, in this case, for the reason that no collateral was available.

A great philosopher once said: *"Initiative is the pass-key that opens the door to opportunity."*

I do not recall who this philosopher was, but I know that he was *great* because of the soundness of his statement.

We will now proceed to outline the exact procedure that you must follow if you are to become a person of *initiative* and *leadership*.

First: You must master the habit of *procrastination* and eliminate it from your make-up. This habit of putting off until tomorrow that which you should have done last week or last year or a score of years ago is gnawing at the very vitals of your being, and you can accomplish nothing until you throw it off.

The method through which you eliminate *procrastination* is based upon a well known and scientifically tested principle of psychology which has been referred to in the two preceding lessons of this course as Auto-suggestion.

Copy the following formula and place it conspicuously in your room where you will see it as you retire at night and as you arise in the morning:

Initiative and Leadership

Having chosen a *definite chief aim* as my life-work I now understand it to be my duty to transform this purpose into reality.

Therefore, I will form the habit of taking some *definite* action each day that will carry me one step nearer the attainment of my *definite chief aim*.

I know that *procrastination* is a deadly enemy of all who would become leaders in any undertaking, and I will eliminate this habit from my make-up by:

(a) Doing some one definite thing each day, that ought to be done, without anyone telling me to do it.

(b) Looking around until I find at least one thing that I can do each day, that I have not been in the habit of doing, and that will be of value to others, without expectation of pay.

(c) Telling at least one other person, each day, of the value of practicing this habit of doing something that ought to be done without being told to do it.

I can see that the muscles of the body become strong in proportion to the extent to which they are used, therefore I understand that the *habit of initiative* also becomes fixed in proportion to the extent that it is practiced.

I realize that the place to begin developing the *habit of initiative* is in the small, commonplace things connected with my daily work, therefore I will go at my work each day as if I were doing it solely for the purpose of developing this necessary *habit of initiative*.

I understand that by practicing this *habit* of taking the *initiative* in connection with my daily work I will be not only developing that habit, but I will also be attracting the attention of those who will place greater value on my services as a result of this practice.

Signed _____

Regardless of what you are now doing, every day brings you face to face with a chance to render some service, outside of the course of your regular duties, that will be of value to others. In rendering this additional service, of your own accord, you of course understand that you are not doing so with the object of receiving monetary pay. You are rendering this service because it provides you with ways and means of exercising, developing and making stronger the aggressive spirit of *initiative* which you must possess before you can ever become an outstanding figure in the affairs of your chosen field of life-work.

Those who work for *money* alone, and who receive for their pay nothing but money, are always underpaid, no matter how much they receive. Money is necessary, but the big prizes of life cannot be measured in dollars and cents.

No amount of money could possibly be made to take the place of the happiness and joy and pride that belong to the person who digs a better ditch, or builds a better chicken coop, or sweeps a cleaner floor, or cooks a better meal. Every normal person loves to create something that is better than the average. The joy of *creating* a work of art is a joy that cannot be replaced by money or any other form of material possession.

I have in my employ a young lady who opens, assorts and answers much of my personal mail. She began in my employ more than three years ago. Then her duties were to take dictation when she was asked to do so. Her salary was about the same as that which others receive for similar service. One day I dictated the following motto which I asked her to typewrite for me:

Remember that your only limitation is the one that you set up in your own mind.

As she handed the typewritten page back to me she said, "Your motto has given me an idea that is going to be of value to both you and me."

I told her I was glad to have been of service to her. The incident made no particular impression on my mind, but from that day on I could see that it had made a *tremendous* impression on her mind. She began to come back to the office after supper and performed service that she was neither paid for nor expected to perform. Without anyone telling her to do it she began to bring to my desk letters that she had answered for me. She had studied my style and these letters were attended to as well as I could have done it; in some instances much better. She kept up this habit until my personal secretary resigned. When I began to look for someone to take his place, what was more natural than to turn to this young woman to fill the place. Before I had time to give her the position *she took it on her initiative*. My personal mail began to come to my desk with a new secretary's name attached, and she was that secretary. On her own time, after hours, without additional pay, she had prepared herself for the best position on my staff.

But that is not all. This young lady became so noticeably efficient that she began to attract the attention of others who offered her attractive positions. I have increased her salary many times and she now receives a salary more than four times as large as the amount she received when she first went to work for me as an ordinary stenographer, and, to tell you the truth, I am helpless in the matter, because she has made herself so valuable to me that I cannot get along without her.

That is initiative transformed into practical, understandable terms. I would be remiss in my duties if I failed to direct your attention to an advantage, other than a greatly increased salary, that this young lady's *initiative* has brought her. It has developed in her a spirit of cheerfulness that brings her happiness which most stenographers never know. Her work is not work—it is a great interesting game at which she is playing. Even though she arrives at the office ahead of the regular stenographers and remains there long after they have watched the clock tick off *five o'clock* and *quitting time*, her hours are shorter by far than are those of the other workers. Hours of labor do not drag on the hands of those who are happy at their work.

This brings us to the next step in our description of the exact procedure that you must follow in developing *initiative* and *leadership*.

Second: You of course understand that the only way to get *happiness* is by giving it away, to others. The same applies to the development of *initiative*. You can best develop this essential quality in yourself by making it your business to interest those around you in doing the same. It is a well known fact that a man learns best that which he endeavors to teach others. If a man embraces a certain creed or religious faith, the first thing he does is to go out and try to "sell" it to others. And in exact proportion to the extent to which he impresses others does he impress *himself*.

In the field of salesmanship it is a well known fact that no salesman is successful in selling others until he has first made a good job of selling *himself*. Stated conversely, no salesman can do his best to sell others without sooner or later selling himself that which he is trying to sell to others.

Any statement that a person repeats over and over again for the purpose of inducing others to believe it, he, also, will come to believe, and this holds good whether the statement is false or true.

Leadership

You can now see the advantage of making it your business to *talk initiative, think initiative, eat initiative, sleep initiative and practice initiative.* By so doing you are becoming a person of *initiative* and *leadership,* for it is a well known fact that people will readily, willingly and voluntarily follow the person who shows by his actions that he is a person of *initiative.*

In the place where you work or the community in which you live you come in contact with other people. Make it your business to interest every one of them who will listen to you, in the development of *initiative.* It will not be necessary for you to give your reasons for doing this, nor will it be necessary for you to announce the fact that you are doing it. *Just go ahead and do it.* In your own mind you will understand, of course, that you are doing it because this practice will help you and will, at least, do those whom you influence in the same practice no harm.

If you wish to try an experiment that will prove both interesting and profitable to you, pick out some person of your acquaintance whom you know to be a person who never does anything that he is not expected to do, and begin selling him your idea of *initiative.* Do not stop by merely discussing the subject once; keep it up every time you have a convenient opportunity. Approach the subject from a different angle each time. If you go at this experiment in a tactful and forceful manner you will soon observe a change in the person on whom you are trying the experiment.

And, you will observe something else of more importance still: *You will observe a change in yourself!*

Do not fail to try this experiment.

You cannot talk *initiative* to others without developing a desire to practice it yourself. Through the operation of the principle of Auto-suggestion every statement that you make to others leaves its imprint on your own subconscious mind, and this holds good whether your statements are false or true.

You have often heard the saying: "He who lives by the sword will die by the sword."

Properly interpreted, this simply means that we are constantly attracting to ourselves and weaving into our own characters and personalities those qualities which our influence is helping to create in others. If we help others develop the habit of initiative, we, in turn, develop this same habit. If we sow the seeds of hatred and envy and discouragement in others, we, in turn, develop these qualities in ourselves. This principle through which a man comes to resemble in his own nature those whom he most admires is fully brought out in Hawthorne's story, *The Great Stone Face*, a story that every parent should have his offspring read.

We come, now, to the next step in our description of the exact procedure that you must follow in developing *initiative* and *leadership*.

Third: Before we go further let it be understood what is meant by the term "Leadership," as it is used in connection with this Reading Course on the Law of Success. There are two brands of *leadership*, and one of them is as deadly and destructive as the other is helpful and constructive. The deadly brand, which leads not to *success*, but to *absolute failure*, is the brand adopted by pseudo-leaders who *force* their leadership on unwilling followers. It will not be necessary here to describe this brand or to point out the fields of endeavor in which it is practiced, with the exception of the field of war, and in this field we will mention but one notable example, that of Napoleon.

Napoleon was a *leader;* there can be no doubt about this, but he led his followers and himself to destruction. The details are recorded in the history of France and the French people, where you may study them if you choose.

It is not Napoleon's brand of *leadership* that is recommended in this course, although I will admit that Napoleon possessed all the necessary fundamentals for great leadership, excepting one—he lacked the spirit of helpfulness to others as an objective. His desire for the power that comes through leadership was based solely upon self-aggrandizement. His desire for leadership was built upon personal ambition and not upon the desire to lift the French people to a higher and nobler station in the affairs of nations.

The brand of *leadership* that is recommended through this course of instruction is the brand which leads to self-determination and freedom and self-development and enlightenment and justice. This is the brand that endures. For example, and as a contrast with the brand of *leadership* through which Napoleon raised himself into prominence, consider our own American commoner, Lincoln. The object of his *leadership* was to bring truth and justice and understanding to the people of the United States. Even though he died a martyr to his belief in this brand of *leadership*, his name has been engraved upon the heart of the world in terms of loving kindliness that will never bring aught but good to the world.

Both Lincoln and Napoleon led armies in warfare, but the objects of their *leadership* were as different as night is different from day. If it would give you a better understanding of the principles upon which this Reading Course is based, you could easily be cited to *leadership* of today which resembles both the brand that Napoleon employed and that which Lincoln made the foundation of his life-work, but this is not essential; your own ability to look around and analyze men who take the leading parts in all lines of endeavor is sufficient to enable you to pick out the Lincoln as well as the Napoleon types. Your own judgment will help you decide which type you prefer to emulate.

There can be no doubt in your mind as to the brand of *leadership* that is recommended in this Reading Course, and there should be no question in your mind as to which of the two brands described you will adopt as your brand. We make no recommendations on this subject, however, for the reason that this Reading Course has been prepared as a means of laying before its students the fundamental principles upon which power is developed, and not as a preachment on ethical conduct. We present both the constructive and the destructive possibilities of the principles outlined in this course, that you may become familiar with both, but we leave entirely to your own discretion the choice and application of these principles, believing that your own intelligence will guide you to make a wise selection.

The Penalty of Leadership*

In every field of human endeavor, he that is first must perpetually live in the white light of publicity. Whether the leadership be vested in a man or in a manufactured product, emulation and envy are ever at work.

In art, in literature, in music, in industry, the reward and the punishment are always the same. The reward is widespread recognition; the punishments fierce denial and detraction.

When a man's work becomes a standard for the whole world, it also becomes a target for the shafts of the envious few. If his work be merely mediocre, he will be left severely alone—if he achieve a masterpiece, it will set a million tongues-a-wagging.

Jealousy does not protrude its forked tongue at the artist who produces a commonplace painting.

Whatsoever you write, or paint, or play, or sing or build, no one will strive to surpass or slander you, unless your work be stamped with the seal of a genius.

Long, long after a great work or a good work has been done, those who are disappointed or envious continue to cry out that it cannot be done.

Mean voices were raised against the author of the Law of Success before the ink was dry on the first textbooks. Poisoned pens were released against both the author and the philosophy the moment the first edition of the course was printed.

---

* (With the compliments of the Cadillac Motor Car Co.)

Spiteful little voices in the domain of art were raised against our own Whistler as a mountebank, long after the big world acclaimed him its greatest artistic genius.

Multitudes flocked to Beyreuth to worship at the musical shrine of Wagner, while the little group of those whom he had dethroned and displaced argued angrily that he was no musician at all.

The little world continued to protest that Fulton could never build a steamboat, while the big world flocked to the river banks to see his boat steam by.

Small, narrow voices cried out that Henry Ford would not last another year, but above and beyond the din of their childish prattle Ford went silently about his business and made himself the richest and most powerful man on earth.

The leader is assailed because he is a leader, and the effort to equal him is merely added proof of his leadership.

Failing to equal or to excel, the follower seeks to depreciate and to destroy—but only confirms the superiority of that which he strives to supplant.

There is nothing new in this.

It is as old as the world and as old as the human passions—envy, fear, greed, ambition and the desire to surpass.

And it all avails nothing.

If the leader truly leads, he remains the LEADER! Master-poet, master-painter, master-workman, each in his turn is assailed, and each holds his laurels through the ages.

That which is good or great makes itself known, no matter how loud the clamor of denial.

A real leader cannot be slandered or damaged by lies of the envious, because all such attempts serve only to turn the spot-light on his ability, and real ability always finds a generous following.

Attempts to destroy real Leadership is love's labor lost, because that which deserves to live, lives!

We come back, now, to the discussion of the third step of the procedure that you must follow in developing *initiative* and *leadership*. This third step takes us back for a review of the principle of *organized effort*, as described in the preceding lessons of this course.

You have already learned that no man can accomplish enduring results of a far-reaching nature without the aid and co-operation of others. You have already learned that when two or more persons ally themselves in any undertaking, in a spirit of harmony and understanding, each person in the alliance thereby multiplies his own powers of achievement. Nowhere is this principle more evidenced than it is in an industry or business in which there is perfect team-work between the employer and the employees. Wherever you find this team-work you find prosperity and goodwill on both sides.

Co-operation is said to be the most important word in the English language. It plays an important part in the affairs of the home, in the relationship of man and wife, parents and children. It plays an important part in the affairs of state. So important is this principle of co-operation that no leader can become powerful or last long who does not understand and apply it in his *leadership*.

Lack of Co-operation has destroyed more business enterprises than have all other causes combined. In my twenty-five years of active business experience and observation I have witnessed the destruction of all manner of business enterprises because of dissension and lack of application of this principle of Co-operation. In the practice of law I have observed the destruction of homes and divorce cases without end as a result of the lack of Co-operation between man and wife. In the study of the histories of nations it becomes alarmingly obvious that lack of Co-operative effort has been a curse to the human race all back down the ages. Turn back the pages of these histories and study them and you will learn a lesson in Co-operation, that will impress itself indelibly upon your mind.

You are paying, and your children and your children's children will continue to pay, for the cost of the most expensive and destructive war the world has ever known, because nations have not yet learned that a part of the world cannot suffer without damage and suffering to the whole world.

This same rule applies, with telling effect, in the conduct of modern business and industry. When an industry becomes disorganized and torn asunder by strikes and other forms of disagreement, both the employers and employees suffer irreparable loss. But, the damage does not stop here; this loss becomes a burden to the public and takes on the form of higher prices and scarcity of the necessities of life.

The people of the United States who rent their homes are feeling the burden, at this very moment, of lack of co-operation between contractors and builders and the workers. So uncertain has the relationship between the contractors and their employees become that the contractors will not undertake a building without adding to the cost an arbitrary sum sufficient to protect them in the event of labor troubles. This additional cost increases rents and places unnecessary burdens upon the backs of millions of people. In this instance the lack of co-operation between a few men places heavy and almost unbearable burdens upon millions of people.

The same evil exists in the operation of our railroads. Lack of harmony and co-operation between the railroad management and the workers has made it necessary for the railroads to increase their freight and passenger rates, and this, in turn, has increased the cost of life's necessities to almost unbearable proportions. Here, again, lack of co-operation between a few leads to hardship for millions of people.

These facts are cited without effort or desire to place the responsibility for this lack of co-operation, since the object of this Reading Course is to help its students get at facts.

It may be truthfully stated that the high cost of living that everywhere manifests itself today has grown out of lack of application of the principle of co-operative *leadership*. Those who wish to decry present systems of government and industrial management may do so, but in the final analysis it becomes obvious to all except those who are not seeking the *truth* that the evils of government and of industry have grown out of lack of *co-operation*.

Nor can it be truthfully said that all the evils of the world are confined to the affairs of state and industry. Take a look at the churches and you will observe the damaging effects of lack of co-operation. No particular church is cited, but analyze any church or group of churches where lack of co-ordination of effort prevails and you will see evidence of disintegration that limits the service those churches could render. For example, take the average town or small city where rivalry has sprung up between the churches and notice what has happened; especially those towns in which the number of churches is far out of proportion to the population.

Through harmonized effort and through co-operation, the churches of the world could wield sufficient influence to render war an impossibility. Through this same principle of co-operative effort the churches and the leaders of business and industry could eliminate rascality and sharp practices, and all this could be brought about speedily.

These possibilities are not mentioned in a spirit of criticism, but only as a means of illustrating the power of co-operation, and to emphasize my belief in the potential power of the churches of the world. So there will be no possibility of misinterpretation of my meaning in the reference that I have here made to the churches I will repeat that which I have so often said in person; namely, that had it not been for the influence of the churches no man would be safe in walking down the street. Men would be at each other's throat like wolves and civilization would still be in the pre-historic age.

My complaint is not against the work that the churches have done, but the work that *they could have done* through *leadership* that was based upon the principle of co-ordinated, co-operative effort which would have carried civilization at least a thousand years ahead of where it is today. It is not yet too late for such leadership.

That you may more fully grasp the fundamental principle of co-operative effort you are urged to go to the public library and read The Science of Power, by Benjamin Kidd. Out of scores of volumes by some of the soundest thinkers of the world that I have read during the past fifteen years, no single volume has given me such a full understanding of the possibilities of co-operative effort as has this book. In recommending that you read this book it is not my purpose to endorse the book in its entirety, for it offers some theories with which I am not in accord. If you read it, do so with an open mind and take from it only that which you feel you can use to advantage in achieving the object of your *definite chief aim*. The book will stimulate *thought,* which is the greatest service that any book can render. As a matter of fact the chief object of this Reading Course on the Law of Success is to stimulate deliberate *thought*: particularly that brand of *thought* that is free from bias and prejudice and is seeking *truth* no matter where or how or when it may be found.

During the World War I was fortunate enough to listen to a great soldier's analysis of how to be a *leader.* This analysis was given to the student-officers of the Second Training Camp at Fort Sheridan, by Major C. A. Bach, a quiet, unassuming army officer acting as an instructor. I have preserved a copy of this address because I believe it to be one of the finest lessons on *leadership* ever recorded.

The wisdom of Major Bach's address is so vital to the business man aspiring to *leadership,* or to the section boss, or to the stenographer, or to the foreman of the shop, or to the president of the works, that I have preserved it as a part of this Reading Course. It is my earnest hope that through the agency of this course this remarkable dissertation on *leadership* will find its way into the hands of every employer and every worker and every ambitious person who aspires to leadership in any walk of life. The principles upon which the address is based are as applicable to *leadership* in business and industry and finance as they are in the successful conduct of warfare.

Major Bach spoke as follows:

In a short time each of you men will control the lives of a certain number of other men. You will have in your charge loyal but untrained citizens, who look to you for instruction and guidance. Your word will be their law. Your most casual remark will be remembered. Your mannerisms will be aped. Your clothing, your carriage, your vocabulary, your manner of command will be imitated.

When you join your organization you will find there a willing body of men who ask from you nothing more than the qualities that will command their respect, their loyalty and their obedience.

They are perfectly ready and eager to follow you so long as you can convince them that you have these qualities. When the time comes that they are satisfied you do not possess them you might as well kiss yourself good-bye. Your usefulness in that organization is at an end.

[How remarkably true this is in all manner of *leadership*.]

From the standpoint of society, the world may be divided into leaders and followers. The professions have their leaders, the financial world has its leaders. In all this leadership it is difficult, if not impossible, to separate from the element of pure leadership that selfish element of personal gain or advantage to the individual, without which any leadership would lose its value.

It is in military service only, where men freely sacrifice their lives for a faith, where men are willing to suffer and die for the right or the prevention of a wrong, that we can hope to realize leadership in its most exalted and disinterested sense. Therefore, when I say *leadership*, I mean *military leadership*.

In a few days the great mass of you men will receive commissions as officers. These commissions will not make you leaders; they will merely make you officers. They will place you in a position where you can become leaders if you possess the proper attributes. But you must make good, not so much with the men over you as with the men under you.

Men must and will follow into battle officers who are not leaders, but the driving power behind these men is not enthusiasm but discipline. They go with doubt and trembling that prompts the unspoken question, "What will he do next?" Such men obey the letter of their orders but no more. Of devotion to their commander, of exalted enthusiasm which scorns personal risk, of *self-sacrifice* to insure his personal safety, they know nothing. Their legs carry them forward because their brain and their training tell them they must go. Their spirit does not go with them.

Great results are not achieved by cold, passive, unresponsive soldiers. They don't go very far and they stop as soon as they can. Leadership not only demands but receives the willing, unhesitating, unfaltering obedience and loyalty of other men; and a devotion that will cause them, when the time comes, to follow their uncrowned king to hell and back again, if necessary.

You will ask yourselves: "Of just what, then, does *leadership* consist? What must I do to become a leader? What are the attributes of leadership, and how can I cultivate them?"

Leadership is a composite of a number of qualities. [Just as success is a composite of the fifteen factors out of which this Reading Course was built.] Among the most important I would list Self-confidence, Moral Ascendency, Self-Sacrifice, Paternalism, Fairness, Initiative, Decision, Dignity, Courage.

Self-confidence results, first, from exact knowledge; second, the ability to impart that knowledge; and third, the feeling of superiority over others that naturally follows. All these give the officer poise. To lead, you must *know!* You may bluff all of your men some of the time, but you can't do it all the time. Men will not have confidence in an officer unless he knows his business, and he must know it from the ground up.

The officer should know more about paper work than his first sergeant and company clerk put together; he should know more about messing than his mess sergeant; more about diseases of the horse than his troop farrier. He should be at least as good a shot as any man in his company.

If the officer does not know, and demonstrates the fact that he does not know, it is entirely human for the soldier to say to himself, "To hell with him. He doesn't know as much about this as I do," and calmly disregard the instructions received.

There is no substitute for accurate knowledge!

Become so well informed that men will hunt you up to ask questions; that your brother officers will say to one another, "Ask Smith—he knows."

And not only should each officer know thoroughly the duties of his own grade, but he should study those of the two grades next above him. A two-fold benefit attaches to this. He prepares himself for duties which may fall to his lot any time during battle; he further gains a broader viewpoint which enables him to appreciate the necessity for the issuance of orders and join more intelligently in their execution.

Not only must the officer know but he must be able to put what he knows into grammatical, interesting, forceful English. He must learn to stand on his feet and speak without embarrassment.

I am told that in British training camps student-officers are required to deliver ten minute talks on any subject they choose. That is excellent practice. For to speak clearly one must think clearly, and clear, logical thinking expresses itself in definite, positive orders.

While self-confidence is the result of knowing more than your men, Moral Ascendency over them is based upon your belief that you are the better man. To gain and maintain this ascendency you must have self-control, physical vitality and endurance and moral force. You must have yourself so well in hand that, even though in battle you be scared stiff, you will never show fear. For if by so much as a hurried movement or a trembling of the hands, or a change of expression, or a hasty order hastily revoked, you indicate your mental condition it will be reflected in your men in a far greater degree.

In garrison or camp many instances will arise to try your temper and wreck the sweetness of your disposition. If at such times you "fly off the handle" you have no business to be in charge of men. For men in anger say and do things that they almost invariably regret afterward.

An officer should never apologize to his men; also an officer should never be guilty of an act for which his sense of justice tells him he should apologize.

Another element in gaining Moral Ascendency lies in the possession of enough physical vitality and endurance to withstand the hardships to which you and your men are subjected, and a dauntless spirit that enables you not only to accept them cheerfully but to minimize their magnitude.

Make light of your troubles, belittle your trials and you will help vitally to build up within your organization an esprit whose value in time of stress cannot be measured.

Moral force is the third element in gaining Moral Ascendency. To exert moral force you must live clean; you must have sufficient brain power to see the right and the will to do right.

Be an example to your men!

An officer can be a power for good or a power for evil. Don't preach to them—that will be worse than useless. Live the kind of life you would have them lead, and you will be surprised to see the number that will imitate you.

A loud-mouthed, profane captain who is careless of his personal appearance will have a loud-mouthed, profane, dirty company. *Remember what I tell you. Your company will be the reflection of yourself!* If you have a rotten company it will be because you are a rotten captain.

Self-sacrifice is essential to leadership. You will give, give, all the time. You will give of yourself physically, for the longest hours, the hardest work and the greatest responsibility are the lot of the captain. He is the first man up in the morning and the last man in at night. He works while others sleep.

You will give of yourself mentally, in sympathy and appreciation for the troubles of men in your charge. This one's mother has died, and that one has lost all his savings in a bank failure. They may desire help, but more than anything else they desire *sympathy*. Don't make the mistake of turning such men down with the statement that you have troubles of your own, for every time you do that you *knock a stone out of the foundation of your house*.

Your men are your foundation, and your house of *leadership* will tumble about your ears unless it rests securely upon them. Finally, you will give of your own slender financial resources. You will frequently spend your own money to conserve the health and well-being of your men or to assist them when in trouble. Generally you get your money back. Very frequently you must charge it off to profit and loss.

Even so, it is worth the cost.

When I say that paternalism is essential to leadership I use the term in its better sense. I do not now refer to that form of paternalism which robs men of *initiative, self-reliance* and *self-respect*. I refer to the paternalism that manifests itself in a watchful care for the comfort and welfare of those in your charge.

Soldiers are much like children. You must see that they have shelter, food and clothing, the best that your utmost efforts can provide. You must see that they have food to eat before you think of your own; that they have each as good a bed as can be provided before you consider where you will sleep. You must be far more solicitous of their comfort than of your own. You must look after their health. You must conserve their strength by not demanding needless exertion or useless labor.

And by doing all these things you are breathing life into what would be otherwise a mere machine. You are creating a soul in your organization that will make the mass respond to you as though it were one man. And that is esprit.

And when your organization has this esprit you will wake up some morning and discover that the tables have been turned; that instead of your constantly looking out for them they have, without even a hint from you, taken up the task of looking out for you. You will find that a detail is always there to see that your tent, if you have one, is promptly pitched; that the most and the cleanest bedding is brought to your tent; that from some mysterious source two eggs have been added to your supper when no one else has any; that an extra man is helping your men give your horse a super grooming; that your wishes are anticipated; that every man is "Johnny-on-the-spot." And then you have *arrived!*

You cannot treat all men alike! A punishment that would be dismissed by one man with a shrug of the shoulders is mental anguish for another. A company commander who, for a given offense, has a standard punishment that applies to all is either too indolent or too stupid to study the personality of his men. In his case justice is certainly blind.

Study your men as carefully as a surgeon studies a difficult case. And when you are sure of your diagnosis apply the remedy. And remember that you apply the remedy to effect a cure, not merely to see the victim squirm. It may be necessary to cut deep, but when you are satisfied as to your diagnosis don't be diverted from your purpose by any false sympathy for the patient.

Hand in hand with fairness in awarding punishment walks fairness in giving credit. Everybody hates a human hog. When one of your men has accomplished an especially creditable piece of work see that he gets the proper reward. *Turn heaven and earth upside down to get it for him.* Don't try to take it away from him and hog it for yourself. You may do this and get away with it, but you have lost the respect and loyalty of your men. Sooner or later your brother officers will hear of it and shun you like a leper. In war there is glory enough for all. Give the man under you his due. *The man who always takes and never gives is not a leader.* He is a parasite.

There is another kind of fairness—that which will prevent an officer from abusing the privileges of his rank. When you exact respect from soldiers be sure you treat them with equal respect. Build up their manhood and self-respect. Don't try to pull it down.

For an officer to be overbearing and insulting in the treatment of enlisted men is the act of a coward. He ties the man to a tree with the ropes of discipline and then strikes him in the face knowing full well that the man cannot strike back.

Consideration, courtesy and respect from officers toward enlisted men are not incompatible with discipline. They are parts of our discipline. Without initiative and decision no man can expect to lead.

In maneuvers you will frequently see, when an emergency arises, certain men calmly give instant orders which later, on analysis, prove to be, if not exactly the right thing, very nearly the right thing to have done. You will see other men in emergency become badly rattled; their brains refuse to work, or they give a hasty order, revoke it; give another, revoke that; in short, show every indication of being in a blue funk.

Regarding the first man you may say: "That man is a genius. He hasn't had time to reason this thing out. He acts intuitively." Forget it! Genius is merely the capacity for taking infinite pains. The man who was ready is the man who has prepared himself. He has studied beforehand the possible situations that might arise; he has made tentative plans covering such situations. When he is confronted by the emergency he is ready to meet it. He must have sufficient mental alertness to appreciate the problem that confronts him and the power of quick reasoning to determine what changes are necessary in his already formulated plan. He must also have the decision to order the execution and stick to his orders.

Any reasonable order in an emergency is better than no order. The situation is there. Meet it. It is better to do something and do the wrong thing than to hesitate, hunt around for the right thing to do and wind up by doing nothing at all. And, having decided on a line of action, stick to it. Don't vacillate. Men have no confidence in an officer who doesn't know his own mind.

Occasionally you will be called upon to meet a situation which no reasonable human being could anticipate. If you have prepared yourself to meet other emergencies which you could anticipate, the mental training you have thereby gained will enable you to act promptly and with calmness.

You must frequently act without orders from higher authority. Time will not permit you to wait for them. Here again enters the importance of studying the work of officers above you. If you have a comprehensive grasp of the entire situation and can form an idea of the general plan of your superiors, that and your previous emergency training will enable you to determine that the responsibility is yours and to issue the necessary orders without delay.

The element of *personal dignity* is important in military leadership. Be the friend of your men, but do not become their intimate. Your men should stand in awe of you—not *fear!* If your men presume to become familiar it is your fault, and not theirs. Your actions have encouraged them to do so. And, above all things, don't cheapen yourself by courting their friendship or currying their favor. They will despise: you for it. If you are worthy of their loyalty and respect and devotion they will surely give all these without asking. If you are not, nothing that you can do will win them.

It is exceedingly difficult for an officer to be dignified while wearing a dirty, spotted uniform and a three days' stubble of whiskers on his face. Such a man lacks self-respect, and self-respect is an essential of dignity.

There may be occasions when your work entails dirty clothes and an unshaved face. Your men all look that way. At such times there is ample reason for your appearance. In fact, it would be a mistake to look too clean—they would think that you were, not doing your share. But as soon as this unusual occasion has passed set an example for personal neatness.

And then I would mention courage. Moral courage you need as well as mental courage—that kind of moral courage which enables you to adhere without faltering to a determined course of action, which your judgment has indicated is the one best suited to secure the desired results.

You will find many times, especially in action, that, after having issued your orders to do a certain thing, you will be beset by misgivings and doubts; you will see, or think you see, other and better means for accomplishing the object sought. You will be strongly tempted to change your orders. Don't do it until it is clearly manifested that your first orders were radically wrong. For, if you do, you will be again worried by doubts as to the efficacy of your second orders.

Every time you change your orders without obvious reason you weaken your authority and impair the confidence of your men. Have the moral courage to stand by your order and see it through.

Moral courage further demands that you assume the responsibility for your own acts. If your subordinates have loyally carried out your orders and the movement you directed is a failure the failure is *yours*, not theirs. Yours would have been the honor had it been successful. Take the blame if it results in disaster. Don't try to shift it to a subordinate and make him the goat. That is a cowardly act. Furthermore, you will need moral courage to determine the fate of those under you. You will frequently be called upon for recommendations for promotion or demotion of officers and non-commissioned officers in your immediate command.

Keep clearly in mind your *personal integrity* and the duty you owe your country. Do not let yourself be deflected from a strict sense of justice by feelings of personal friendship. If your own brother is your second lieutenant, and you find him unfit to hold his commission, eliminate him. If you don't your lack of moral courage may result in the loss of valuable lives.

If, on the other hand, you are called upon for a recommendation concerning a man whom, for personal reasons, you thoroughly dislike, do not fail to do him full justice. Remember that your aim is the general good, not the satisfaction of an individual grudge.

I am taking it for granted that you have physical courage. I need not tell you how necessary that is. Courage is more than bravery. Bravery is fearlessness—the absence of fear. The merest dolt may be brave, because he lacks the mentality to appreciate his danger; he doesn't know enough to be afraid.

Courage, however, is that firmness of spirit, that moral backbone which, while fully appreciating the danger involved, nevertheless goes on with the undertaking. Bravery is physical; courage is mental and moral. You may be cold all over; your hands may tremble; your legs may quake; your knees be ready to give way—that is fear. If, nevertheless, you go forward; if, in spite of this physical defection you continue to lead your men against the enemy, you have courage. The physical manifestations of fear will pass away. You may never experience them but once. They are the "buck fever" of the hunter who tries to shoot his first deer. You must not give way to them.

A number of years ago, while taking a course in demolitions, the class of which I was a member was handling dynamite. The instructor said, regarding its manipulation: "I must caution you gentlemen to be careful in the use of these explosives. One man has but one accident." And so I would caution you. If you give way to fear that will doubtless beset you in your first action; if you show the white feather; if you let your men go forward while you hunt a shell crater, you will never again have the opportunity of leading those men.

Use judgment in calling on your men for displays of physical courage or bravery. *Don't ask any man to go where you would not go yourself.* If your common sense tells you that the place is too dangerous for you to venture into, then it is too dangerous for him. You know his life is as valuable to him as yours is to you.

Occasionally some of your men must be exposed to danger which you cannot share. A message must be taken across a fire-swept zone. You call for volunteers. If your men know you and know that you are "right" you will never lack volunteers, for they will know your heart is in your work, that you are giving your country the best you have, that you would willingly carry the message yourself if you could. Your example and enthusiasm will have inspired them.

And, lastly, if you aspire to leadership, I would urge you to study men.

Get under their skins and find out what is inside. Some men are quite different from what they appear to be on the surface. Determine the workings of their mind.

Much of General Robert E. Lee's success as a leader may be ascribed to his ability as a psychologist. He knew most of his opponents from West Point days; knew the workings of their minds; and he believed that they would do certain things under certain circumstances. In nearly every case he was able to anticipate their movements and block the execution.

You cannot know your opponent in this war in the same way. But you can know your own men. You can study each to determine wherein lies his strength and his weakness; which man can be relied upon to the last gasp and which cannot.

Know your men, know your business, know yourself!

In all literature you will not find a better description of *leadership* than this. Apply it to yourself, or to your business, or to your profession, or to the place where you are employed, and you will observe how well it serves as your guide.

Major Bach's address is one that might well be delivered to every boy and girl who graduates in high school. It might well be delivered to every college graduate. It might well become the book of rules for every man who is placed in a position of leadership over other men, no matter in what calling, business or profession.

In Lesson Two you learned the value of a *definite chief aim*. Let it be here emphasized that your aim must be active and not passive. A *definite aim* will never be anything else but a mere wish unless you become a person of initiative and *aggressively* and *persistently* pursue that aim until it has been fulfilled.

You can get nowhere without persistence, a fact which cannot be too often repeated.

The difference between persistence and lack of it is the same as the difference between wishing for a thing and positively determining to get it.

To become a person of initiative you must form the habit of *aggressively* and *persistently* following the object of your *definite chief aim* until you acquire it, whether this requires one year or twenty years. You might as well have no *definite chief aim* as to have such an aim without *continuous* effort to achieve it.

You are not making the most of this course if you do not take some step each day that brings you nearer realization of your *definite chief aim*. Do not fool yourself, or permit yourself to be misled to believe that the object of your *definite chief aim* will matter—alive if you only wait. The materialization will come through your own determination, backed by your own carefully laid plans and your own initiative in putting those plans into action, or it will not come at all.

One of the major requisites for Leadership is the power of quick and firm DECISION!

Analysis of more than 16,000 people disclosed the fact that Leaders are always men of ready decision, even in matters of small importance, while the follower is NEVER a person of quick decision.

This is worth remembering!

The follower, in whatever walk of life you find him, is a man who seldom knows what he wants. He vacillates, procrastinates, and actually refuses to reach a decision, even in matters of the smallest importance, unless a Leader induces him to do so.

To know that the majority of people cannot and will not reach decisions quickly, if at all, is of great help to the Leader who knows what he wants and has a plan for getting it.

Here it will be observed how closely allied are the two laws covered by Lesson Two and this lesson.

The Leader not only works with A DEFINITE CHIEF AIM, but he has a very definite plan for attaining the object of that aim. It will be seen, also, that the Law of Self-confidence becomes an important part of the working equipment of the Leader.

The chief reason why the follower does not reach decisions is that he lacks the Self-confidence to do so. Every Leader makes use of the Law of a Definite Purpose, the Law of Self-confidence and the Law of Initiative and Leadership. And if he is an outstanding, successful Leader he makes use, also, of the Laws of Imagination, Enthusiasm, Self-Control, Pleasing Personality, Accurate Thinking, Concentration and Tolerance. Without the combined use of all these Laws no one may become a really great Leader. Omission of a single one of these Laws lessens the power of the Leader proportionately.

A salesman for the LaSalle Extension University called on a real estate dealer, in a small western town, for the purpose of trying to sell the real estate man a course in Salesmanship and Business Management.

When the salesman arrived at the prospective student's office he found the gentleman pecking out a letter by the two-finger method, on an antiquated typewriter. The salesman introduced himself, then proceeded to state his business and describe the course he had come to sell.

The real estate man listened with apparent interest.

After the sales talk had been completed the salesman hesitated, waiting for some signs of "yes" or "no" from his prospective client. Thinking that perhaps he had not made the sales talk quite strong enough, he briefly went over the merits of the course he was selling, a second time. Still there was no response from the prospective student.

The salesman then asked the direct question, "You want this course, do you not?"

In a slow, drawling tone of voice, the real estate man replied:

"Well, I hardly know whether I do or not."

No doubt he was telling the truth, because he was one of the millions of men who find it hard to reach decisions.

Being an able judge of human nature the salesman then arose, put on his hat, placed his literature back in his brief case and made ready to leave. Then he resorted to tactics which were somewhat drastic, and took the real estate man by surprise with this startling statement:

"I am going to take it upon myself to say something to you that you will not like, but it may be of help to you.

"Take a look at this office in which you work! The floor is dirty; the walls are dusty; the typewriter you are using looks as if it might be the one Mr. Noah used in the Ark during the big flood; your pants are bagged at the knees; your collar is dirty; your face is unshaved, and you have a look in your eyes that tells me you are defeated.

"Please go ahead and get mad—that's just what I want you to do, because it may shock you into doing some thinking that will be helpful to you and to those who are dependent upon you.

"I can see, in my imagination, the home in which you live. Several little children, none too well dressed, and perhaps none too well fed; a mother whose dress is three seasons out of style, whose eyes carry the same look of defeat that yours do. This little woman whom you married has stuck by you but you have not made good in life as she had hoped, when you were first married, that you would.

"Please remember that I am not now talking to a prospective student, because I would not sell you this course at THIS PARTICULAR MOMENT if you offered to pay cash in advance, because if I did you would not have the initiative to complete it, and we want no failures on our student list.

"The talk I am now giving you will make it impossible, perhaps, for me ever to sell you anything, but it is going to do something for you that has never been done before, providing it makes you think.

"Now, I will tell you in a very few words exactly why you are defeated; why you are pecking out letters on an old typewriter, in an old dirty office, in a little town: IT IS BECAUSE YOU DO NOT HAVE THE POWER TO REACH A DECISION!

"All your life you have been forming the habit of dodging the responsibility of reaching decisions, until you have come, now, to where it is well-nigh impossible for you to do so.

"If you had told me that you wanted the course, or that you did not want it, I could have sympathized with you, because I would have known that lack of funds was what caused you to hesitate, but what did you say? Why, you admitted you did not know whether you wanted it or not.

"If you will think over what I have said I am sure you will acknowledge that it has become a habit with you to dodge the responsibility of reaching clear-cut decisions on practically all matters that affect you."

The real estate man sat glued in his chair, with his under jaw dropped, his eyes bulged in astonishment, but he made no attempt to answer the biting indictment.

The salesman said good-bye and started for the door.

After he had closed the door behind him he again opened it, walked back in, with a smile on his face, took his seat in front of the astonished real estate man, and explained his conduct in this way:

"I do not blame you at all if you feel hurt at my remarks. In fact I sort of hope that you have been offended, but now let me say this, man to man, that I think you have intelligence and I am sure you have ability, but you have fallen into a habit that has whipped you. No man is ever down and out until he is under the sod. You may be temporarily down, but you can get up again, and I am just sportsman enough to give you my hand and offer you a lift, if you will accept my apologies for what I have said.

"You do not belong in this town. You would starve to death in the real estate business in this place, even if you were a Leader in your field. Get yourself a new suit of clothes, even if you have to borrow the money with which to do it, then go over to St. Louis with me and I will introduce you to a real estate man who will give you a chance to earn some money and at the same time teach you some of the important things about this line of work that you can capitalize later on.

"If you haven't enough credit to get the clothes you need I will stand good for you at a store in St. Louis where I have a charge account. I am in earnest and my offer to help you is based upon the highest motive that can actuate a human being. I am successful in my own field, but I have not always been so. I went 'through just what you are now going through, but, the important thing is that I WENT THROUGH IT, and got it over with, JUST AS YOU ARE GOING TO DO IF YOU WILL FOLLOW MY ADVICE.

"Will you come with me?"

The real estate man started to arise, but his legs wobbled and he sank back into his chair. Despite the fact that he was a great big fellow, with rather pronounced manly qualities, known as the "he-man" type, his emotions got the better of him and he actually wept.

He made a second attempt and got on his feet, shook hands with the salesman, thanked him for his kindness, and said he was going to follow the advice, but he would do so in his own way.

Calling for an application blank he signed for the course on Salesmanship and Business Management, made the first payment in nickels and dimes, and told the salesman he would hear from him again.

Three years later this real estate man had an organization of sixty salesmen, and one of the most successful real estate businesses in the city of St. Louis. The author of this course (who was advertising manager of the LaSalle

Extension University at the time this incident happened) has been in this real estate man's office many times and has observed him over a period of more than fifteen years. He is an entirely different man from the person interviewed by the LaSalle salesman over fifteen years ago, and the thing that made him different is the same that will make YOU different: it is the power of DECISION which is so essential to Leadership.

This real estate man is now a Leader in the real estate field. He is directing the efforts of other salesmen and helping them to become more efficient. This one change in his philosophy has turned temporary defeat into success. Every new salesman who goes to work for this man is called into his private office, before he is employed, and told the story of his own transformation, word for word just as it occurred when the LaSalle salesman first met him in his shabby little real estate office.

Some eighteen years ago the author of this course made his first trip to the little town of Lumberport, W. Va. At that time the only means of transportation leading from Clarksburg, the largest near-by center, to Lumberport, was the Baltimore & Ohio Railroad and an interurban electric line which ran within three miles of the town; one could walk the three miles if he chose.

Upon arrival at Clarksburg I found that the only train going to Lumberport in the forenoon had already gone, and not wishing to wait for the later afternoon train I made the trip by trolley, with the intention of walking the three miles.

On the way down the rain began to pour, and those three miles had to be navigated on foot, through deep yellow mud. When I arrived at Lumberport my shoes and pants were muddy, and my disposition was none the better for the experience.

The first person I met was V. L. Hornor, who was then cashier of the Lumberport Bank. In a rather loud tone of voice I asked of him, "Why do you not get that trolley line extended from the junction over to Lumberport so your friends can get in and out of town without drowning in mud?"

"Did you see a river with high banks, at the edge of the town, as you came in?" he asked. I replied that I had seen it. "Well," he continued, "that's the reason we have no street cars running into town. The cost of a bridge would be about $100,000, and that is more than the company owning the trolley line is willing to invest. We have been trying for ten years to get them to build a line into town."

"Trying!" I exploded. "How hard have you tried?"

"We have offered them every inducement we could afford, such as free right of way from the junction into the town, and free use of the streets, but that bridge is the stumbling block. They simply will not stand the expense. Claim they cannot afford such an expense for the small amount of revenue they would receive from the three mile extension."

Then the Law of Success philosophy began to come to my rescue!

I asked Mr. Hornor if he would take a walk over to the river with me, that we might look at the spot that was causing so much inconvenience. He said he would be glad to do so.

Leadership

When we got to the river I began to take inventory of everything in sight. I observed that the Baltimore & Ohio Railroad tracks ran up and down the river banks, on both sides of the river; that the county road crossed the river on a rickety wooden bridge, both approaches to which were over several strands of railroad track, as the railroad company had its switching yards at that point.

While we were standing there a freight train blocked the crossing and several teams stopped on both sides of the train, waiting for an opportunity to get through. The train kept the road blocked for about twenty-five minutes.

With this combination of circumstances in mind it required but little imagination to see that THREE DIFFERENT PARTIES were or could be interested in the building of the bridge such as would be needed to carry the weight of a streetcar.

It was obvious that the Baltimore & Ohio Railroad Company would be interested in such a bridge, because that would remove the county road from their switching tracks, and save them a possible accident on the crossing, to say nothing of much loss of time and expense in cutting trains to allow teams to pass.

It was also obvious that the County Commissioners would be interested in the bridge, because it would raise the county road to a better level and make it more serviceable to the public. And, of course the street railway company was interested in the bridge, but IT DID NOT WISH TO PAY THE ENTIRE COST. All these facts passed through my mind as I stood there and watched the freight train being cut for the traffic to pass through.

A DEFINITE CHIEF AIM took place in my mind. Also, a definite plan for its attainment. The next day I got together a committee of townspeople, consisting of the mayor, councilmen and some leading citizens, and called on the Division Superintendent of the Baltimore & Ohio Railroad Company, at Grafton. We convinced him that it was worth one third of the cost of the bridge to get the county road off his company's tracks. Next we went to the County Commissioners and found them to be quite enthusiastic over the possibility of getting a new bridge by paying for only one third of it. They promised to pay their one third providing we could arrange for the other two thirds.

We then went to the president of the Traction Company that owned the trolley line, at Fairmont, and laid before him an offer to donate all the rights of way and pay for two thirds of the cost of the bridge providing he would begin building the line into town promptly. We found him receptive, also.

Three weeks later a contract had been signed between the Baltimore & Ohio Railroad Company, the Monongahela Valley Traction Company and the County Commissioners of Harrison County, providing for the construction of the bridge, one third of its cost to be paid by each.

Two months later the right of way was being graded and the bridge was under way, and three months after that street cars were running into Lumberport on regular schedule.

This incident meant much to the town of Lumberport, because it provided transportation that enabled people to get in and out of the town without undue effort.

It also meant a great deal to me, because it served to introduce me as one who "got things done." Two very definite advantages resulted from this transaction. The Chief Counsel for the Traction Company gave me a position as his assistant, and later on it was the means of an introduction which led to my appointment as the advertising manager of the LaSalle Extension University.

Lumberport, W. Va., was then, and still is a small town, and Chicago was a large city and located a considerable distance away, but news of Initiative and Leadership has a way of taking on wings and traveling.

Four of the Fifteen Laws of Success were combined in the transaction described, namely: A DEFINITE CHIEF AIM, SELF-CONFIDENCE, IMAGINATION and INITIATIVE and LEADERSHIP.

The Law of DOING MORE THAN PAID FOR also entered, somewhat, into the transaction, because I was not offered anything and in fact did not expect pay for what I did.

To be perfectly frank I appointed myself to the job of getting the bridge built more as a sort of challenge to those who said it could not be done than I did with the expectation of getting paid for it. By my attitude I rather intimated to Mr. Hornor that I could get the job done, and he was not slow to snap me up and put me to the test.

It may be helpful to call attention here to the part which IMAGINATION played in this transaction. For ten years the townspeople of Lumberport had been trying to get a street car line built into town. It must not be concluded that the town was without men of ability, because that would be inaccurate. In fact there were many men of ability in the town, but they had been making the mistake which is so commonly made by us all, of trying to solve their problem through one single source, whereas there were actually THREE SOURCES of solution available to them.

One hundred thousand dollars was too much for one company to assume, for the construction of a bridge, but when the cost was distributed between three interested parties the amount to be borne by each was more reasonable.

The question might be asked: "Why did not some of the local townsmen think of this three-way solution?"

In the first place they were so close to their problem that they failed to take a perspective, bird's-eye view of it, which would have suggested the solution. This, also, is a common mistake, and one that is always avoided by great Leaders. In the second place these townspeople had never before co-ordinated their efforts or worked as an organized group with the sole purpose in mind of finding a way to get a street car line built into town. This, also, is another common error made by men in all walks of life—that of failure to work in unison, in a thorough spirit of cooperation.

I, being an outsider, had less difficulty in getting cooperative action than one of their own group might have had. Too often there is a spirit of selfishness in small communities which prompts each individual to think that his ideas should prevail. It is an important part of the Leader's responsibility to induce people to subordinate their own ideas and interests for the good of the whole, and this applies to matters of a civic, business, social, political, financial or industrial nature.

Success, no matter what may be one's conception of that term, is nearly always a question of one's ability to get others to subordinate their own individualities and follow a Leader. The Leader who has the Personality and the Imagination to induce his followers to accept his plans and carry them out faithfully is always an able Leader.

The next lesson, on IMAGINATION, will take you still further into the art of tactful Leadership. In fact Leadership and Imagination are so closely allied and so essential for success that one cannot be successfully applied without the other. Initiative is the moving force that pushes the Leader ahead, but Imagination is the guiding spirit that tells him which way to go.

Imagination enabled the author of this course to analyze the Lumberport bridge problem, break it up into its three component parts, and assemble these parts in a practical working plan. Nearly every problem may be so broken up into parts which are more easily managed, as parts, than they are when assembled as a whole. Perhaps one of the most important advantages of Imagination is that it enables one to separate all problems into their component parts and to reassemble them in more favorable combinations.

It has been said that all battles in warfare are won or lost, not on the firing line, after the battle begins, but back of the lines, through the sound strategy, or the lack of it, used by the generals who plan the battles.

What is true of warfare is equally true in business, and in most other problems which confront us throughout life. We win or lose according to the nature of the plans we build and carry out, a fact which serves to emphasize the value of the Laws of Initiative and Leadership, Imagination, Self-confidence and a Definite Chief Aim. *With the intelligent use of these four laws one may build plans, for any purpose whatsoever, which cannot be defeated by any person or group of persons who do not employ or understand these laws.*

There is no escape from the truth here stated!

ORGANIZED EFFORT is effort which is directed according to a plan that was conceived with the aid of Imagination, guided by a Definite Chief Aim, and given momentum with Initiative and Self-confidence. These four laws blend into one and become a power in the hands of a Leader. Without their aid effective leadership is impossible.

> # VI
> ## The Master Mind
>
> *The Master Mind,*
> article from
> *Napoleon Hill's Magazine*
> (March 1922)

I have included this short magazine article from 1922 because it provides one of Hill's earliest references to the Master Mind. The Master Mind, Hill writes, occurs when a harmonious, like-minded group of people meet regularly for the furtherance of a common goal. Their combined efforts increase the energy and acumen of each participant. In later writing, Hill's teaching on the Master Mind evolved so that each group member can possess his or her own individual goal.

Although it is crucial to maintain a regular schedule for your Master Mind group, the Master Mind effect, as Hill notes in this article, occurs everywhere, in any organization, community, group setting, or congregation where there is a unified sense of aim, values, and purpose.

Forming a Master Mind group is simple. Two or more people join together (and as many as seven, and possibly more, though you don't want things to get unwieldy) and meet at regular intervals of at least once a week to support one another's aims, wishes, and needs. The meetings can occur in person or by video or conference call.

My Master Mind group consists of four people spread from New Hampshire to Southern California. We meet Tuesday mornings at 11:30 a.m. eastern by conference call. We begin by reading a statement of group principles. Each member then offers a piece of good news from the previous week. Each participant then states his wants and needs for the coming week and is responded to individually. The group offers advice, support, or suggestions. We hold one other's needs in mind during the coming week. We sometimes offer support outside of meetings too. We are friends as well as Master Mind colleagues.

The key ingredient is group harmony. So long as there is an atmosphere of mutual support and comity, and at least two people, you have a Master Mind group. Harmony and cooperation are the essentials.

As noted, the Master Mind pools and heightens each member's intellectual, intuitive, and psychical abilities. Hill describes the Master Mind producing flashes of insight and synchronous events for each member. I have found this to be true. In essence, the Master Mind is Infinite Intelligence localized. When you and your Master Mind colleagues gather in a spirit of trust and support, an additional something is added to the proceedings. That something is what Hill called Infinite Intelligence.

Hill called the Master Mind crucial to his program. Do not neglect it. If you wish to learn more about the Master Mind in practice and effects, you can read my book The Power of the Master Mind.

—MH

THE MASTER MIND

Through organized effort comes power.
If you would attain financial success,
you must get a firm hold on this principle
of organized, cooperative effort.

Fourteen years ago Andrew Carnegie made a statement that I did not hear until ten years later.

During a newspaper interview with the great steel magnate, I asked him to what he attributed his success. He replied by asking me to define the term *success*. When I told him I had reference to his money, he said:

"Well, if you want to know how I got my money, I will refer you to these men here on my staff; they got it for me. We have here in this business a master mind. It is not my mind, and it is not the mind of any other man on my staff, but the sum total of all these minds that I have gathered around me that constitute a master mind in the steel business. I have been many years gathering these men around me and building this mind. Each man contributes an important part to the building of this mind. I do not always agree with all the men on my staff, on all matters, nor do they always agree with me. Perhaps some of us do not like each other from a personal viewpoint, but I know that I need these men and they know that they need me in the maintenance of this master mind that is necessary in carrying on this steel business."

For years afterward I wondered just what Carnegie meant by "master mind." In the light of more mature years, it began to dawn on me that he had stated a whole life's philosophy in a few words. Carnegie knew the value of organized effort. He knew that no one man could accomplish very much without the coordinated effort of other minds. He knew the value of cooperation. He had on his staff men who did not always agree with him. He had men whom he did not always admire in every respect, and who, perhaps, did not always admire him, but each knew that he needed the others, therefore they harmonized their efforts toward a common end, with the result that all profited.

I wonder if there is not a great lesson for the remainder of us in the history of Carnegie s accumulation of one of the greatest fortunes this country has ever seen? I wonder if his plan of making use of organized effort could not be applied to all walks of life? Following in Mr. Carnegie's footsteps, and making use of exactly the same philosophy, Mr. Chas. M. Schwab is rapidly duplicating Carnegie's success. Is it not possible for anyone else to apply the same principle in any legitimate business undertaking with equal success?

What remarkable strength is shown by the man who can lay aside personal prejudices and work without friction with a group of men with whom he is not in accord on many subjects. What remarkable genius it shows when a man can exercise sufficient self-control, as did Carnegie and as Mr, Schwab is now doing, in working side by side with men of different racial and religious viewpoints, with never a thought of friction, with never a sign of intolerance. I would give a considerable sum if I could purchase from Mr. Schwab the privilege of working with him for a few months for the purpose of studying his simple procedure in applying this principle of organized effort that has raised him from the work of humble coachman to the head of one of America's greatest industries, employing thousands of men.

Out of organized effort comes power, and the process of organization begins, always, in the mind of some one man who organizes the faculties of his own mind and then gathers other minds around him and teaches them how to organize themselves and how to do team work. Oh to be such a genius, with the self-control and the spirit of tolerance to work with others toward a definite goal, without selfishness or haughtiness.

VII
Sex Energy: Your Magic Elixir

The Mystery of Sex Transmutation,
from
Think and Grow Rich
(1937)

Sex transmutation is perhaps the most esoteric but also the most practical technique in Napoleon Hill's work. In short, when you feel sexual desire you shift your thoughts away from physical satisfaction and toward the accomplishment of a cherished task. You do this at times of your own choosing. By doing so you place enormous energy at the back of your efforts. As Hill describes it, sex energy is the creative energy of life seeking expression.

Although we think of sexuality as a matter of procreation, physical pleasure, or both, the sexual urge is the universal creative impulse—sex energy is at back of all your efforts whether artistic, financial, athletic, or otherwise. You often use sex energy unconsciously, like when making a sales pitch or arguing for something. Hill's exercise makes you aware of what you're doing, and helps you enlist these energies at will.

It is important to note that Hill's exercise requires no fundamental change in your intimate life. You are not asked to practice abstention. Rather at times that you select, you simply shift your thoughts away from physical satisfaction and toward any vital task. This is a private exercise to try at your discretion.

This practice has much in common with teachings about sexuality in a wide range of esoteric traditions, including Tantra, Kabbalah, and sex magick. Its inclusion in Think and Grow Rich *marks Hill as a true pioneer in popularizing occult methods.*

—MH

THE MYSTERY OF SEX TRANSMUTATION

The meaning of the word "transmute" is, in simple language, "the changing, or transferring of one element, or form of energy, into another."

The emotion of sex brings into being a state of mind.

Because of ignorance on the subject, this state of mind is generally associated with the physical, and because of improper influences, to which most people have been subjected, in acquiring knowledge of sex, things essentially physical have highly biased the mind.

The emotion of sex has back of it the possibility of three constructive potentialities, they are:

1. The perpetuation of mankind.
2. The maintenance of health, (as a therapeutic agency, it has no equal).
3. The transformation of mediocrity into genius through transmutation.

Sex transmutation is simple and easily explained. It means the switching of the mind from thoughts of physical expression, to thoughts of some other nature.

Sex desire is the most powerful of human desires. When driven by this desire, men develop keenness of imagination, courage, will-power, persistence, and creative ability unknown to them at other times. So strong and impelling is the desire for sexual contact that men freely run the risk of life and reputation to indulge it. When harnessed, and redirected along other lines, this motivating force maintains all of its attributes of keenness of imagination, courage, etc., which may be used as powerful creative forces in literature, art, or in any other profession or calling, including, of course, the accumulation of riches.

The transmutation of sex energy calls for the exercise of will-power, to be sure, but the reward is worth the effort. The desire for sexual expression is inborn and natural. The desire cannot, and should not be submerged or eliminated. But it should be given an outlet through forms of expression which enrich the body, mind, and spirit of man. If not given this form of outlet, through transmutation, it will seek outlets through purely physical channels.

A river may be dammed, and its water controlled for a time, but eventually, it will force an outlet. The same is true of the emotion of sex. It may be submerged and controlled for a time, but its very nature causes it to be ever seeking means of expression. If it is not transmuted into some creative effort it will find a less worthy outlet.

Fortunate, indeed, is the person who has discovered how to give sex emotion an outlet through some form of creative effort, for he has, by that discovery, lifted himself to the status of a genius. Scientific research has disclosed these significant facts:

1. The men of greatest achievement are men with highly developed sex natures; men who have learned the art of sex transmutation.
2. The men who have accumulated great fortunes and achieved outstanding recognition in literature, art, industry, architecture, and the professions, were motivated by the influence of a woman.

The research from which these astounding discoveries were made, went back through the pages of biography and history for more than two thousand years. Wherever there was evidence available in connection with the lives of men and women of great achievement, it indicated most convincingly that they possessed highly developed sex natures.

The emotion of sex is an "irresistible force," against which there can be no such opposition as an "immovable body." When driven by this emotion, men become gifted with a super power for action. Understand this truth, and you will catch the significance of the statement that sex transmutation will lift one to the status of a genius.

The emotion of sex contains the secret of creative ability.

Destroy the sex glands, whether in man or beast, and you have removed the major source of action. For proof of this, observe what happens to any animal after it has been castrated. A bull becomes as docile as a cow after it has been altered sexually. Sex alteration takes out of the male, whether man or beast, all the FIGHT that was in him. Sex alteration of the female has the same effect.

The Ten Mind Stimuli

The human mind responds to stimuli, through which it may be "keyed up" to high rates of vibration, known as enthusiasm, creative imagination, intense desire, etc. The stimuli to which the mind responds most freely are:

1. The desire for sex expression
2. Love
3. A burning desire for fame, power, or financial gain, MONEY
4. Music
5. Friendship between either those of the same sex, or those of the opposite sex.
6. A Master Mind alliance based upon the harmony of two or more people who ally themselves for spiritual or temporal advancement.
7. Mutual suffering, such as that experienced by people who are persecuted.
8. Auto-suggestion
9. Fear
10. Narcotics and alcohol.

The desire for sex expression comes at the head of the list of stimuli, which most effectively "step-up" the vibrations of the mind and start the "wheels" of physical action. Eight of these stimuli are natural and constructive. Two are destructive. The list is here presented for the purpose of enabling you to make a comparative study of the major sources of mind stimulation. From this study, it will be readily seen that the emotion of sex is, by great odds, the most intense and powerful of all mind stimuli.

This comparison is necessary as a foundation for proof of the statement that transmutation of sex energy may lift one to the status of a genius. Let us find out what constitutes a genius.

Some wiseacre has said that a genius is a man who "wears long hair, eats queer food, lives alone, and serves as a target for the joke makers." A better definition of a genius is, "a man who has discovered how to increase the vibrations of thought to the point where he can freely communicate with sources of knowledge not available through the ordinary rate of vibration of thought."

The person who thinks will want to ask some questions concerning this definition of genius. The first question will be, "How may one communicate with sources of knowledge which are not available through the ORDINARY rate of vibration of thought?"

The next question will be, "Are there known sources of knowledge which are available only to genii, and if so, WHAT ARE THESE SOURCES, and exactly how may they be reached?"

We shall offer proof of the soundness of some of the more important statements made in this book—or at least we shall offer evidence through which you may secure your own proof through experimentation, and in doing so, we shall answer both of these questions.

"Genius" is Developed Through the Sixth Sense

The reality of a "sixth sense" has been fairly well established. This sixth sense is "Creative Imagination." The faculty of creative imagination is one which the majority of people never use during an entire lifetime, and if used at all, it usually happens by mere accident. A relatively small number of people use, WITH DELIBERATION AND PURPOSE AFORETHOUGHT, the faculty of creative imagination. Those who use this faculty voluntarily, and with understanding of its functions, are GENII.

The faculty of creative imagination is the direct link between the finite mind of man and Infinite Intelligence. All so-called revelations, referred to in the realm of religion, and all discoveries of basic or new principles in the field of invention, take place through the faculty of creative imagination.

When ideas or concepts flash into one's mind, through what is popularly called a "hunch," they come from one or more of the following sources:

1. Infinite Intelligence
2. One's subconscious mind, wherein is stored every sense impression and thought impulse which ever reached the brain through any of the five senses

Sex Energy: Your Magic Elixir

3. From the mind of some other person who has just released the thought, or picture of the idea or concept, through conscious thought, or
4. From the other person's subconscious storehouse.

There are no other KNOWN sources from which "inspired" ideas or "hunches" may be received.

The creative imagination functions best when the mind is vibrating (due to some form of mind stimulation) at an exceedingly high rate. That is, when the mind is functioning at a rate of vibration higher than that of ordinary, normal thought.

When brain action has been stimulated, through one or more of the ten mind stimulants, it has the effect of lifting the individual far above the horizon of ordinary thought, and permits him to envision distance, scope, and quality of THOUGHTS not available on the lower plane, such as that occupied while one is engaged in the solution of the problems of business and professional routine.

When lifted to this higher level of thought, through any form of mind stimulation, an individual occupies, relatively, the same position as one who has ascended in an airplane to a height from which he may see over and beyond the horizon line which limits his vision, while on the ground. Moreover, while on this higher level of thought, the individual is not hampered or bound by any of the stimuli which circumscribe and limit his vision while wrestling with the problems of gaining the three basic necessities of food, clothing, and shelter. He is in a world of thought in which the ORDINARY, work-a-day thoughts have been as effectively removed as are the hills and valleys and other limitations of physical vision, when he rises in an airplane.

While on this exalted plane of THOUGHT, the creative faculty of the mind is given freedom for action. The way has been cleared for the sixth sense to function, it becomes receptive to ideas which could not reach the individual under any other circumstances. The "sixth sense" is the faculty which marks the difference between a genius and an ordinary individual.

The creative faculty becomes more alert and receptive to vibrations, originating outside the individual's subconscious mind, the more this faculty is used, and the more the individual relies upon it, and makes demands upon it for thought impulses. This faculty can be cultivated and developed only through use.

That which is known as one's "conscience" operates entirely through the faculty of the sixth sense.

The great artists, writers, musicians, and poets become great, because they acquire the habit of relying upon the "still small voice" which speaks from within, through the faculty of creative imagination. It is a fact well known to people who have "keen" imaginations that their best ideas come through so-called "hunches."

There is a great orator who does not attain to greatness, until he closes his eyes and begins to rely entirely upon the faculty of Creative Imagination. When asked why he closed his eyes just before the climaxes of his oratory, he replied, "I do it, because, then I speak through ideas which come to me from within."

One of America's most successful and best known financiers followed the habit of closing his eyes for two or three minutes before making a decision. When asked why he did this, he replied, "With my eyes closed, I am able to draw upon a source of superior intelligence."

The late Dr. Elmer R. Gates, of Chevy Chase, Maryland, created more than 200 useful patents, many of them basic, through the process of cultivating and using the creative faculty. His method is both significant and interesting to one interested in attaining to the status of genius, in which category Dr. Gates, unquestionably belonged. Dr. Gates was one of the really great, though less publicized scientists of the world.

In his laboratory, he had what he called his "personal communication room." It was practically sound proof, and so arranged that all light could be shut out. It was equipped with a small table, on which he kept a pad of writing paper. In front of the table, on the wall, was an electric pushbutton, which controlled the lights. When Dr. Gates desired to draw upon the forces available to him through his Creative Imagination, he would go into this room, seat himself at the table, shut off the lights, and CONCENTRATE upon the KNOWN factors of the invention on which he was working, remaining in that position until ideas began to "flash" into his mind in connection with the UNKNOWN factors of the invention.

On one occasion, ideas came through so fast that he was forced to write for almost three hours. When the thoughts stopped flowing, and he examined his notes, he found they contained a minute description of principles which had not a parallel among the known data of the scientific world. Moreover, the answer to his problem was intelligently presented in those notes. In this manner Dr. Gates completed over 200 patents, which had been begun, but not completed, by "halfbaked" brains. Evidence of the truth of this statement is in the United States Patent Office.

Dr. Gates earned his living by "sitting for ideas" for individuals and corporations. Some of the largest corporations in America paid him substantial fees, by the hour, for "sitting for ideas."

The reasoning faculty is often faulty, because it is largely guided by one's accumulated experience. Not all knowledge, which one accumulates through "experience," is accurate. Ideas received through the creative faculty are much more reliable, for the reason that they come from sources more reliable than any which are available to the reasoning faculty of the mind.

The major difference between the genius and the ordinary "crank" inventor, may be found in the fact that the genius works through his faculty of creative imagination, while the "crank" knows nothing of this faculty. The scientific inventor (such as Mr. Edison, and Dr. Gates), makes use of both the synthetic and the creative faculties of imagination.

For example, the scientific inventor, or "genius," begins an invention by organizing and combining the known ideas, or principles accumulated through experience, through the synthetic faculty (the reasoning faculty). If he finds this accumulated knowledge to be insufficient for the completion of

Sex Energy: Your Magic Elixir

his invention, he then draws upon the sources of knowledge available to him through his creative faculty. The method by which he does this varies with the individual, but this is the sum and substance of his procedure:

1. He *stimulates his mind* so that it vibrates on a higher-than-average plane, using one or more of the ten mind stimulants or some other stimulant of his choice.
2. He *Concentrates* upon the known factors (the finished part) of his invention, and creates in his mind a perfect picture of unknown factors (the unfinished part), of his invention. He holds this picture in mind until it has been taken over by the subconscious mind, then relaxes by clearing his mind of ALL thought, and waits for his answer to "flash" into his mind.

Sometimes the results are both definite and immediate. At other times, the results are negative, depending upon the state of development of the "sixth sense," or creative faculty.

Mr. Edison tried out more than 10,000 different combinations of ideas through the synthetic faculty of his imagination before he "tuned in" through the creative faculty, and got the answer which perfected the incandescent light. His experience was similar when he produced the talking machine.

There is plenty of reliable evidence that the faculty of creative imagination exists. This evidence is available through accurate analysis of men who have become leaders in their respective callings, without having had extensive educations. Lincoln was a notable example of a great leader who achieved greatness, through the discovery, and use of his faculty of creative imagination. He discovered, and began to use this faculty as the result of the stimulation of love which he experienced after he met Anne Rutledge, a statement of the highest significance, in connection with the study of the source of genius.

The pages of history are filled with the records of great leaders whose achievements may be traced directly to the influence of women who aroused the creative faculties of their minds, through the stimulation of sex desire. Napoleon Bonaparte was one of these. When inspired by his first wife, Josephine, he was irresistible and invincible. When his "better judgment" or reasoning faculty prompted him to put Josephine aside, he began to decline. His defeat and St. Helena were not far distant.

If good taste would permit, we might easily mention scores of men, well known to the American people, who climbed to great heights of achievement under the stimulating influence of their wives, only to drop back to destruction AFTER money and power went to their heads, and they put aside the old wife for a new one. Napoleon was not the only man to discover that sex influence, *from the right source*, is more powerful than any substitute of expediency, which may be created by mere reason.

The human mind responds to stimulation!

Among the greatest, and most powerful of these stimuli is the urge of sex. When harnessed and transmuted, this driving force is capable of lifting men into that higher sphere of thought which enables them to master the sources of worry and petty annoyance which beset their pathway on the lower plane.

Unfortunately, only the genii have made the discovery. Others have accepted the experience of sex urge, without discovering one of its major potentialities—a fact which accounts for the great number of "others" as compared to the limited number of genii.

For the purpose of refreshing the memory, in connection with the facts available from the biographies of certain men, we here present the names of a few men of outstanding achievement, each of whom was known to have been of a highly sexed nature. The genius which was their's, undoubtedly found its source of power in transmuted sex energy:

George Washington	Elbert H. Gary
Napoleon Bonaparte	Oscar Wilde
Abraham Lincoln	Woodrow Wilson
Ralph Waldo Emerson	John H. Patterson
Robert Burns	Andrew Jackson
Thomas Jefferson	Enrico Caruso
Elbert Hubbard	

Your own knowledge of biography will enable you to add to this list. Find, if you can, a single man, in all history of civilization, who achieved outstanding success in any calling, who was not driven by a well developed sex nature.

If you do not wish to rely upon biographies of men not now living, take inventory of those whom you know to be men of great achievement, and see if you can find one among them who is not highly sexed.

Sex energy is the creative energy of all genii. *There never has been, and never will be a great leader, builder, or artist lacking in this driving force of sex.*

Surely no one will misunderstand these statements to mean that ALL who are highly sexed are genii! Man attains to the status of a genius ONLY when, and IF, he stimulates his mind so that it draws upon the forces available, through the creative faculty of the imagination. Chief among the stimuli with which this "stepping up" of the vibrations may be produced is sex energy. The mere *possession* of this energy is not sufficient to produce a genius. The energy must be *transmuted* from desire for physical contact, into some *other* form of desire and action, before it will lift one to the status of a genius.

Far from becoming genii, because of great sex desires, the majority of men *lower* themselves, through misunderstanding and misuse of this great force, to the status of the lower animals.

Why Men Seldom Succeed before Forty

I discovered, from the analysis of over 25,000 people, that men who succeed in an outstanding way, seldom do so before the age of forty, and more often they do not strike their real pace until they are well beyond the age of fifty. This fact was so astounding that it prompted me to go into the study of its cause most carefully, carrying the investigation over a period of more than twelve years.

This study disclosed the fact that the major reason why the majority of men who succeed do not begin to do so before the age of forty to fifty, is their tendency to DISSIPATE their energies through over indulgence in physical expression of the emotion of sex. The majority of men never learn that the urge of sex has other possibilities, which far transcend in importance, that of mere physical expression. The majority of those who make this discovery, do so *after having wasted many years* at a period when the sex energy is at its height, prior to the age of forty-five to fifty. This usually is followed by noteworthy achievement.

The lives of many men up to, and sometimes well past the age of forty, reflect a continued dissipation of energies, which could have been more profitably turned into better channels. Their finer and more powerful emotions are sown wildly to the four winds. Out of this habit of the male, grew the term, "sowing his wild oats."

The desire for sexual expression is by far the strongest and most impelling of all the human emotions, and for this very reason this desire, when *harnessed and transmuted* into action, other than that of physical expression, may raise one to the status of a genius.

One of America's most able business men frankly admitted that his attractive secretary was responsible for most of the plans he created. He admitted that her presence lifted him to heights of creative imagination, such as he could experience under no other stimulus.

One of the most successful men in America owes most of his success to the influence of a very charming young woman, who has served as his source of inspiration for more than twelve years. Everyone knows the man to whom this reference is made, but not everyone knows the REAL SOURCE of his achievements.

History is not lacking in examples of men who attained to the status of genii, as the result of the use of artificial mind stimulants in the form of alcohol and narcotics. Edgar Allen Poe wrote the "Raven" while under the influence of liquor, "dreaming dreams that mortal never dared to dream before." James Whitcomb Riley did his best writing while under the influence of alcohol. Perhaps it was thus he saw "the ordered intermingling of the real and the dream, the mill above the river, and the mist above the stream." Robert Burns wrote best when intoxicated, "For Auld Lang Syne, my dear, we'll take a cup of kindness yet, for Auld Lang Syne."

But let it be remembered that many such men have destroyed themselves in the end. Nature has prepared her own potions with which men may safely stimulate their minds so they vibrate on a plane that enables them to tune in to fine and rare thoughts which come from—no man knows where! No satisfactory substitute for Nature's stimulants has ever been found.

It is a fact well known to psychologists that there is a very close relationship between sex desires and spiritual urges—a fact which accounts for the peculiar behavior of people who participate in the orgies known as religious "revivals," common among the primitive types.

The world is ruled, and the destiny of civilization is established, by the human emotions. People are influenced in their actions, not by reason so much as by "feelings." The creative faculty of the mind is set into action entirely by emotions, and *not by cold reason*. The most powerful of all human emotions is that of sex. There are other mind stimulants, some of which have been listed, but no one of them, nor all of them combined, can equal the driving power of sex.

A mind stimulant is any influence which will either temporarily, or permanently, increase the vibrations of thought. The ten major stimulants, described, are those most commonly resorted to. Through these sources one may commune with Infinite Intelligence, or enter, at will, the storehouse of the subconscious mind, either one's own, or that of another person, a procedure *which is all there is of genius*.

A teacher, who has trained and directed the efforts of more than 30,000 sales people, made the astounding discovery that highly sexed men are the most efficient salesmen. The explanation is, that the factor of personality known as "personal magnetism" is nothing more nor less than sex energy. Highly sexed people always have a plentiful supply of magnetism. Through cultivation and understanding, this vital force may be drawn upon and used to great advantage in the relationships between people. This energy may be communicated to others through the following media:

1. The hand-shake. The touch of the hand indicates, instantly, the presence of magnetism, or the lack of it.
2. The tone of voice. Magnetism, or sex energy, is the factor with which the voice may be colored, or made musical and charming.
3. Posture and carriage of the body. Highly sexed people move briskly, and with grace and ease.

4. The vibrations of thought. Highly sexed people mix the emotion of sex with their thoughts, or may do so at will, and in that way, may influence those around them.
5. Body adornment. People who are highly sexed are usually very careful about their personal appearance. They usually select clothing of a style becoming to their personality, physique, complexion, etc.

When employing salesmen, the more capable sales manager looks for the quality of personal magnetism as the *first requirement* of a salesman. People who lack sex energy will never become enthusiastic nor inspire others with enthusiasm, and enthusiasm is one of the most important requisites in salesmanship, no matter what one is selling.

The public speaker, orator, preacher, lawyer, or salesman who is lacking in sex energy is a "flop," as far as being able to influence others is concerned. Couple with this the fact, that most people can be influenced only through an appeal to their emotions, and you will understand the importance of sex energy as a part of the salesman's native ability. Master salesmen attain the status of mastery in selling, because they, either consciously, or unconsciously, *transmute* the energy of sex into SALES ENTHUSIASM! In this statement may be found a very practical suggestion as to the actual meaning of sex transmutation.

The salesman who knows how to take his mind off the subject of sex, and direct it in sales effort with as much enthusiasm and determination as he would apply to its original purpose, has acquired the art of sex transmutation, whether he knows it or not. The majority of salesmen who transmute their sex energy do so without being in the least aware of what they are doing, or how they are doing it.

Transmutation of sex energy calls for more will power than the average person cares to use for this purpose. Those who find it difficult to summon will-power sufficient for transmutation, may gradually acquire this ability. Though this requires will-power, the reward for the practice is more than worth the effort.

The entire subject of sex is one with which the majority of people appear to be unpardonably ignorant. The urge of sex has been grossly misunderstood, slandered, and burlesqued by the ignorant and the evil minded, for so long that the very word sex is seldom used in polite society. Men and women who are known to be blessed—yes, BLESSED—with highly sexed natures, are usually looked upon as being people who will bear watching. Instead of being called blessed, they are usually called cursed.

Millions of people, even in this age of enlightenment, have inferiority complexes which they developed because of this false belief that a highly sexed nature is a curse. These statements, of the virtue of sex energy, should not be construed as justification for the libertine. The emotion of sex is a virtue ONLY when used intelligently, and with discrimination. It may be misused, and often is, to such an extent that it debases, instead of enriches, both body and mind. The better use of this power is the burden of this chapter.

It seemed quite significant to the author, when he made the discovery that practically every great leader, whom he had the privilege of analyzing, was a man whose achievements were largely inspired by a woman. In many instances, the "woman in the case" was a modest, self-denying wife, of whom the public had heard but little or nothing. In a few instances, the source of inspiration has been traced to the "other woman." Perhaps such cases may not be entirely unknown to you.

Intemperance in sex habits is just as detrimental as intemperance in habits of drinking and eating. In this age in which we live, an age which began with the world war, intemperance in habits of sex is common. This orgy of indulgence may account for the shortage of great leaders. No man can avail himself of the forces of his creative imagination, while dissipating them. Man is the only creature on earth which violates Nature's purpose in this connection. Every other animal indulges its sex nature in moderation, and with purpose which harmonizes with the laws of nature. Every other animal responds to the call of sex only in "season." Man's inclination is to declare "open season."

Every intelligent person knows that stimulation in excess, through alcoholic drink and narcotics, is a form of intemperance which destroys the vital organs of the body, including the brain. Not every person knows, however, that over indulgence in sex expression may become a habit as destructive and as detrimental to creative effort as narcotics or liquor.

A sex-mad man is not essentially different than a dope-mad man! Both have lost control over their faculties of reason and will-power. Sexual overindulgence may not only destroy reason and willpower, but it may also lead to either temporary, or permanent insanity. Many cases of hypochondria (imaginary illness) grow out of habits developed in ignorance of the true function of sex.

From these brief references to the subject, it may be readily seen that ignorance on the subject of sex transmutation, forces stupendous penalties upon the ignorant on the one hand, and withholds from them equally stupendous benefits, on the other.

Widespread ignorance on the subject of sex is due to the fact that the subject has been surrounded with mystery and beclouded by dark silence. The conspiracy of mystery and silence has had the same effect upon the minds of young people that the psychology of prohibition had. The result has been increased curiosity, and desire to acquire more knowledge on this "verboten" subject; and to the shame of all lawmakers, and most physicians—by training best qualified to educate youth on that subject—information has not been easily available.

Seldom does an individual enter upon highly creative effort in any field of endeavor before the age of forty. The average man reaches the period of his greatest capacity to create between forty and sixty. These statements are based upon analysis of thousands of men and women who have been carefully observed. They should be encouraging to those who fail to arrive before the age of forty, and to those who become frightened at the approach of "old age," around the forty-year mark. The years between forty and fifty are, as a rule, the most fruitful. Man should approach this age, not with fear and trembling, but with hope and eager anticipation.

If you want evidence that most men do not begin to do their best work before the age of forty, study the records of the most successful men known to the American people, and you will find it. Henry Ford had not "hit his pace" of achievement until he had passed the age of forty. Andrew Carnegie was well past forty before he began to reap the reward of his efforts. James J. Hill was still running a telegraph key at the age of forty. His stupendous achievements took place after that age. Biographies of American industrialists and financiers are filled with evidence that the period from forty to sixty is the most productive age of man.

Between the ages of thirty and forty, man begins to learn (if he ever learns), the art of sex transmutation. This discovery is generally accidental, and more often than otherwise, the man who makes it is totally unconscious of his discovery. He may observe that his powers of achievement have increased around the age of thirty-five to forty, but in most cases, he is not familiar with the cause of this change; that Nature begins to harmonize the emotions of love and sex in the individual, between the ages of thirty and forty, so that he may draw upon these great forces, and apply them jointly as stimuli to action.

Sex, alone, is a mighty urge to action, but its forces are like a cyclone—they are often uncontrollable. When the emotion of love begins to mix itself with the emotion of sex, the result is calmness of purpose, poise, accuracy of judgment, and balance. What person, who has attained to the age of forty, is so unfortunate as to be unable to analyze these statements, and to corroborate them by his own experience?

Sex Energy: Your Magic Elixir

When driven by his desire to please a woman, based solely upon the emotion of sex, a man may be, and usually is, capable of great achievement, but his actions may be disorganized, distorted, and totally destructive. When driven by his desire to please a woman, based upon the motive of sex alone, a man may steal, cheat, and even commit murder. But when the emotion of LOVE is mixed with the emotion of sex, that same man will guide his actions with more sanity, balance, and reason.

Criminologists have discovered that the most hardened criminals can be reformed through the influence of a woman's *love*. There is no record of a criminal having been reformed solely through the sex influence. These facts are well known, but their cause is not. Reformation comes, if at all, through the *heart*, or the emotional side of man, *not* through his head, or reasoning side. Reformation means, "a change of heart." It does not mean a "change of head." A man may, because of reason, make certain changes in his personal conduct to avoid the consequences of undesirable effects, but GENUINE REFORMATION comes only through a change of heart—through a DESIRE to change.

Love, Romance, and Sex are all emotions capable of driving men to heights of super achievement. Love is the emotion which serves as a safety valve, and insures balance, poise, and constructive effort. When combined, these three emotions may lift one to an altitude of a genius. There are genii, however, who know but little of the emotion of love. Most of them may be found engaged in some form of action which is destructive, or at least, not based upon justice and fairness toward others. If good taste would permit, a dozen genii could be named in the field of industry and finance, who ride ruthlessly over the rights of their fellow men. They seem totally lacking in conscience. The reader can easily supply his own list of such men.

The emotions are states of mind. Nature has provided man with a "chemistry of the mind" which operates in a manner similar to the principles of chemistry of matter. It is a well known fact that, through the aid of chemistry of matter, a chemist may create a deadly poison by mixing certain elements, none of which are—in themselves—harmful in the right proportions. The emotions may, likewise, be combined so as to create a deadly poison. The emotions of sex and jealousy, when mixed, may turn a person into an insane beast.

The presence of any one or more of the destructive emotions in the human mind, through the chemistry of the mind, sets up a poison which may destroy one's sense of justice and fairness. In extreme cases, the presence of any combination of these emotions in the mind may destroy one's reason.

The road to genius consists of the development, control, and use of sex, love, and romance. Briefly, the process may be stated as follows:

Encourage the presence of these emotions as the dominating thoughts in one's mind, and discourage the presence of all the destructive emotions. The mind is a creature of habit. It thrives upon the *dominating* thoughts fed it. Through the faculty of will-power, one may discourage the presence of any emotion, and encourage the presence of any other. Control of the mind, through the power of will, is not difficult.

Control comes from persistence, and habit. The secret of control lies in understanding the process of transmutation. When any negative emotion presents itself in one's mind, it can be transmuted into a positive, or constructive emotion, by the simple procedure of changing one's thoughts.

THERE IS NO OTHER ROAD TO GENIUS THAN THROUGH VOLUNTARY SELF EFFORT! A man may attain to great heights of financial or business achievement, solely by the driving force of sex energy, but history is filled with evidence that he may, and usually does, carry with him certain traits of character which rob him of the ability to either hold, or enjoy his fortune. This is worthy of analysis, thought, and meditation, for it states a truth, the knowledge of which may be helpful to women as well as men. Ignorance of this has cost thousands of people their privilege of HAPPINESS, even though they possessed riches.

The emotions of love and sex leave their unmistakable marks upon the features. Moreover, these signs are so visible, that all who wish may read them. The man who is driven by the storm of passion, based upon sex desires alone, plainly advertises that fact to the entire world, by the expression of his eyes, and the lines of his face. The emotion of love, when mixed with the emotion of sex, softens, modifies, and beautifies the facial expression. No character analyst is needed to tell you this—you may observe it for yourself.

The emotion of love brings out, and develops, the artistic and the aesthetic nature of man. It leaves its impress upon one's very soul, even after the fire has been subdued by time and circumstance.

Memories of love never pass. They linger, guide, and influence long after the source of stimulation has faded. There is nothing new in this. Every person, who has been moved by GENUINE LOVE, knows that it leaves enduring traces upon the human heart. The effect of love endures, because love is spiritual in nature. The man who cannot be stimulated to great heights of achievement by love, is hopeless—he is dead, though he may seem to live.

Even the memories of love are sufficient to lift one to a higher plane of creative effort. The major force of love may spend itself and pass away, like a fire which has burned itself out, but it leaves behind indelible marks as evidence that it passed that way. Its departure often prepares the human heart for a still greater love.

Go back into your yesterdays, at times, and bathe your mind in the beautiful memories of past love. It will soften the influence of the present worries and annoyances. It will give you a source of escape from the unpleasant realities of life, and maybe—who knows?—your mind will yield to you, during this temporary retreat into the world of fantasy, ideas, or plans which may change the entire financial or spiritual status of your life.

If you believe yourself unfortunate, because you have "loved and lost," perish the thought. One who has loved truly, can never lose entirely. Love is whimsical and temperamental. Its nature is ephemeral, and transitory. It comes when it pleases, and goes away without warning. Accept and enjoy it while it remains, but spend no time worrying about its departure. Worry will never bring it back.

Dismiss, also, the thought that love never comes but once. Love may come and go, times without number, but there are no two love experiences which affect one in just the same way. There may be, and there usually is, one love experience which leaves a deeper imprint on the heart than all the others, but all love experiences are beneficial, except to the person who becomes resentful and cynical when love makes its departure.

There should be no disappointment over love, and there would be none if people understood the difference between the emotions of love and sex. The major difference is that love is spiritual, while sex is biological. No experience, which touches the human heart with a spiritual force, can possibly be harmful, except through ignorance, or jealousy.

Love is, without question, life's greatest experience. It brings one into communion with Infinite Intelligence. When mixed with the emotions of romance and sex, it may lead one far up the ladder of creative effort. The emotions of love, sex, and romance, are sides of the eternal triangle of achievement-building genius. Nature creates genii through no other force.

Love is an emotion with many sides, shades, and colors. The love which one feels for parents, or children is quite different from that which one feels for one's sweetheart. The one is mixed with the emotion of sex, while the other is not.

The love which one feels in true friendship is not the same as that felt for one's sweetheart, parents, or children, but it, too, is a form of love.

Then, there is the emotion of love for things inanimate, such as the love of Nature's handiwork. But the most intense and burning of all these various kinds of love, is that experienced in the blending of the emotions of love and sex. Marriages, not blessed with the eternal affinity of love, properly balanced and proportioned, with sex, cannot be happy ones—and seldom endure. Love, alone, will not bring happiness in marriage, nor will sex alone. When these two beautiful emotions are blended, marriage may bring about a state of mind, closest to the spiritual that one may ever know on this earthly plane.

When the emotion of romance is added to those of love and sex, the obstructions between the finite mind of man and Infinite Intelligence are removed. Then a genius has been born!

What a different story is this, than those usually associated with the emotion of sex. Here is an interpretation of the emotion which lifts it out of the commonplace, and makes of it potter's clay in the hands of God, from which He fashions all that is beautiful and inspiring. It is an interpretation which would, when properly understood, bring harmony out of the chaos which exists in too many marriages. The disharmonies often expressed in the form of nagging, may usually be traced to *lack of knowledge* on the subject of sex. Where love, romance and the proper understanding of the emotion and function of sex abide, there is no disharmony between married people.

Fortunate is the husband whose wife understands the true relationship between the emotions of love, sex, and romance. When motivated by this holy triumvirate, no form of labor is burdensome, because even the most lowly form of effort takes on the nature of a labor of love.

Sex Energy: Your Magic Elixir

It is a very old saying that "a man's wife may either make him or break him," but the reason is not always understood. The "making" and "breaking" is the result of the wife's understanding, or lack of understanding of the emotions of love, sex, and romance.

Despite the fact that men are polygamous, by the very nature of their biological inheritance, it is true that no woman has as great an influence on a man as his wife, unless he is married to a woman totally unsuited to his nature. If a woman permits her husband to lose interest in her, and become more interested in other women, it is usually because of her ignorance, or indifference toward the subjects of sex, love, and romance. This statement presupposes, of course, that genuine love once existed between a man and his wife. The facts are equally applicable to a man who permits his wife's interest in him to die.

Married people often bicker over a multitude of trivialities. If these are analyzed accurately, the real cause of the trouble will often be found to be indifference, or ignorance on these subjects.

Man's greatest motivating force is his desire to please woman! The hunter who excelled during prehistoric days, before the dawn of civilization, did so, because of his desire to appear great in the eyes of woman. Man's nature has not changed in this respect. The "hunter" of today brings home no skins of wild animals, but he indicates his desire for her favor by supplying fine clothes, motor cars, and wealth. Man has the same desire to please woman that he had before the dawn of civilization. The only thing that has changed, is his method of pleasing. Men who accumulate large fortunes, and attain to great heights of power and fame, do so, mainly, to satisfy their *desire to please women*. Take women out of their lives, and great wealth would be useless to most men. *It is this inherent desire of man to please woman, which gives woman the power to make or break a man.*

The woman who understands man's nature and tactfully caters to it, need have no fear of competition from other women. Men may be "giants" with indomitable will-power when dealing with other men, but they are easily managed by the women of their choice.

Most men will not admit that they are easily influenced by the women they prefer, because it is in the nature of the male to want to be recognized as the stronger of the species. Moreover, the intelligent woman recognizes this "manly trait" and very wisely makes no issue of it.

Some men know that they are being influenced by the women of their choice—their wives, sweethearts, mothers or sisters—but they tactfully refrain from rebelling against the influence because they are intelligent enough to know that NO MAN IS HAPPY OR COMPLETE WITHOUT THE MODIFYING INFLUENCE OF THE RIGHT WOMAN. The man who does not recognize this important truth deprives himself of the power which has done more to help men achieve success than all other forces combined.

VIII
Rebounding from Failure

How Success Grows from Failure,
article from
Napoleon Hill's Magazine
(April 1921)

Failure is painful but it is also our primary channel of growth. This is one of Hill's core principles. This concept appears in many ethical and spiritual systems. For example:

Poet William Blake wrote, "Opposition is True Friendship."

Nietzsche famously observed, "What does not kill me, makes me stronger."

Spiritual philosopher G.I. Gurdjieff observed, "Every stick has two ends."

In his essay "Compensation," Ralph Waldo Emerson described the compensatory laws of life and how every mishap brings proportionate consolation.

This compensating dynamic also appears within the many meanings of the Hermetic principle, "As above, so below."

It is a fundamental truth: life is a polarity.

The traits that you most admire in yourself—qualities of maturity, perseverance, self-sufficiency—grow from times when you are challenged, frustrated, or blocked. I can recall painful episodes in life, including betrayals, calumny, loss of cherished projects, which ultimately made me clearer, stronger, and more capable. I wouldn't want to repeat such experiences, but I also wouldn't want to have not gone through them.

It is only when pressed by opposition that we grow. If you didn't suffer you would remain a mental and emotional child. This may be the esoteric meaning behind the expulsion from Eden. Friction is the cause and the inevitable price of growth.

Obviously you've come to this book because you want to success. But setbacks and failures are as basic to life as the seasonal cycles. And they are just as purposeful.

Even the sting of foolish criticism or the edge of an insult can make you stronger. Perhaps your detrac-

tor ("Opposition is True Friendship") has identified a weak spot, which your friends are too kind to voice. We are conventionally told to ignore bullies and their jibes. I reject that advice. First off, it is impossible; I regard it the ultimate cliché in self-development. Second, your adversary, cruel and unreasonable though he may be, may hit a soft spot or chink in your armor. Resolve to fortify that gap. Use every resource you possess. Seen on the sliding scale of polarity, friendship and adversity cosmically mirror each other. Each serves a purpose. Each is inevitable.

The following article is one of Hill's earliest statements on the constructive uses of failure. Read his words with care, and allow them to inform every twisted ankle that you experience.

—MH

HOW SUCCESS GROWS
FROM FAILURE

Turn back the pages of history, back to the very beginning of all that we know of civilization, and you will find that the men and women whose names lived after they passed on were those whose efforts were born of struggle, hardship, and failure.

Men may leave behind them monuments of marble without struggle, hardship, and failure, but those who would build monuments in the hearts of their fellowmen, where neither the disintegrating forces of the elements nor the degrading hand of man can destroy them, must pay the price in sacrifice and struggle!

Ten years ago a baby was born into one of the wealthiest families in America. The whole world showered the little fellow with gifts it did not need and could not use. One foolish king sent, as his offering to the useless collection, a gold crib that cost $40,000.

I was going to law school in the city where that baby was born, therefore I know considerable about the event. That bountiful shower of gifts reminded me of the passage in the Bible that reads something along these lines: "To him that hath it shall be given, and to him that hath not it shall be taken away, even that which he hath."

Nothing more true to human nature was ever said than this. Like attracts like. Wealth attracts wealth and poverty attracts poverty. It is the way of human nature.

By and by, this little baby grew old enough to be taken on the streets. When he was taken out, he was flanked by a coterie of servants and private detectives whose business it was to see that no misfortune overtook him. Never in all this baby's life was he permitted outside the protecting influence of these servants. He could not go on the street alone. He was watched over with care that would lead one to believe he might have been made of superior clay.

This little fellow had no cares. He experienced no hardships. He never knew what struggle meant. All he knew was that he was not born to toil. He did not have to dress himself; he had servants for that purpose. He did not have to use his eyes; he had servants' eyes to use. He did not have to use his hands; he had servants' hands to use. In fact he did not have to do anything.

Each winter he went with his army of servants to play in the rolling waters of the warm Gulf of Mexico, where he was not bothered with the cold blizzards of the north. When he went out to swim he was surrounded by this same army of servants, who flanked him and watched to see that no harm befell him.

Two years ago this little fellow, now a boy of ten years, had just returned to the north from his wintering place in Florida. He was out in the gardens with his servants when he noticed that the gates were open, and he saw beyond the much longed-for freedom that every normal child is constantly seeking. While the servants' vigilance had slackened for a moment, he saw his chance and made a run for the street He got outside and into the middle of the street when he was run down and instantly killed by a Ford automobile.

At the very moment this was happening, there were no less than a million little urchins located in the crowded streets of the great cities, not one of which could have been run down by an automobile in an open ten-acre field, because these little "unfortunates" had learned the art of self-defense. Out of struggle—struggle born of necessity—they had learned to get out of the way of automobiles.

Verily do we repeat that out of struggle and hardship come endurance and power!

Servants and private detectives can watch over a baby and possibly keep him from being stolen; they can even keep him from being run down by automobiles, if they attend to their duties properly, but the eternal law of compensation takes its toll when the little fellow grows up to maturity and commences to take his place among men. He pays dearly for the early protection that relieved him of struggle the very first time he is called upon to rely entirely on his own resources, because he finds that he has no real "resources."

The strong-armed blacksmith developed his strength out of "resistance." The greater the resistance, the greater his strength. By wielding a heavy hammer day in and day out, he finally grew a mighty arm that serves him wherever physical strength is needed. He developed his strong arm in exactly the same manner that all strength must be developed: by overcoming resistance.

We point with pride to Lincoln as being one of the really great Americans of the past, yet how many stop to consider that his strength, both physical and moral, grew out of hardship and struggle! No doubt Nancy Hanks would have given Lincoln as royal a birth as that of the little boy mentioned above, if she had been financially able, but if she had done so there is but little doubt that Lincoln would never have risen to the heights to which he attained!

Much of Lincolns greatness grew out of his early struggles and hardships, because out of these grew strength, that mighty strength which carried him through one of the most trying crises of this country.

The most dangerous handicap with which any child could be surrounded is the handicap of money, provided it is used to relieve the child of struggle.

Twenty-odd years ago I was secretary to a wealthy man whose two sons were away at college. It was a part of my duty to make out a check for $100 for each of these boys on the first of the month. This was their "spending money," and spend it they did!

Well do I remember how I envied these boys the easy time this monthly remittance provided. By and by, they returned home with their "sheep skins" and other things too, among them being the capacity for great quantities of whiskey.

One of those boys is now under the sod and the other is in an insane asylum, a victim of "D.T.'s."

Last year I had the privilege of speaking in the college where one of the boys went to school. The principal of the school told me that the $100 check which came monthly for that boy was the influence that undermined him. With that check he had money to be a "good fellow." This led to the drink habit, and that led to ruination!

I can see now that fate dealt me a lucky blow when it placed the great cosmic urge of necessity behind me, in my early childhood, and forced me to struggle for a schooling and for existence itself. That struggle seemed hard then, but I know now that it was the strengthening process I needed to prepare me for a mans work in life.

My own boys are coming along now, and in spite of the powerful moral which I have drawn from my own experience and from my observation of the two boys mentioned, I see myself inclined to "make it easy" for my boys when I can. This is a common tendency—a human sort of tendency, perhaps—which can lead nowhere but to distress and grief when the child is called upon for the reserve strength that is not there because he has never met with the necessary resistance.

It may seem like a trite statement, but it is nonetheless true on that account, to say the only permanent good that can come to a child comes out of what he does for himself. The greatest service that can be rendered any person on earth is the service which causes that person to rely upon himself.

When you pitch a dime to a beggar you may benefit him temporarily, but in the long run you have done him a decided injury, because you have taken away from him the necessity of struggle.

I met a man in Lawton, Oklahoma, on my recent tour of the country, who gave me much food for thought. I had ridden around with him all afternoon in an automobile before I learned that he was stone blind. His dark glasses covered his eyes, and not a sign of his affliction was to be seen on his face or detected from his voice. He laughingly carried on one of the most interesting conversations I have ever listened to, and entertained me so splendidly that I did not notice his blindness.

Afterward I learned of this mans early struggles. He had lost his eyes at the age of four. Several years ago he presented himself at Northwestern University, in the city of Chicago, for matriculation as a student. The officials refused to accept him, urging him not to undertake a stiff course such as tried the strength of able-bodied young men and women to the utmost.

But this young fellow knew no defeat! He was persistent Finally the university officials asked him how much money he had with which to pay his way through school, and he replied, "Thirty-five dollars."

They told him he would only be wasting his time to start in school with his handicap without sufficient funds, and advised him not to try it. He went out and walked around the block a time or two and then came back and said, "Now, look here. Let me enter for the first semester, and if I do not keep up with my classes and pay my way, you can turn me out." They consented, largely, I suspect, because they did not have the heart to refuse.

This young man not only completed the first semester with honors, at the head of his classes, but he finished the entire course—leading all the way through.

But this is not all. He paid his way by taking notes in the lecture rooms, transcribing them on the typewriter, and selling copies to his fellow students—those who had two perfectly good eyes and money in the bank besides!

Rarely does a person ever have opportunity to test the limits of his ability. We can accomplish pretty much whatever we make up our minds to accomplish. If we are not forced to test our strength through dire necessity, through struggle, through hardship, we seldom discover our possibilities. Lay it down as a general rule—and a sound one at that—that real strength comes from struggle, hardship, adversity, and handicaps imposed upon us by causes beyond our immediate control. If we could "control" these causes, they would not exist because we would eliminate them, thereby depriving ourselves of the most beneficial experience that can come to a human being.

Twenty-odd years ago I found myself forced to work as a laborer in the coal mines. Nothing short of necessity would have induced me to perform such work, yet out of that very work came experience that has played, and is now playing, no small part in the very best service I have rendered and will continue to render my fellowmen. We are in the midst of a great industrial crisis, not alone in America but throughout the world, and much of our effort is directed toward the elimination of the "cause" out of which this crisis grew. These efforts have not been without visible results, something that would not have been possible except for the "forced service" rendered in the coal mines years ago. This brought me close to the people who labor in those mines and gave me a splendid chance to study the conditions under which they work, the grievances of which they complain, their faults, and their virtues.

Now when I presume to write for or about those who perform the most lowly sort of labor, I write not as one whose hands were never covered with the grime and dust of honest toil, but as one who has worked shoulder to shoulder with these men whose voices are now crying out for justice and fair treatment.

And when I send back the message to the laborers out of whose ranks I came, urging them to "perform more work and better work than actually paid for," I know that I am not leading them astray or counseling them unwisely, because it has been this one practice, more than any other, that has helped me to throw off an undesirable, unprofitable environment and get into the work that I love. The reason why this is sound practice is obvious. It develops greater and greater ability until, finally, a man just naturally bursts out of his cramped environment by attracting the attention of men in a more desirable walk of life. Out of effort and resistance comes strength! The greater the effort, the greater the compensating strength, and the man who foolishly withholds the best service he is capable of rendering because he may not be receiving what it is worth, is only prolonging the time of failure.

I know of no other single quality that has paid me greater dividends and carried me further toward my ultimate goal in life than has the habit of performing more service and better service than was actually paid for!

But lay stress on that word *habit*.

This practice must become a habit, and recognition must be gained before the real results begin to show. To merely perform more service and better service than is paid for one day, and refrain from doing it the other five working days of the week, would be something like training one hour a week for a prize fight and resting the remainder of the time.

Out of resistance comes strength!

A man may be "born to the weary treadmill of toil" but if he understands that out of toil, out of resistance, out of effort, out of adversity comes strength, he will not long remain a victim of this handicap. Instead, he will soon burst the cords of circumstances and environment, no matter how strong they may seem, and rise to claim his own—his own that is born of struggle and hardship.

A Toast to the Man Who Fails!

As my fingers begin to play upon the keyboard of my typewriter, I look and see before me a great army of men whose faces show the lines of care and despair.

Some are in rags, having reached the last stage of that long, long trail which all men fight to avoid: failure!

Others are in better circumstances, but the fear of starvation shows plainly on their faces, the smile of courage has left their lips, and they, too, seem to have given up the fight.

The scene shifts. I look again and am carried backward into the events of history past, and there I see, also, the failures of the past—failures which have meant more to the human race than all the successes recorded in the history of the world.

I see the homely face of Socrates as he stood at the very end of that trail which men call failure, waiting, with upturned eyes, through those moments that must have seemed like an eternity, just before he drank the poisoned hemlock.

I see Christopher Columbus standing in a Spanish dungeon, a prisoner in chains, the tribute paid him for his sacrifice when he set sail on an unknown ocean to discover an unknown world, knowing that the chances were greatly in favor of his never returning to his native land.

I see the face of Thomas Paine, the man whom the English sought to capture and put to death as the real instigator of the American Revolution. I see him lying in a filthy prison in France, waiting calmly under the shadow of the guillotine, a reprieve from death, and writing—as he waited—many pages dedicated to the advancement of human liberty.

And I see, also, the face of the man from Galilee suffering on the cross at Calvary, the reward for his efforts to interest men in being decent with one another here on earth.

Failures, all!

Oh, to be such a failure. Oh, to go down in history, as these men did, as being brave enough to place humanity above the individual and principle above pecuniary gain. On such failures rest the hopes of the world.

The Test of a Man!

The measure of a real man is in his ability to see, with clear eyes, all the beauty and the good and all the injustice and the wrong there is in the world and still maintain an even sense of proportion in all things, toward all people.

I bow to the man who can see the imperfections of mankind without becoming cynical; who can temper justice with mercy; who can see the good there is in men who disagree with him; who can work in harmony with those whom he does not admire; who exercises self-control and lets reason instead of emotion govern his actions toward others.

Such a man was the immortal Lincoln!

He was a man with a message when he had sufficient provocation to have become a man with a grievance instead. As a reward for his greatness, the world has erected an everlasting monument to Lincoln's name. A monument that the elements can never disintegrate, that no depredating hand can destroy; a monument built in the heart of the people—built not of stone but of love, sympathy, patience, tolerance, and forgiveness for mankind—those gentle qualities that memory attaches to his name and which are now the real test of a man!

The Damaging Effects of Subterfuge and Deceit

Nothing really seems so very bad until someone tries to cover it up through subterfuge and deceit.

We may not agree with the man who boldly admits his shortcomings, but we cannot withhold from him a certain healthy respect on account of his boldness.

On the other hand, the moment a person resorts to secrecy or to subterfuge, even in connection with matters of small importance, that person becomes immediately marked as unworthy of trust.

If there is a skeleton in the closet which is apt to crawl out to plague one at the most inopportune time, a mighty good plan is to voluntarily drag it out and say, "There it is; what are you going to do about it?"

People will forgive most anything unless there is an attempt to cover it up and clothe it in secrecy. In that event forgiveness comes reluctantly, if at all.

Many a solid friend has been made by open frankness in connection with matters that, within themselves, were of small importance, while on the other hand lifelong enemies have been made by lack of this frankness.

If a person is secretive and resorts to deceit and subterfuge in small matters, the supposition is that in matters of greater import the same tactics will prevail.

Deliver More Service and Better Service than You Are Paid For

This simple injunction comes from a man who started at the very bottom, in the most lowly sort of labor.

It constitutes the keynote of almost every public address this man delivers; it permeates nearly everything he writes; it creeps into his everyday conversation.

There are many reasons why this is sound counsel, only one of which need be mentioned—namely, every person who forms the habit of delivering this sort of service soon attracts the attention of competitive bidders for his services. He stands out above the common crowd like a skyscraper above the ordinary buildings, and there is keen competition for his labor.

Give the best service you know how to render, regardless of the amount you receive for it, and soon—much sooner than you might imagine—you will become a "marked" person and greater responsibilities and higher wages will be thrusting themselves upon you.

Deliver the best services you can, not necessarily out of consideration for the purchaser but out of consideration for yourself. Failure to practice this habit is the chief obstacle that stands between 95 percent of the people and success, but of course this does not apply to you. Or does it?

Aimlessness is a sin and it leads straight to poverty, misery, want, and failure. A man without a definite, constructive purpose in life is simply one of natures mistakes, because she did not intend to create such a being, in all probability.

IX
How Cosmic Law Helps You

The Law of Cosmic Habitforce,
from
The Master Key to Riches
(1945)

I consider this chapter the most important in this book. It may be the most important piece of Hill's writing that you ever encounter.

Hill's theory of "Cosmic Habit Force" is one of his most vital insights. He developed it several years after writing The Law of Success *and* Think and Grow Rich. *Cosmic Habit Force is the cycle of positive repeat behaviors by which creation maintains itself, such as the rotation of the planets, the ebb and flow of tides, and the cycle of seasons. Humans are the only beings that possess the ability to choose their habits, thereby playing a self-selecting role in creation. If you select habits that build your generative forces, you merge with the flow of nature and place enormous power behind your efforts.*

You are never truly without resources. With the cultivation of right habits—which means steady, beneficial behaviors and intentions—you join with spiritual, natural, and cosmic laws, and, barring some equally powerful intervention, you are delivered to the destination you seek like a twig carried downstream in a river. But unlike the twig, the sentient being possesses the possibility of choice, attention, and selection. Choose intelligently (no easy thing), and you enter this stream.

In this chapter, similar to the previous one, Hill identifies failure as a necessary course-correction within the scheme of Cosmic Habit Force. Failure breaks up calcified, unsuccessful thought patterns, plans, and relationships. This entire anthology is dedicated to inculcating you with the right kinds of habits.

Hill also endorses crafting what might be called a "total environment," to borrow Anton LaVey's phrase. This is an environment in which you surround yourself with ideas, voices, imagery, décor, and people who affirm your ideal. This is no small point. You are profoundly affected by your surroundings, which serve as a kind of autosuggestive trigger. Harvard psychologist Ellen Langer has conducted experiments in which elderly people demonstrate renewed physical and mental vitality in surroundings of nostalgia, which evoke their youth. (You can read about this in The Miracle Club*). And this does not even touch upon the importance of sound relationships, about which Hill writes:*

> *One must remove himself from the range of influence of every person and every circumstance which has even a slight tendency to cause him to feel inferior or incapable of attaining the object of his purpose. Positive egos do not grow in negative environments. On this point there can be no excuse from compromise, and failure to observe it will prove fatal to the chance of success.*

At the risk of sounding heterodox, I believe that too much has been made of forgiveness and acceptance (both of self and others) within our spiritual and motivational culture. Sometimes it is vital, first and foremost, to physically separate yourself from cruel or depleting people. No amount of self-acceptance will build immunity to a relative, parent, boss, coworker, or "friend" who makes sport of running you down or who chronically directs passive-aggressive barbs at you.

Hostility is a widespread and under-acknowledged fact of human nature. More important than analyzing or understanding hostility is getting away from it. You cannot survive sustained hostility, and should not be expected to. This is true inasmuch as a houseplant cannot survive chronic absence of sunlight or water. Such conditions are unnatural and unnecessary. Questions of forgiveness, understanding, and acceptance, whether of self or another, can be explored after you've gotten to safety and protected yourself and your psyche.

Some people feel unable to separate from a cruel person due to familial ties or financial needs. I sympathize with that—and offer this three-part formula:

1. *Be certain that the bonds you feel are actual and not artificial. Fear of disapproval is not a valid excuse for remaining in proximity to a cruel person. Just because someone else will disapprove of your decision to separate is not a real bind. Every*

decision carries consequences; the positive consequences of moving away from cruelty almost invariably outweigh the negative. Another person's judgment must not deter you. If it does, that is self-created.

2. *If you've determined that you authentically wish to separate but feel financially or otherwise bound, vow first to separate from the person internally. Acknowledge to yourself their cruelty and admit its grotesque and destructive nature. Do not tell the other person what you're doing or thinking. Do not share your insight. Cruel people always have plausible denial. It is part of how they maintain their hold on people. Just knowing this makes you more powerful. But there is one last and vital step.*

3. *Vow to separate from this person as a physical fact at the first possible opportunity. This opportunity will come, and probably sooner than you think. Because Cosmic Habit Force sustains and fortifies growth. When you place yourself within its schema, which these steps are designed to*

do, opportunities for expansion and separation will reach and carry you. But the first and most important step is determining that this is want you want.

—MH

THE LAW OF COSMIC HABITFORCE

*Habit is a cable; we weave a thread of it every day,
and at last we cannot break it.*
—*Horace Mann.*

So, we come now to the analysis of the greatest of all of Nature's laws, the law of Cosmic Habitforce!

Briefly described, the law of Cosmic Habitforce is Nature's method of giving fixation to all habits so that they may carry on automatically once they have been set into motion—the habits of men the same as the habits of the universe.

Every man is where he is and what he is because of his established habits of thoughts and deeds. The purpose of this entire philosophy is to aid the individual in the formation of the kind of habits that will transfer him from where he is to where he wishes to be in life.

Every scientist, and many laymen, know that Nature maintains a perfect balance between all the elements of matter and energy throughout the universe; that the entire universe is operated through an inexorable system of orderliness and habits which never vary, and cannot be altered by any form of human endeavor; that the five known realities of the universe are (1) Time, (2) Space, (3) Energy, (4) Matter, and (5) Intelligence, which shape the other known realities into orderliness and system based upon *fixed habits.*

These are Nature's building-blocks with which she creates a grain of sand or the largest stars that float through space, and every other thing known to man, or that the mind of man can conceive.

These are the known realities, but not every one has taken the time or the interest to ascertain the fact that Cosmic Habitforce is the particular application of Energy with which Nature maintains the relationship between the atoms of matter, the stars and the planets in their ceaseless motion onward toward some unknown destiny, the seasons of the year, night and day, sickness and health, life and death. Cosmic Habitforce is the medium through which all habits and all human relationships are maintained in varying degrees of permanence, and the medium through which thought is translated into its physical equivalent in response to the desires and purposes of individuals.

But these are truths capable of proof, and one may count that hour sacred during which he discovers the unescapable truth that man is only an instrument through which higher powers than his own are projecting themselves. This entire philosophy is designed to lead one to this important discovery, and to enable him to make use of the knowledge it reveals, *by placing himself in harmony with the unseen forces of the universe which may carry him inevitably into the success side of the great River of Life.*

The hour of this discovery should bring him within easy reach of the Master-Key to all Riches!

Cosmic Habitforce is Nature's Comptroller through which all other natural laws are coordinated, organized and operated through orderliness and system. Therefore it is the greatest of all natural laws.

We see the stars and the planets move with such precision that the astronomers can predetermine their exact location and their relationship to one another scores of years hence.

We see the seasons of the year come and go with a clock-like regularity.

We know that an oak tree grows from an acorn, and a pine tree grows from the seed of its ancestor; that an acorn never makes a mistake and produces a pine tree; nor does a pine seed produce an oak tree. We know that nothing is ever produced that does not have its antecedents in something similar which preceded it; that the nature and the purpose of one's thoughts produce fruits after their kind, just as surely as fire produces smoke.

Cosmic Habitforce is the medium by which every living thing is forced to take on and become a part of the environmental influences in which it lives and moves. Thus it is clearly evident that success attracts more success, and failure attracts more failure—a truth that has long been known to men, although but few have understood the reason for this strange phenomenon.

It is known that the person who has been a failure may become a most outstanding success by close association with those who think and act in terms of success, but not every one knows that this is true because the law of Cosmic Habitforce transmits the "success consciousness" from the mind of the successful man to the mind of the unsuccessful one who is closely related to him in the daily affairs of life.

Whenever any two minds contact each other there is born of that contact a third mind patterned after the stronger of the two. Most successful men recognize this truth and frankly admit that their success began with their close association with some person whose positive mental attitude they either consciously or unconsciously appropriated.

Cosmic Habitforce is silent, unseen and unperceived through any of the five physical senses. That is why it has not been more widely recognized, for most men do not attempt to understand the intangible forces of Nature, nor do they interest themselves in abstract principles. However, these intangibles and abstractions represent the real powers of the universe, and they are the real basis of everything that is tangible and concrete, the source from which tangibility and concreteness are derived.

Understand the working principle of Cosmic Habitforce and you will have no difficulty in interpreting Emerson's essay on Compensation, for he was rubbing elbows with the law of Cosmic Habitforce when he wrote this famous essay.

And Sir Isaac Newton likewise came near to the complete recognition of this law when he made his discovery of the law of gravitation. Had he gone but a brief distance beyond where his discovery ended he might have helped to reveal the same law which holds our little earth in space and relates it systematically to all other planets in both Time and Space; the same law that relates human beings to each other and relates every individual to himself through his *thought habits*.

The term "Habitforce" is self-explanatory. It is a force which works through established habits. And every living thing below the intelligence of man lives, reproduces itself and fulfills its earthly mission in direct response to the power of Cosmic Habitforce through what we call "instinct."

Man alone has been given the privilege of choice in connection with his living habits, and these he may fix by the patterns of his thoughts—the one and only privilege over which any individual has been given complete right of control.

Man may think in terms of self-imposed limitations of fear and doubt and envy and greed and poverty, and Cosmic Habitforce will translate these thoughts into their material equivalent. Or he may think in terms of opulence and plenty, and this same law will translate his thoughts into their physical counterpart.

In this manner may one control his earthly destiny to an astounding degree—simply by exercising his privilege of shaping his own thoughts. But once these thoughts have been shaped into definite patterns they are taken over by the law of Cosmic Habitforce and are made into permanent habits, and they remain as such unless and until they have been supplanted by *different and stronger* thought patterns.

Now we come to the consideration of one of the most profound of all truths; the fact that most men who attain the higher brackets of success seldom do so until they have undergone some tragedy or emergency which reached deeply into their souls and reduced them to that circumstance of life which men call "failure."

The reason for this strange phenomenon is readily recognized by those who understand the law of Cosmic Habitforce, for it consists in the fact that these disasters and tragedies of life serve to break up the established habits of man—habits which have led him eventually to the inevitable results of failure—and thus break the grip of Cosmic Habitforce and allow him to formulate new and better habits.

We see the same phenomenon in the results of warfare!

When nations or large groups of people so relate themselves that their efforts do not harmonize with the Divine Plan of Nature, they are forced to break up their habits, by warfare or some other equally disturbing circumstances, such as business depressions or epidemics of disease, so that a new start may be made which conforms more nearly to Nature's ultimate and overall scheme.

This conclusion is not intended to provide a justification for warfare, but rather to serve as an indictment of mankind on the charge of ignorance of a law which, if it were universally understood and respected would make warfare unnecessary and impossible!

Wars grow out of maladjustments in the relationships of men! These maladjustments are the results of the negative thoughts of men which have grown until they assume *mass proportions*. The spirit of any nation is but the sum total of the dominating thought-habits of its people.

And the same is true of individuals, for here too the spirit of the individual is determined by his dominating thought habits. Most individuals are at war, in one way or another, throughout their lives. They are at war with their own conflicting thoughts and emotions. They are at war in their family relationships and in their occupational and social relationships.

Recognize this truth and you will understand the real power and the benefits which are available to those who live by the Golden Rule, for this great rule *will save you from the conflicts of personal warfare.*

Recognize it and you will understand also the real purpose and benefits of a Definite Major Purpose, for once that purpose has been fixed in the consciousness, by one's thought habits, it will be taken over by Cosmic Habitforce and carried out to its logical conclusion, *by whatever practical means that may be available.*

Cosmic Habitforce does not suggest to an individual what he shall desire, or whether his thought habits shall be positive or negative, but it does act upon all his thought habits by crystalizing them into varying degrees of permanency and translating them into their physical equivalent, through inspired motivation to action.

It not only fixes the thought-habits of individuals, but it fixes also the thought-habits of groups and masses of people, according to the pattern established by the preponderance of their individual dominating thoughts. For example, the whole world began, soon after the end of World War I, to speak of "the next war," until that war was crystalized into action.

In a similar manner epidemics of disease are thought and talked into existence. When the Department of Health of a city begins posting large red-lettered signs, warning people to be on the lookout for the measles, or diphtheria, or some other disease, an epidemic of that particular disease is the very next manifestation of this expression of thought. It is almost sure to follow.

Here too the same rule applies to the individual who thinks and talks of disease. At first he is regarded as a hypochondriac—one who suffers with imaginary illness—but when the habit is maintained the disease thus manifested, or one very closely akin to it, generally makes its appearance. Cosmic Habitforce attends to this! For it is true that any thought held in the mind through repetition begins immediately to translate itself into its physical equivalent, by every practical means that may be available.

It is a sad commentary on the intelligence of people to observe that more than three-fourths of the people who have the full benefits of a great country such as ours, should go all the way through life in poverty and want, but the reason for this is not difficult to understand if one recognizes the working principle of Cosmic Habitforce.

Poverty is the direct result of a "poverty consciousness" which results from thinking in terms of poverty, fearing poverty, and talking of poverty.

It would be difficult to imagine Henry Ford thinking in terms of that which he does not want, or in terms of poverty! He lives on the side of the street opposite the things he does not want, but he never crosses over, and that is why he is carried onward to success by the positive side of the great River of Life!

His education and general ability have nothing to do with his success, for he has less of each than have millions of men who remain poverty-stricken all their lives, some of them men with a string of college degrees after their names.

The world has thought and spoken of cancer as an incurable disease for so long that Cosmic Habitforce has transmuted this *thought-pattern* into a major fixation which is difficult to break. But the time is at hand when groups of the better informed people are beginning to set up thought patterns which may serve as an antidote for this disease.

When this kind of "mass thinking" becomes sufficiently extensive cancer will go the way of all human ills which have been starved to death because people stopped talking and thinking of them. And let us all join in the hope that the time will come, and soon, when people will stop "enjoying poor health," and will regard the admission of sickness as a disgrace rather than something to serve as the major topic of polite conversation wherever friends and acquaintances meet.

Sound health is the result of a carefully cultivated "health consciousness" that has been created by constant thoughts of sound health and is made permanent by the law of Cosmic Habitforce. If you desire sound health, give orders to your subconscious mind to create it and Cosmic Habitforce will carry out the order.

If you desire opulence, give orders to your subconscious mind to produce opulence, thus developing a "prosperity consciousness," and see how quickly your economic condition will improve.

First comes the "consciousness" of that which you desire; then follows the physical or mental manifestation of your desires. The "consciousness" is your responsibility. It is something you must create by your daily thoughts, or by meditation if you prefer to make known your desires in that manner. In this manner one may ally himself with no less a power than that of the Creator of all things.

"I have come to the conclusion," said a great philosopher, "that the acceptance of poverty, or the acceptance of ill health, is an open confession of the lack of Faith."

We do a lot of proclaiming of Faith, but our actions belie our words. Faith is a state of mind that may become permanent only by actions. Belief alone is not sufficient, for as the great Philosopher has said, "Faith without works is dead."

The law of Cosmic Habitforce is Nature's own creation. It is the one universal principle through which order and system and harmony are carried out in the entire operation of the universe, from the largest star that hangs in the heavens to the smallest atoms of matter.

It is a power that is equally available to the weak and the strong, the rich and the poor, the sick and the well. It provides the solution to all human problems.

The major purpose of the seventeen principles of this philosophy is that of aiding the individual to adapt himself to the power of Cosmic Habitforce by self-discipline in connection with the formation of his habits of thought.

Let us turn now to a brief review of these principles, so that we may understand their relationship to Cosmic Habit' force. Let us observe how these principles are so related that they blend together and form the Master Key which unlocks the doors to the solution of all problems.

The analysis begins with the first principle of the philosophy:

(a) THE HABIT OF GOING THE EXTRA MILE.

This principle is given first position because it aids in conditioning the mind for the rendering of useful service. And this conditioning prepares the way for the second principle—

(b) DEFINITENESS OF PURPOSE

With the aid of this principle one may give organized direction to the principle of Going The Extra Mile, and make sure that it leads in the direction of his major purpose and becomes cumulative in its effects. These two principles alone will take anyone very far up the ladder of achievement, but those who are aiming for the higher goals of life will need much help on the way, and this help is available through the application of the third principle—

(c) THE MASTER MIND.

Through the application of this principle one begins to experience a new and a greater sense of power which is not available to the individual mind, as it bridges one's personal deficiencies and provides him, when necessary, with any portion of *the combined knowledge of mankind* which has been accumulated down through the ages. But this sense of power will not be complete until one acquires the art of receiving guidance through the fourth principle—

(d) APPLIED FAITH.

Here the individual begins to tune in on the powers of Infinite Intelligence, which is a benefit that is available only to the person who has conditioned his mind to receive it. Here the individual begins to take full possession of his own mind by mastering all fears, worries and doubts, by recognizing his oneness with the source of all power.

These four principles have been rightly called the "Big Four" because they are capable of providing more power than the average man needs to carry him to great heights of personal achievement. But they are adequate only for the very few who have other needed qualities of success, such as those which are provided by the fifth principle.

(e) PLEASING PERSONALITY.

A pleasing personality enables a man to sell himself and his ideas to other men. Hence it is an essential for all who desire to become the guiding influence in a Master Mind alliance. But observe carefully how definitely the four preceding principles tend to give one a pleasing personality. These five principles are capable of providing one with stupendous personal power, but not enough power to insure him against defeat, for defeat is a circumstance that every man meets many times throughout his lifetime; hence the necessity of understanding and applying the sixth principle—

(f) HABIT OF LEARNING FROM DEFEAT.
Notice that this principle begins with the word "habit," which means that it must be accepted and applied as a matter of habit, under all the circumstances of defeat. In this principle may be found hope sufficient to inspire a man to make a fresh start when his plans go astray, as go astray they must at one time or another.

Observe how greatly the source of personal power has increased through the application of these six principles. The individual has found out where he is going in life; he has acquired the friendly cooperation of all whose services are needed to help him reach his goal; he has made himself pleasing, thereby insuring for himself the continued cooperation of others; be has acquired the art of drawing upon the source of Infinite Intelligence and of expressing that power through applied faith; and he has learned to make stepping stones of the stumbling blocks of personal defeat. Despite all of these advantages, however, the man whose Definite Major Purpose leads in the direction of the higher brackets of personal achievement will come many times to the point in his career when he will need the benefits of the seventh principle—

(g) CREATIVE VISION.
This principle enables one to look into the future and to judge it by a comparison with the past, and to build new and better

plans for attaining his hopes and aims through the wort shop of his imagination. And here, for the first time perhaps, a man may discover his sixth sense and begin to draw upon it for the knowledge which is not available through the organized sources of human experience and accumulated knowledge. But, in order to make sure that he puts this benefit to practical use he must embrace and apply the eighth principle—

(h) PERSONAL INITIATIVE.

This is the principle that starts action and keeps it moving toward definite ends. It insures one against the destructive habits of procrastination, indifference and laziness. An approximation of the importance of this principle may be had by recognizing that it is the "habit-producer" in connection with the seven preceding principles, for it is obvious that the application of no principle may become a *habit* except by the application of personal initiative. The importance of this principle may be further evaluated by recognition of the fact that it is the sole means by which a man may exercise full and complete control over the only thing that the Creator has given him to control, *the power of his own thoughts*.

Thoughts do not organize and direct themselves. They need guidance, inspiration and aid which can be given only by one's personal initiative.

But personal initiative is sometimes misdirected. Therefore it needs the supplemental guidance that is available through the ninth principle—

(i) ACCURATE THINKING.

Accurate thinking not only insures one against the misdirection of personal initiative, but it also insures one against errors of judgment, guess-work and premature decisions. It also protects one against the influence of his own *undependable emotions* by modifying them through the power of reason commonly known as the "head."

Here the individual who has mastered these nine principles will find himself in possession of tremendous power, but personal power may be, and often it is, a dangerous power if it is not controlled and directed through the application of the tenth principle—

(j) SELF-DISCIPLINE.

Self-discipline cannot be had for the mere asking, nor can it be acquired quickly. It is the product of carefully established and carefully maintained habits which in many instances can be acquired only by many years of painstaking effort. So we have come to the point at which the power of the will must be brought into action, *for self-discipline is solely a product of the mill*.

Numberless men have risen to great power by the application of the preceding nine principles, only to meet with disaster, or they carry others to defeat by their lack of self-discipline in the use of their power.

This principle, when mastered and applied, gives one complete control over his greatest enemy, himself!

Self-discipline must begin with the application of the eleventh principle—

(k) CONCENTRATION OF ENDEAVOR.

The power of concentration is also a product of the will. It is so closely related to self-discipline that the two have been called the "twin-brothers" of this philosophy. Concentration saves one from the dissipation of his energies, and aids him in keeping his mind focused upon the object of his Definite Major Purpose until it has been taken over by the sub-conscious section of the mind and there made ready for translation into its physical equivalent, through the law of Cosmic Habitforce. It is the camera's eye of the imagination through which the detailed outline of one's aims and purposes are recorded in the sub-conscious section of the mind; hence it is indispensable.

Now look again, and see how greatly one's personal power has grown by the application of these eleven principles. But even these are not sufficient for every circumstance of life, for there are times when one must have the friendly co-operation of many people, such as customers in business, or clients in a profession, or votes in an election to public office, all of which may be had through the application of the twelfth principle—

(l) COOPERATION.

Co-operation differs from the Master Mind principle in that it is a human relationship that is needed, and may be had, without a definite alliance with others, based upon a complete fusion of the minds for the attainment of a definite purpose.

Without the co-operation of others one cannot attain success in the higher brackets of personal achievement, for co-operation is the means of major value by which one may extend the space he occupies in the minds of others, which is sometimes known as "good-will." Friendly co-operation brings the merchant's customers back as repeat purchasers of his wares, and insures a continuance of patronage from the clients of the professional man. Hence it is a principle that belongs definitely in the philosophy of successful men, regardless of the occupation they may follow.

Co-operation is attained more freely and willingly by the application of the thirteenth principle—

(m) ENTHUSIASM.

Enthusiasm is a contagious state of mind which not only aids one in gaining the co-operation of others, but more important than this, it inspires the individual to draw upon and use the power of his own imagination. It inspires action also in the expression of personal initiative, and leads to the habit of concentration of endeavor. Moreover, it is one of the qualities of major importance of a pleasing personality, and it makes easy the application of the principle of Going The Extra Mile. In addition to all these benefits, enthusiasm gives force and conviction to the spoken word.

Enthusiasm is the product of *motive*, but it is difficult of ranee without the aid of the fourteenth principle—

(n) THE HABIT OF HEALTH.

Sound physical health provides a suitable housing place for aeration of the mind; hence it is an essential for enduring success, assuming that the word "success" shall embrace all of the requirements for happiness.

Here again the word "habit" comes into prominence, for sound health begins with a "health consciousness" that can be developed only by the right habits of living, sustained through self-discipline.

Sound health provides the basis for enthusiasm, and enthusiasm encourages sound health; so the two are like the hen and the egg; no one can determine which came into existence first, but everyone knows that both are essential for the production of either. Health and enthusiasm are like that. Both are essential for human progress and happiness.

Now take inventory again and count up the gains in power which the individual has attained by the application of these fourteen principles. It has reached proportions so stupendous that it staggers the imagination. Yet it is not sufficient to insure one against failure; therefore we shall have to add the fifteenth principle—

(o) BUDGETING TIME AND MONEY.

Oh! what a headache one gets at the mention of saving of time and the conservation of money. Nearly everyone wishes to spend both time and money freely, but budget and conserve them, never! However, independence and freedom of body and mind, the two great desires of all mankind, cannot become enduring realities without the self-discipline of a strict budgeting system. Hence this principle is of necessity an important essential of the philosophy of individual achievement.

Now we are reaching the ultimate in the attainment of personal power. We have learned the sources of power and how we may tap them and apply them at will to any desired end; and that power is so great that nothing can resist it save only the fact that the individual may unwisely apply it to his own destruction and the destruction of others. Hence, to guide one in the right use of power it is necessary to add the sixteenth principle—

(p) THE GOLDEN RULE *APPLIED*.

Observe the emphasis on the word "applied." Belief in the soundness of the Golden Rule is not enough. To be of enduring benefit, and in order that it may serve as a safe guide in the use of personal power, it must be applied as a matter of habit, in all human relationships.

Quite an order, this! But the benefits which are available through the application of this profound rule of human relationship are worthy of the efforts necessary to develop it into a habit. The penalties for failure to live by this rule are too numerous for description in detail.

Now we have attained the ultimate in personal power, and we have provided ourselves with the necessary insurance against its misuse. What we need from here on out is the means by which this power may be made permanent during our entire lifetime. We shall climax this philosophy, therefore, with the only known principle by which we may attain this desired end—the seventeenth and last principle of this philosophy—

(q) COSMIC HABITFORCE.

Cosmic Habitforce is the principle by which all habits are fixed and made permanent in varying degrees. As stated, it is the comptrolling principle of this entire philosophy, into which the preceding sixteen principles blend and become a part. And it is the comptrolling principle of all natural laws of the universe. It is the principle that gives the *fixation of habit* in the preceding principles of this philosophy. Thus it is the controlling factor in conditioning the individual mind for the development and the expression of the "prosperity consciousness" which is so essential in the attainment of personal success.

Mere understanding of the sixteen preceding principles will not lead anyone to the attainment of personal power. The principles must be understood and applied as a matter of strict habit, and habit is the sole work of the law of Cosmic Habitforce.

Cosmic Habitforce is synonymous with the great River of Life to which frequent references have been made previously, for it consists of a negative and a positive potentiality, as do all forms of energy.

The negative application is called "hypnotic rhythm" because it has a hypnotic effect on everything that it contacts. We may see its effects, in one way or another, on every human being.

It is the sole means by which the "poverty consciousness" becomes fixed as a habit!

It is the builder of all established *habits* of fear, and envy, and greed, and revenge, and of desire for something for nothing.

It fixes the *habits* of hopelessness and indifference.

And it is the builder of the *habit* of hypochondria, through which millions of people suffer all through their lives with imaginary illness.

It is also the builder of the "failure consciousness" which undermines the self-confidence of millions of people.

In brief, it fixes all *negative habits*, regardless of their nature or effects. Thus it is the "failure" side of the great River of Life.

The "success" side of the River—the positive side—fixes all constructive habits, such as the habit of Definiteness of Purpose, the habit of Going The Extra Mile, the habit of applying the Golden Rule in human relationships, and all the other habits which one must develop and apply in order to get the benefits of the sixteen preceding principles of this philosophy.

Now let us examine this word "habit"!

Webster's dictionary gives the word many definitions, among them: "Habit implies a settled disposition or tendency *due to repetition*; custom suggests the fact of repetition rather than the tendency to repeat; usage (applying only to a considerable body of people) adds the implication of long acceptance or standing; both custom and usage often suggest authority; as, we do many things mechanically from force of habit."

Webster's definition runs on into considerable additional detail, but no part of it comes within sight of describing the law that fixes all habits; this omission being due no doubt to the fact that the law of Cosmic Habitforce had not been revealed to the editors of this dictionary. But we observe one significant and important word in the Webster definition—the word "repetition." It is important because it describes the means by which any habit is begun.

The habit of Definiteness of Purpose, for example, becomes a habit only by repetition of the thought of that purpose, by bringing the thought into the mind repeatedly; by *repeatedly* submitting the thought to the imagination with a burning desire for its fulfillment, until the imagination creates a practical plan for attaining this desire; by applying the *habit* of Faith in connection with the desire, and doing it so intensely and repeatedly that one may see himself already in possession of the object of his desires, *even before he begins to attain it.*

The building of voluntary positive habits calls for the application of self-discipline, persistence, willpower and Faith, all of which are available to the person who has assimilated the sixteen preceding principles of this philosophy.

Voluntary habit-building is self-discipline in its highest and noblest form of application!

And all voluntary positive habits are the products of willpower directed toward the attainment of definite ends. *They originate with the individual,* not with Cosmic Habitforce. And they must be grounded in the mind through repetition of thoughts and deeds until they are taken over by Cosmic Habitforce and are given fixation, after which they operate automatically.

The word *habit is* an important word in connection with this philosophy of individual achievement, for it represents the real cause of every man's economic, social, professional, occupational and spiritual condition in life. We are where we are and what we are because of our fixed habits. And we may be where we wish to be and what we wish to be only by the development and the maintenance of our *voluntary habits*.

Thus we see that this entire philosophy leads inevitably to an understanding and application of the law of Cosmic Habitforce—the power of fixation of all habits!

The major purpose of each of the sixteen preceding principles of this philosophy is that of aiding the individual in the development of a particular, specialized form of habit that is necessary as a means of enabling him to *take full possession of his own mind!* This too must become a habit!

Mind-power is always actively engaged on one side of the River of Life or the other. The purpose of this philosophy is to enable one to develop and maintain habits of thought and of deed which keep his mind concentrated upon the "success" side of the River. This is the sole burden of the philosophy.

Mastery and assimilation of the philosophy, like every other desirable thing, has a definite price which must be paid before its benefits may be enjoyed. That price, among other things, is eternal vigilance, determination, persistence and the will to make Life pay off on one's own terms instead of accepting substitutes of poverty and misery and disillusionment.

There are two ways of relating one's self to Life.

One is that of playing horse while Life rides. The other is that of becoming the rider while Life plays horse. The choice as to whether one becomes the horse or the rider is the privilege of every person, but this much is certain: if one does not choose to become the rider of Life, he is sure to be forced to become the horse. Life either rides or is ridden. It never stands still.

The Relationship of the "Ego" and Cosmic Habitforce

As a student of this philosophy you are interested in the method by which one may transmute the power of thought into its physical equivalent. And you are interested in learning how to relate yourself to others in a spirit of harmony.

Unfortunately our public schools have been silent on both of these important needs. "Our educational system," said Dr. Henry C. Link, "has concentrated on mental development and has failed to give any understanding of the way emotional and personality habits are acquired or corrected."

His indictment is not without a sound foundation. The public school system has failed in the obligation of which Dr. Link complains, because the law of Cosmic Habitforce was but recently revealed, and even now it has not been recognized by the great mass of educators.

Everyone knows that practically everything we do, from the time we begin to walk, is the result of habit. Walking and talking are habits. Our manner of eating and drinking is a habit. Our sex activities are the results of habit. Our relationships with others, whether they are positive or negative, are the results of habits, but few people understand why or how we form habits.

Habits are inseparably related to the human ego. Therefore, let us turn to the analysis of this greatly misunderstood subject of the ego. But first let us recognize that the ego is the medium through which faith and all other states of mind operate.

Throughout this philosophy great emphasis has been placed upon the distinction between passive faith and active faith. The ego is the medium of expression of all action. Therefore we must know something of its nature and possibilities in order that we may make the best use of it. We must learn how to stimulate the ego to action and how to control and guide it to the attainment of definite ends.

Above all, we must disabuse our minds of the popular error of believing the ego to be only a medium for expression of vanity. The word "ego" is of Latin origin, and it means "I." But it also connotes a driving force which may be organized and made to serve as the medium for translating desire into faith, through action.

The Misunderstood Power of the Ego

The word ego has reference to all the factors of one's personality!

Therefore it is obvious that the ego is subject to development, guidance and control through voluntary habits—habits which we deliberately and with purpose aforethought develop.

A great philosopher who devoted his entire life to the study of the human body and the mind, provided us with a practical foundation for the study of the ego when he stated:

"Your body, whether living or dead, is a collection of millions of little energies that can never die.

"These energies are separate and individual; at times they act in some degree of harmony.

"The human body is a drifting mechanism of life, capable but not accustomed to control the forces within, except as habit, will, cultivation or special excitement (through the emotion) may marshal these forces to the accomplishment of some important end.

"We are satisfied from many experiments that this power of marshalling and using these energies can be, in every person, cultivated to a high degree.

"The air, sunlight, food and water you take, are agents of a force which comes from the sky and earth. You idly float upon the tide of circumstances to make up your day's life, and the opportunities of being something better than you are drift beyond your reach and pass away.

"Humanity is hemmed in by so many influences that, from time immemorial, no real effort has been made to gain control of the impulses that run loose in the world. It has been, and still is, easier to let things go as they will rather than exert the will to direct them.

"But the dividing line between success and failure is found at the stage where aimless drifting ceases. (Where Definiteness of Purpose begins.)

"We are all creatures of emotions, passions, circumstances and accident. What the mind will be, what the heart will be, what the body will be, are problems which are shaped to the drift of life, even when special attention is given to any of them.

"If you will sit down and think for a while, *you will be surprised to know how much of your life has been mere drift.*"

"Look at any created life, and see its efforts to express itself. The tree sends its branches toward the sunlight, struggles through its leaves to inhale air; and even underground sends forth its roots in search of water and the minerals it needs for food. This you call inanimate life; but it represents a force that comes from some source and operates for some purpose.

"There is no place on the globe where energy is not found.

"The air is so loaded with it that in the cold north the sky shines in boreal rays; and wherever the frigid temperature yields to the warmth, the electric conditions may alarm man. Water is but a liquid union of gases, and is charged with electrical, mechanical and chemical energies, any one of which is capable of doing great service and great damage to man.

"Even ice, in its coldest phase, has energy, for it is not subdued, nor even still; its force has broken mountain rocks into fragments. This energy about us we are drinking in water, eating in food and breathing in air. Not a chemical molecule is free from it; not an atom can exist without it. We are a combination of individual energies."

Man consists of two forces, one tangible, in the form of his physical body, with its myriad individual cells numbering billions, each of which is endowed with intelligence and energy; and the other intangible, in the form of an ego—the organized dictator of the body which may control man's thoughts and deeds.

Science teaches us the tangible portion of a man weighing one hundred and sixty pounds is composed of about seventeen chemical elements, all of which are known. They are:

- 95 pounds of oxygen.
- 38 pounds of carbon.
- 15 pounds of hydrogen.
- 4 pounds of nitrogen.
- 4½ pounds of calcium.
- 6 ounces of chlorine.
- 4 ounces of sulphur.
- ¾ ounces of potassium.
- 3 ounces of sodium.
- ¼ ounce of iron.
- 2½ ounces of fluorin.
- 2 ounces of magnesium.
- 1½ ounces of silicon.
- Small traces of arsenic, iodine and aluminum.

These tangible parts of man are worth commercially approximately eighty cents, and may be purchased in any modem chemical plant.

Add to these chemical elements a well developed and properly organized and controlled ego, and they may be worth any price the owner sets upon them. The ego is a power which cannot be purchased at any price, but it can be developed and shaped to fit any desired pattern. The development takes place through organized habits which are made permanent by the law of Cosmic Habitforce, which carries out the thought patterns one develops through controlled thought.

An Edison develops and guides his ego in the field of creative investigation, and the world finds a genius whose worth cannot be estimated in dollars alone.

A Henry Ford guides his ego in the field of automotive transportation and gives it such a stupendous value that it changes the trend of civilization by removing frontiers and converting mountain trails into public highways.

A Marconi magnetizes his ego with a keen desire to harness the ether and lives to see his wireless communication system evolve into the discovery of radio through which the world becomes akin, through instantaneous exchange of thought.

These men, and all others who have contributed to the march of progress, have given the world a demonstration of the power of a well-developed and carefully controlled ego.

One of the major differences between men who make valuable contributions to mankind and those who merely take up space in the world, is mainly a difference in egos, because the ego is the driving force behind all forms of human action.

Liberty and freedom of body and mind—the two major desires of all people—are available in exact proportion to the development and use one makes of the ego. Every person who has properly related himself to his own ego has both liberty and freedom in whatever proportions he desires.

A man's ego determines the manner in which he relates himself to all other people. More important than this, it determines the policy under which a man relates his own body and mind, wherein is patterned every hope, aim and purpose by which he fixes his destiny in life.

A man's ego is his greatest asset or his greatest liability, according to the way he relates himself to it. The ego is the sum total of one's thought habits which have been fastened upon him through the automatic operation of the law of Cosmic Habitforce.

Every highly successful person possesses a well-developed and highly disciplined ego, but there is a third factor associated with the ego which determines its potency for good or evil—the self-control necessary to enable one to transmute its power into any desired purpose.

The starting point of all individual achievements is some plan by which one's ego can be inspired with a "success consciousness." The person who succeeds must do so by properly developing his own ego, impressing it with the object of his desires, and removing from it all forms of limitation, fear and doubt which lead to the dissipation of the power of the ego.

Auto-suggestion (or self-hypnosis) is the medium by which one may attune his ego to any desired rate of vibration and charge it with the attainment of any desired purpose.

Unless you catch the full significance of the principle of auto-suggestion you will miss the most important part of this analysis, because the power of the ego is fixed entirely by the application of self-suggestion.

When this self-suggestion attains the status of faith the ego becomes limitless in its power.

The ego is kept alive and active, and it is given power by constant feeding. Like the physical body, the ego cannot and will not subsist without food.

It must be fed with Definiteness of Purpose.

It must be fed with Personal Initiative.

It must be fed with continuous action, through well organized plans.

It must be supported with Enthusiasm.

It must be fed by Controlled Attention, directed to a definite end.

It must be controlled and directed through Self-discipline.

And it must be supported with Accurate Thought.

No man can become the master of anything or anyone until he becomes the master of his own ego.

No man can express himself in terms of opulence while most of his thought-power is given over to the maintenance of a "poverty consciousness." Nevertheless, one should not lose sight of the fact that many men of great wealth began in poverty—a fact which suggests that this and all other fears can be conquered and removed from interference with the ego.

In the one word, ego, may be found the composite effects of all the principles of individual achievement described in this philosophy, co-ordinated into one single unit of power which may be directed to any desired end by any individual who is the complete master of his ego.

We are preparing you to accept the fact that the most important power which is available to you—the one power which will determine whether you succeed or fail in your life's ambition—is that which is represented by your own ego.

We are also preparing you to brush aside that time-worn belief which associates the ego with self-love, vanity and vulgarity, and to recognize the truth that the ego is all there is of a man outside of the eighty cents' worth of chemicals, of which his physical body is composed.

Sex is the great creative force of man. It is definitely associated with and is an important part of one's ego. Both sex and the ego got their bad reputations from the fact that both are subject to destructive as well as constructive application, and both have been abused by the ignorant, from the beginning of the history of mankind.

The egoist who makes himself offensive through the expression of his ego is one who has not discovered how to relate himself to his ego in a manner which gives it constructive use.

Constructive application of the ego is made through the expressions of one's hopes, desires, aims, ambitions and plans, and not by boastfulness or self-love. The motto of the person who has his ego under control is, "Deeds, not words."

The desire to be great, to be recognized and to have personal power, is a healthy desire; but an open expression of one's belief in his own greatness is an indication that he has not taken possession of his ego, that he has allowed it to take possession of him; and you may be sure that his proclamations of greatness are but a cloak with which to shield some fear or inferiority complex.

The Relationship Between the Ego and Mental Attitude.

Understand the real nature of your ego and you will understand the real significance of the Master Mind principle.

Moreover, you will recognize that to be of the greatest service to you, the members of your Master Mind alliance must be in complete sympathy with your hopes, aims and purposes; that they must not be in competition with you in any manner whatsoever. They must be willing to subordinate their own desires and personal ties entirely for the attainment of your major purpose in life.

They must have confidence in you and your integrity, and they must respect you. They must be willing to pander to your virtues and make allowances for your faults. They must be willing to permit you to be yourself and live your own life in your own way at all times. Lastly, they must receive from you some form of benefit which will make you as beneficial to them as they are to you.

Failure to observe the last mentioned requirement will bring an end to the power of your Master Mind alliance.

Men relate themselves to one another in whatever capacities they may be associated because of a motive or motives. There can be no permanent human relationship based upon an indefinite or vague motive, or upon no motive at all. Failure to recognize this truth has cost many men the difference between penury and opulence.

The power which takes over the ego and clothes it with the material counterparts of the thoughts which give it shape, is the law of Cosmic Habitforce. This law does not give quality or quantity to the ego; it merely takes what it finds and translates it into its physical equivalent.

The men of great achievement are, and they have always been, those who deliberately feed, shape and control their own egos, leaving no part of the task to luck or chance, or to the varying vicissitudes of life.

Every person may control the shaping of his own ego, but from that point on he has no more to do with what happens than does the farmer have anything to do with what happens to the seed he sows in the soil of the earth. The inexorable law of Cosmic Habitforce causes every living thing to perpetuate itself after its kind, and it translates the picture which a man paints of his ego into its physical equivalent, as definitely as it develops an acorn into an oak tree, and no outside aid whatsoever is required, except time.

From these statements it is obvious that we are not only advocating the deliberate development and control of the ego, but also we are definitely warning that no man can hope to succeed in any calling without such control over his ego.

So that there may be no misunderstanding as to what is meant by the term "a properly developed ego" we shall describe briefly the factors which enter into its development, viz:

First, one must ally himself with one or more persons who will co-ordinate their minds with his in a spirit of perfect harmony for the attainment of a definite purpose, and that alliance must be continuous and active.

Moreover, the alliance must consist of people whose spiritual and mental qualities, education, sex and age are suited for aiding in the attainment of the purpose of the alliance. For example, Andrew Carnegie's Master Mind alliance was made up of more than twenty men, each of whom brought to the alliance some quality of mind, experience, education or knowledge which was directly related to the object of the alliance and not available through any of the other members of the alliance.

Second, having placed himself under the influence of the proper associates, one must adopt some definite plan by which to attain the object of the alliance and proceed to put that plan into action. The plan may be a composite plan created by the joint efforts of all the members of the Master Mind group.

If one plan proves to be unsound or inadequate, it must be supplemented or supplanted by others, until a plan is found which will work. But there must be no change in the purpose of the alliance.

Third, one must remove himself from the range of influence of every person and every circumstance which has even a slight tendency to cause him to feel inferior or incapable of attaining the object of his purpose. Positive egos do not grow in negative environments. On this point there can be no excuse for a compromise, and failure to observe it will prove fatal to the chances of success.

The line must be so clearly drawn between a man and those who exercise any form of negative influence over him that he closes the door tightly against every such person, no matter what previous ties of friendship or obligation or blood relationship may have existed between them.

Fourth, one must close the door tightly against every thought of any past experience or circumstance which tends to make him feel inferior or unhappy. Strong, vital egos cannot be developed by dwelling on thoughts of past unpleasant experiences. Vital egos thrive on the hopes and desires of the yet unattained objectives.

Thoughts are the building-blocks from which the human ego is constructed. Cosmic Habitforce is the cement which binds these blocks together in permanency, through fixed habits. When the job is finished it represents, right down to the smallest detail, the nature of the thoughts which went into the building.

It was Henry Ford's recognition of this truth which prompted him to remove from his business family every person who was out of step with his business policy.

It was Andrew Carnegie's complete understanding of this truth which caused him to insist upon complete harmony between himself and the members of his Master Mind group.

Fifth, one must surround himself with every possible physical means of impressing his mind with the nature and the purpose of the ego he is developing. For example, the author should set up his workshop in a room decorated with pictures and the works of authors in his field whom he most admires. He should fill his book shelves with books related to his own work. He should surround himself with every possible means of conveying to his ego the exact picture of himself which he expects to express, because that picture is the pattern which the law of Cosmic Habitforce will pick up; the picture which it translates into its physical equivalent.

Sixth, the properly developed ego is at all times under the control of the individual. There must be no over-inflation of the ego in the direction of "egomania" by which some men destroy themselves.

Egomania reveals itself by a mad desire to control others by force. Striking examples of such men are Adolph Hitler,

Benito Mussolini and William Hohenzollern, the former kaiser of Germany.

In the development of the ego, one's motto might well be, "Not too much, not too little, of anything." When men begin to thirst for control over others, or begin to accumulate large sums of money which they cannot or do not use constructively, they are treading upon dangerous grounds. Power of this nature grows of its own accord and soon gets out of control.

Nature has provided man with a safety-valve through which she deflates the ego and relieves the pressure of its influence when an individual goes beyond certain limits in the development of the ego. Emerson called it the law of Compensation, but whatever it is, it operates with inexorable definiteness.

Napoleon Bonaparte began to die, because of his crushed ego, on the day he landed on St. Helena Island.

People who quit work and retire from all forms of activity, after having led active lives, generally atrophy and die soon thereafter. If they live they are usually miserable and unhappy. A healthy ego is one which is always in use and under complete control.

Seventh, the ego is constantly undergoing changes, for better or for worse, because of the nature of one's thought habits. The two factors which force these changes upon one are Time and the law of Cosmic Habitforce.

We are here concerned with the desire to bring to your attention the importance of Time as a significant factor in the operation of Cosmic Habitforce. Just as seed which are planted in the soil of the earth require definite periods of

Time for their germination, development and growth, so do ideas, impulses of thought and desires which are planted in the mind require definite periods of Time during which the law of Cosmic Habitforce gives them life and action.

There is no adequate means of describing or predetermining the exact period of Time which is required for the transformation of a desire into its physical equivalent. The nature of the desire, the circumstances which are related to it, and the intensity of the desire, are all determining factors in connection with the Time required for transformation from the thought stage to the physical stage.

The state of mind known as faith is so favorable for the quick change of desire into its physical equivalent that it has been known to make the change almost instantaneously.

Man matures physically within about twenty years, but mentally—which means the ego—he requires from thirty-five to sixty years for maturity. This fact explains why men seldom begin to accumulate material riches in great abundance, or to attain outstanding records of achievement in other directions, until they are about fifty years of age.

The ego which can inspire a man to acquire and retain great material wealth is of necessity one which has undergone self-discipline, through which he acquires self-confidence, definiteness of purpose, personal initiative, imagination, accuracy of judgment and other qualities, without which no ego has the power to procure and hold wealth in abundance.

These qualities come through the proper *use* of Time. Observe that we did not say they come through the lapse of Time. Through the operation of Cosmic Habitforce every individual's thought habits, whether they are negative or positive, whether of opulence or of poverty, are woven into the pattern of his ego, and there they are given permanent form which determines the nature and the extent of his spiritual and physical status.

About the beginning of the 1929 economic depression the owner of a small beauty salon turned over a back room in her place of business to an old man who needed a place to sleep. The man had no money, but he did have considerable knowledge of the methods of compounding cosmetics.

The owner of the salon gave him a place to sleep and provided him with an opportunity to pay for his room by compounding the cosmetics she used in her business.

Soon the two entered into a Master Mind alliance which was destined to bring each of them economic independence. First, they entered into a business partnership, with the object of compounding cosmetics to be sold from house to house; the woman providing the money for the raw materials, the man doing the work.

After a few years the Master Mind arrangement between the two had proved so profitable that they decided to make it permanent by marriage, although there was a difference of more than twenty-five years in their ages.

The man had been in the cosmetic business for the better portion of his adult life, but he had never achieved success. The young woman had barely made a living from her beauty salon. The happy combination of the two brought them into possession of a power which neither had known prior to their alliance, and they began to succeed financially.

At the beginning of the depression they were compounding cosmetics in one small room, and selling their products personally from door to door. By the end of the depression, some eight years later, they were compounding their cosmetics in a large factory which they had bought and paid for, and had more than a hundred employees working steadily, and more than four thousand agents selling their products throughout the nation.

During this period they accumulated a fortune of over two million dollars, despite the fact that they were operating during depression years when such luxuries as cosmetics were naturally hard to sell.

They have placed themselves beyond the need for money for the remainder of their lives. Moreover, they have gained financial freedom on precisely the same knowledge and the same opportunities they possessed prior to their Master Mind alliance, when both were poverty-stricken.

We wish the names of these two interesting people could be revealed, but the circumstances of their alliance and the nature of the analysis we shall now present makes this impractical. Nevertheless we are free to describe what we conceive to be the source of their astounding achievement, viewing every circumstance of their relationship entirely from the viewpoint of an unbiased analyst who is seeking only to present a true picture of the facts.

The motive which brought these two people together in a Master Mind alliance was definitely economic in nature. The woman had previously been married to a man who failed to earn a living for her and who deserted her when her child was an infant. The man also had been previously married.

There was not the slightest indication of the emotion of love as a motive for their marriage. The motive was entirely a mutual desire for economic freedom.

The business and the elaborate home in which the couple live are entirely dominated by the old man, who sincerely believes that he is responsible for both.

Their house is expensively furnished, but no one—not even invited guests—is permitted to take a turn at the piano, or to sit in one of the chairs in the living room, without special invitation from the "lord and master" of the household.

The main dining room is equipped with ornate furniture, including a long dining table which is suitable for use on "state" occasions, but the family is never permitted to use it on other occasions. They dine in the breakfast room, and nothing may be served at the table at any time except food of the "master's" choice.

A gardener is employed to attend the gardens, but no one is permitted to cut a flower without special invitation from the head of the house.

Such conversations as are carried on by the family are conducted entirely by the head of the house, and no one may intervene, not even to ask a question or to offer a remark, unless he invites it. His wife never speaks unless she is definitely requested to do so, and then her speech is very brief and carefully weighed so as not to irritate her "master."

Their business is incorporated and the man is the president of the company. He has an elaborate office which is furnished with a large hand-carved desk and overstuffed chairs.

On the wall, directly in front of his desk, is an enormous oil painting of himself at which he gazes, sometimes for an hour at a time, with obvious approval.

When he speaks of the business, and particularly of the unusual success it has enjoyed during the country's worst business depression, the man takes full credit for all that has been accomplished, and he never mentions his wife's name in connection with the business.

While the wife goes to business daily, she has no office and no desk. She is apt to be found strolling around among the workers, or assisting one of the girls in wrapping packages as nonchalantly as if she were an ordinary paid employee.

The man's name is on every package of merchandise which leaves the factory. It is printed in large letters on every delivery truck they operate, and it appears in large type on every piece of sales literature and in every advertisement they publish. The wife's name is conspicuous by its total absence.

The man believes that he built the business; that he operates it; that it could not operate without him. The truth of the matter is precisely the opposite. His ego built the business, runs it, and the business might continue to run as well or better with out his presence as with it, for the very good reason that his wife developed that ego, and she could have done the same for any other man under similar circumstances.

Patiently, wisely and with purpose aforethought, this man's wife completely submerged her own personality into that of her husband, and step by step she fed his ego the type of food which removed from it every trace of his former inferiority complex, which was born of a lifetime of deprivation and failure. She hypnotized her husband into believing himself to be a great business tycoon.

Whatever degree of ego this man may have possessed before it came under the influence of a clever woman, had died of starvation. She revived his ego, nurtured it, fed it and developed it into a power of stupendous proportions despite his eccentric nature and his lack of business ability.

In truth every business policy, every business move, and every forward step the business has taken was the result of the wife's ideas, which she so cleverly planted in her husband's mind that he failed to recognize their source. In reality she is the brains of the business, he the mere window dressing; *but the combination is unbeatable*, as evidenced by their astounding financial achievements.

The manner in which this woman completely effaced herself was not only convincing evidence of her complete self-control, but it was evidence of her wisdom, for she probably knew she could not have accomplished the same results alone, or by any other methods than those she adopted.

This woman has very little formal education, and we have no idea how or where she learned enough about the operation of the human mind to inspire her to merge her entire personality with that of her husband for the purpose of developing in him the ego he now has. Perhaps the natural intuition which many women possess was responsible for her successful procedure. Whatever it was, she did a thorough job, and it served the ends she sought by bringing her economic security.

Here then is evidence that the major difference between poverty and riches is merely the difference between an ego that is dominated by an inferiority complex and one that is dominated by a feeling of superiority. This old man might have died a homeless pauper if a clever woman had not blended her mind with his in such a way as to feed his ego with thoughts of, and belief in, his ability to attain opulence.

This is a conclusion from which there is no escape. Moreover, this case is only one of many that could be cited which prove that the human ego must be fed, organized and directed to definite ends if one is to succeed in any walk of life.

The Henry Ford ego—famous because of what the public at large does not know about it—is a combination of his own ego and that of his wife. The definiteness and singleness of purpose, persistence, self-reliance and self-control—so obviously important parts of the Ford ego—can be traced largely to the influence of Mrs. Ford.

The Ford ego—quite unlike that of the cosmetician described—functions without glamor or ostentation of any kind. It functions in an obvious spirit of humility of the heart.

There are no large pictures of Henry Ford hanging on the walls of his office, but make no mistake about this: Mr. Ford's influence is felt by every person associated directly or indirectly with his vast industrial empire, and something of Henry Ford himself goes into every automobile which leaves his factories.

These are the means whereby he expresses his ego:

Through mechanical perfection; through transportation service which is dependable, at a popular price; through the satisfaction he gets from giving employment, directly and indirectly, to millions of men and women.

Mr. Ford is not above appreciating a word of praise, but he has never gone out of his way to attract it. His ego does not require constant pampering such as that which was given the cosmetician by his wife.

Mr. Ford's method of appropriating the knowledge and experience of other men is entirely different from that of Andrew Carnegie and most other business magnates. His ego is so modest and unassuming that he neither encourages favorable comment upon his work nor goes out of his way to express any form of appreciation of the compliments which are paid him.

Henry Ford has one of the truly great minds of the world.

He has a great mind because he has learned to recognize the laws of nature and to adapt himself to them in a manner beneficial to himself, but many believe that his greatness is derived in a large measure from the influence of his wife and his association with other great minds, including those of Thomas A. Edison, Luther Burbank, John Burroughs and Harvey Firestone, with whom he had a Master Mind alliance for a great number of years.

For many years these five men left their respective businesses and went away together to some quiet spot where they exchanged thoughts and fed their egos on the food which each needed and craved.

Henry Ford's personality, his business policies, and even his physical appearance began to show a decided improvement from year to year because of his association with these four men. Their influence upon him was definite, deep, profound and enduring.

Henry Ford has his ego completely under his control. By studying men of great achievement one may observe that the space they occupy in the world is in exact proportion to the extent to which they dominate their egos.

The cosmetician occupies and controls only the space bounded by his own business and his household. It does not extend beyond these bounds, and it never can. His own mental attitude has fixed these limits and Cosmic Habitforce has made the fixation permanent.

Henry Ford occupies, in one way or another, practically all of the space of the world, and he influences in many ways the entire trend of civilization. Because he is master of his ego, Henry Ford is capable of acquiring any material thing he may set his heart upon. In fact he has already done so.

The cosmetician expresses his ego in many forms of childish, petty selfishness. Consequently he has limited his influence to the mere accumulation of a few million dollars, and the domination (without their consent) of a few hundred people, including his own household and his employees.

Henry Ford expresses his ego in ever expanding and increasing terms of benefit to mankind and, without making a bid for it, finds himself an influencing factor throughout the world.

This is an astounding thought!

It provides vitally important suggestions as to the type of ego one should endeavor to develop.

Henry Ford has developed an ego which extends itself into plans which belt the entire earth. He thinks in terms of the manufacture and distribution of millions of automobiles.

He thinks in terms of tens of thousands of men and women working for him.

He thinks in terms of millions of dollars of working capital.

He thinks in terms of a business he dominates by establishing his own policies for procuring working capital by which he keeps his business out of the control of others.

He thinks in terms of economy through efficient coordination of the efforts of the thousands of men and women who work for him, by setting up pay schedules and working conditions far more favorable to his employees than they could reasonably demand.

He thinks in terms of harmonious cooperation between himself and his business associates, and puts his thoughts into action by removing from his organization any man who does not see eye to eye with him.

These are the qualities and traits of character which nourish, feed and maintain the Ford ego. There is nothing about any of these qualities which is difficult to understand. They are qualities which any man may have by simply adopting them and using them.

Turn the spotlight on the many men who began to build automobiles after Henry Ford began; study each of the men carefully and you will learn quickly why one remembers but few of those men, or the brands of automobiles they temporarily produced.

You will discover that every one of the Ford competitors who fell by the wayside did so because of self-imposed limitations or dissipation of the ego. You will also find that practically every one of these forgotten men apparently possessed as much intelligence as Henry Ford. The majority of them not only had better educations than he, but many of them had more dynamic personalities.

The major difference between Henry Ford and his competitors of the past is this: He developed an ego which extended itself far beyond his personal achievements; the others so limited their egos that they soon caught up with them, and their plans went on the rocks for want of that something which an extended, flexible ego does to lead a man forward.

Among the hundreds of Ford competitors who started to make automobiles soon after he began, there was one man who made such rapid progress that he probably would have eclipsed Ford's achievements in the industry if something had not gone wrong with his ego.

That man's outstanding qualities were: a magnetic personality, a well rounded formal education, marvelous capacity as a salesman and sales organizer, and a record of achievement in a great industrial enterprise outside of the automotive field of such magnitude as to enable him to procure all the working capital he needed.

When he was at the height of his career he was the head of his own company, manufacturing an automobile which led the field in its price class. Even at the outset of his career he had before him a future far more promising than that of Henry Ford. His name was then a national by-word in the automotive field.

His ego was dynamic, powerful and ambitious. According to the rules by which men are usually judged, he should have out-distanced Henry Ford in a few more years of operations. But something happened to him at the very height of his career which sent him into financial oblivion and quickly erased his name from the list of automobile manufacturers.

The tragedy which happened was this:

Success went to his head and he allowed his ego to become so greatly over inflated that it literally blew up and burst!

Had he acquired humility of the heart, as did Henry Ford, he would have equaled Ford's achievements, or perhaps he would have excelled them. He had everything which was required for success except the self-discipline necessary to shape his ego and control it. Therefore his ego took possession of him and led him to ruin.

The well-balanced ego is not subject to serious influence by either commendation or condemnation. The man with a well-balanced ego sets his sails in the direction of his Definite Major Purpose, moves on his personal initiative in the direction of that purpose, and never looks to the right or to the left. He accepts both defeat and victory as the natural essentials of life, but he does not allow either to modify his plans.

No one ever heard of Henry Ford spending an evening among social butterflies and cocktail glasses. No one ever read a newspaper account of Ford having boasted of his achievements. The Ford ego was not evolved from such influences, and that is why it became powerful and healthy, hale and rich, at an age when most men consider themselves ready for the scrap heap.

The Ford ego is exactly as Mr. Ford desires it to be. He is in control of it at all times; therefore he occupies more space and carries more influence in the world than any other industrialist. What an astounding fact; and all the more so when one considers the lowly beginning from which Mr. Ford started, with but little education, no working capital, no extensive influence, no credit privileges; with nothing but a Definite Major Purpose plus the qualities he acquired by the application of the seventeen principles of this philosophy. These were enough!

Henry Ford's power and fortune are not based upon knowledge alone. They are not based upon intelligence alone. They are not based upon education. They are in no way associated with luck, good fortune, or his having been born under the "right star." The Ford power is only the expression of the self-made ego which is absolutely free from all manner of fear, and which is not fettered by any self-imposed limitations.

Henry Ford has taken possession of his own mind and has learned to direct it to the attainment of his desires.

When Mr. Ford told a group of newspaper men, who accosted him on a visit to the White House, that he had come to Washington to let the President see a man who did not come to ask any favors and who did not want anything, he was neither egotistical nor facetious. He spoke a truth with stupendous connotations.

Henry Ford can get any material thing he desires, or its adequate equivalent, because he has developed and controls his own ego! There is no other mystery to his great power.

Henry Ford has long been a resident of Happy Valley.

He attained a place in that great estate by the proper organization and usage of his own ego. He developed that ego by the application of the principles of this philosophy, through which he came into possession of the great Master Key To Riches.

And you who are learning to assimilate this philosophy may reach that estate in the same manner. You have, in the seventeen principles of this philosophy, all that is required to place you in possession of the Master-Key!

You are now in possession of all the practical knowledge which has been used by successful men from the dawn of civilization to the present.

This is a complete philosophy of life—sufficient for every human need. It holds the secret to the solution of all human problems. And it has been presented in terms which the humblest person may understand.

You may not aspire to become a Henry Ford, or a Thomas A. Edison, but you can and you should aspire to make yourself useful in order that you may occupy as much space in the world as your ego desires.

Every man comes finally to resemble those who make the strongest impression upon his ego. We are all creatures of imitation, and naturally we endeavor to imitate the heroes of our choice. This is a natural and healthful trait.

Fortunate indeed is the man whose hero is a person of great Faith, because hero-worship carries with it something of the nature of the hero one worships.

In conclusion let us summarize what has been said on the subject of the ego by calling attention to the fact that it represents the fertile garden spot of the mind wherein one may develop all the stimuli which inspire active Faith, or by neglecting to do so he may allow this fertile soil to produce a negative crop of fear and doubt and indecision which will lead to failure.

The amount of space you occupy in the world is now a matter of choice with you. The Master-Key To Riches is in your hands. You stand before the last gate which separates you from Happy Valley. The gate will not open to you without your demand that it do so. You must use the Master-Key by making the seventeen principles of this philosophy *your own!*

You now have at your command a *complete philosophy* of life that is sufficient for the solution of every individual problem.

It is a philosophy of principles, some combination of which has been responsible for every individual success in every occupation or calling, although many may have used the philosophy successfully without recognizing the seventeen principles by the names we have given them.

No essential factor of successful achievement has been omitted. The philosophy embraces them all and describes them in words and similes that are well within the understanding of a majority of the people.

It is a philosophy of concreteness that touches only rarely the abstractions, and then only when necessary. It is free from academic terms and phrases which all too often serve only to confuse the average person.

The overall purpose of the philosophy is to enable one to get from where he stands to where he wishes to be, *both economically and spiritually*; thus it prepares one to enjoy the abundant life which the Creator intended all people to enjoy.

And it leads to the attainment of "riches" in the broadest and fullest meaning of the word, *including the twelve most important of all riches*.

The world has been greatly enriched by abstract philosophies, from the days of Plato, Socrates, Copernicus, Aristotle and many others of the same profound caliber of thinkers, on down to the days of Ralph Waldo Emerson and William James.

Now the world has the first complete, concrete philosophy of individual achievement that provides the individual with the practical means by which he may take possession of his own mind and direct it to the attainment of peace of mind, harmony in human relationships, economic security, and the fuller life known as happiness.

Not as an apology, but to serve as an explanation, I shall call your attention to the fact that throughout this analysis of the seventeen principles we have emphasized the more important of these principles by continuous reference to them. The repetition was not accidental!

It was deliberate and necessary because of the tendency of all mankind to be unimpressed by new ideas or new interpretations of old truths.

Repetition has been necessary also because of the interrelationship of the seventeen principles, being connected as they are like the links of a chain, each one extending into and becoming a part of the principle preceding it and the principle following it.

And lastly, let us recognize that repetition of ideas is one of the basic principles of effective pedagogy and the central core of all effective advertising. Therefore it is not only justified, but it is definitely necessary as a means of human progress.

When you have assimilated this philosophy you will have a better education than the majority of people who graduate from college with the Master of Arts degree. You will be in possession of all the more useful knowledge which has been organized from the experiences of the most successful men this nation has produced, and you will have it in a form which you can understand and apply.

But remember that the responsibility for the proper use of this knowledge will be yours. The mere possession of the knowledge will avail you nothing. Its *use* is what will count!

X
Taking it All the Way

Condensation of *Think and Grow Rich* (1937)

What follows is a digest of Think and Grow Rich. *I think you will find it a succinct but also thorough summary of Hill's signature book. If you've read* Think and Grow Rich *already—and if you haven't it's a must—read this condensation anyway as a reminder and reinforcement of Hill's program. You will always benefit from a refresher of Hill's thirteen steps to wealth, which often disclose a new insight.*

I encourage you to return regularly to this primer for reference and inspiration. It includes my original introduction. —MH

Introduction

The Power of a Single Book

The book you are about to experience has probably touched more lives than any other work of modern self-help. Try a small personal experiment: Carry a copy of *Think and Grow Rich* with you through an airport, grocery store, shopping mall, or any public place—and see if more than one person doesn't stop you and say something like, "Now, *that's* a great book..."

I have met artists, business people, doctors, teachers, athletes—people from different professions and possessed of seemingly different outer goals—who have attested that *Think and Grow Rich* made a concrete difference in their lives.

This is because, whatever our individual aims and desires, all motivated people share one common trait: the drive for personal excellence. This book, better than any other I know, breaks down the steps and elements to accomplishing any worthy goal.

When journalist Napoleon Hill published *Think and Grow Rich* in 1937 he had already dedicated more than twenty years of study to discovering and documenting the common traits displayed by high achievers across varying fields. Hill observed and interviewed more than five hundred exceptional people, ranging from statesmen and generals, to inventors and industrialists.

He condensed their shared traits into thirteen principles of accomplishment—and this forms the core of *Think and Grow Rich*.

This book has sold many millions of copies around the world since its first appearance—but that is not the true measure of its success. Lots of books gain popularity for a time, but go unread and sometimes unheard of within a decade or so of their publication. But *Think and Grow Rich* has, if anything, grown in influence since Hill's death in 1970. Its ideas are at the foundation of most of today's philosophies of business motivation and personal achievement.

But there is still more to Hill's book than that—and this brings us back to the little experiment proposed at the start of this preface. *Think and Grow Rich* evokes rare and deeply felt affection among many of its readers. All over America, and in other parts of the world, it is possible to run into friendly strangers who will beckon you aside for a moment to share a brief personal connection, telling you how *Think and Grow Rich* has helped them in life.

In a sense, you are about to join an informal fraternity of strivers, from a wide range of backgrounds, who have benefited from the principles in this book. When you meet them—and you will—many will welcome you with a nod and a smile, as if to say: *We've been waiting for you.*

—Mitch Horowitz

Chapter One
Desire
The First Step to Riches

In the early twentieth century a great American salesman and businessman named Edwin C. Barnes discovered how true it is that men really do *think and grow rich*.

Barnes's discovery did not come in one sitting. It came little by little, beginning with an ALL-CONSUMING DESIRE to become a business associate of inventor Thomas Edison. One of the chief characteristics of Barnes's desire was that it was *definite*. Barnes wanted to work *with* Edison—not just *for* him.

Straight off a freight train, Barnes presented himself in 1905 at Edison's New Jersey laboratory. He announced that he had come to go into business with the inventor. In speaking of their meeting years later, Edison said: "He stood there before me, looking like an ordinary tramp, but there was something in the expression of his face which conveyed the impression that he was determined to get what he had come after."

Barnes did *not* get his partnership with Edison on his first interview. But he *did* get a chance to work in the Edison offices, at a very nominal wage, doing a job that was unimportant to Edison—but *most important* to Barnes, because it gave him an opportunity to display his abilities to his future "partner."

Months passed. Nothing happened outwardly to bring Barnes any closer to his goal. But something important *was* happening in Barnes's mind. He was constantly intensifying his *chief desire* and his *plans* to become Edison's business associate.

Barnes was *determined to remain ready until he got the opportunity he came for.*

When the "big chance" arrived, it was in a different form, and from a different direction, than Barnes had expected. *That is one of the tricks of opportunity.* It has a sly habit of slipping in by the back door, and it often comes disguised as misfortune or temporary defeat. Perhaps this is why so many fail to wait for—or recognize—opportunity when it arrives.

Edison had just perfected a new device, known then as the Edison Dictating Machine. His salesmen were not enthusiastic. But Barnes saw his opportunity hidden in a strange-looking contraption that interested no one. Barnes seized the chance to sell the dictating machine, and did it so successfully that Edison gave him a contract to distribute and market it all over the world.

When Edwin C. Barnes climbed down from that freight train in Orange, New Jersey, he possessed one CONSUMING OBSESSION: to become the business associate of the great inventor. Barnes's desire was not a *hope!* It was not a *wish!* It was a keen, pulsating DESIRE, which transcended everything else. It was DEFINITE.

Wishing will not bring riches or other forms of success. But *desiring* riches with a state of mind that becomes an obsession, then planning definite ways and means to acquire riches, and backing those plans with persistence *that does not recognize failure*, will bring success.

The method by which DESIRE can be transmuted into its financial equivalent, consists of six definite, practical steps.

First

Fix in your mind the *exact* amount of money you desire. It is not sufficient merely to say, "I want plenty of money." Be definite as to the amount.

Second

Determine exactly what you intend to give in return for the money you desire.

Third

Establish a definite date when you intend to *possess* the money you desire.

Fourth

Create *a definite plan* for carrying out your desire, and begin *at once*, whether or not you are ready, to put this plan into *action*.

Fifth

Write out a clear, concise statement of the amount of money you intend to acquire, name the time limit for its acquisition, state what you intend to give in return for the money, and describe clearly the plan through which you intend to accumulate it.

Sixth

Read your written statement aloud, twice daily, once just before retiring at night and once after arising in the morning. AS YOU READ—SEE AND FEEL AND BELIEVE YOURSELF ALREADY IN POSSESSION OF THE MONEY.

It is especially important that you observe and follow number six. You may complain that it is impossible for you to "see yourself in possession of money" before you actually have it. Here is where a BURNING DESIRE will come to your aid. If you truly DESIRE money or another goal so keenly that your desire is an obsession, you will have no difficulty in convincing yourself that you will acquire it. The object is to want it so much and become so determined that you CONVINCE yourself you will have it. In future chapters you will learn why this is so important.

Chapter Two
Faith
The Second Step to Riches

FAITH is the head chemist of the mind. When FAITH is blended with the vibration of thought, the subconscious mind instantly picks up the vibration, translates it into its spiritual equivalent, and transmits it to Infinite Intelligence, as in the case of prayer.

ALL THOUGHTS THAT HAVE BEEN EMOTIONALIZED (given feeling) AND MIXED WITH FAITH begin immediately to translate themselves into their physical equivalent.

If you have difficulty getting a grasp of just what faith is, think of it as a special form of *persistence*—one that we feel when we *know* that we have right at our backs and that helps us persevere through setbacks and temporary failure.

To develop this quality in yourself, use this five-step formula. Promise yourself to read, repeat, and abide by these steps—and write down your promise.

First
I know that I have the ability to achieve the object of my DEFINITE PURPOSE in life, therefore, I *demand* of myself

persistent, continuous action toward its attainment, and I here and now promise to render such action.

Second

I realize the dominating thoughts of my mind will eventually reproduce themselves in outward physical action, and gradually transform themselves into physical reality. Therefore, I will concentrate my thoughts for thirty minutes daily upon the task of thinking of the person I intend to become, thereby creating in my mind a clear mental picture of that person.

Third

I know that through the principle of auto suggestion any desire that I persistently hold in my mind will eventually seek expression through some practical means of attaining the object back of it. Therefore, I will devote ten minutes daily to demanding of myself the development of *self-confidence*.

Fourth

I have clearly written down a description of my DEFINITE CHIEF AIM in life, and I will never stop trying until I have developed sufficient self-confidence for its attainment.

Fifth

I fully realize that no wealth or position can long endure unless built upon truth and justice. Therefore, I will engage in no transaction which does not benefit all whom it affects. I will succeed by attracting to myself the forces I wish to use, and the cooperation of other people. I will induce others to serve me, because of my willingness to serve others. I will eliminate hatred, envy, jealousy, selfishness, and cynicism, by developing love for all humanity, because I know that a negative attitude toward others can never bring me success. I will cause others to believe in me because I will believe in them, and in myself.

I will sign my name to this formula, commit it to memory, and repeat it aloud once a day, with full FAITH that it will gradually influence my THOUGHTS and ACTIONS, so that I will become a self-reliant and successful person.

Chapter Three
Auto Suggestion
The Third Step to Riches

AUTO SUGGESTION is a term that applies to all suggestions and self-administered stimuli that reach one's mind through the five senses. Stated another way: *auto suggestion is self suggestion.*

It is the agency of communication between the conscious and subconscious minds. But your subconscious mind recognizes and acts ONLY upon thoughts that have been well mixed with *emotion or feeling*. This is a fact of such importance as to warrant repetition.

When you begin to use—and keep using—the three-step program for auto suggestion in this chapter, be on the alert for hunches from your subconscious mind—and when they appear, put them into ACTION IMMEDIATELY.

First
Go into some quiet spot (preferably in bed at night) where you will not be disturbed or interrupted, close your eyes, and repeat aloud (so you may hear your own words) the written statement of the amount of money you intend to accumulate, the time limit for its accumulation, and a

description of the service or merchandise you intend to give in return for the money. As you carry out these instructions SEE YOURSELF ALREADY IN POSSESSION OF THE MONEY.

For example: Suppose that you intend to accumulate $50,000 by the first of January, five years hence, and that you intend to give personal services in return for the money in the capacity of a salesman. Your written statement of your purpose should be similar to the following:

"By the first day of January, I will have in my possession $50,000, which will come to me in various amounts from time to time during the interim.

"In return for this money I will give the most efficient service of which I am capable, rendering the fullest possible quantity and the best possible quality of service in the capacity of salesman of... (and describe the service or merchandise you intend to sell).

"I believe that I will have this money in my possession. My faith is so strong that I can now see this money before my eyes. I can touch it with my hands. It is now awaiting transfer to me at the time and in the proportion that I deliver the service I intend to render for it. I am awaiting a plan by which to accumulate this money, and I will follow that plan when it is received."

Second
Repeat this program night and morning until you can see (in your imagination) the money you intend to accumulate.

Third

Place a written copy of your statement where you can see it night and morning, and read it just before retiring and upon arising, until it has been memorized.

Chapter Four
Specialized Knowledge
The Fourth Step to Riches

General knowledge, no matter how great in quantity or variety, is of little use in accumulating money. Knowledge is only *potential* power. It becomes power only when, and if, it is organized into *definite plans of action*, and directed toward a *definite end*.

In connection with your aim, you must decide what sort of specialized knowledge you require, and the purpose for which it is needed. To a large extent, your major purpose in life, and the goal toward which you are working, will help determine what knowledge you need. With this question settled, your next move requires that you have ACCURATE INFORMATION concerning DEPENDABLE SOURCES OF KNOWLEDGE.

Look toward many high-quality sources for the knowledge you seek: people, courses, partnerships, books—look everywhere. Some of this knowledge will be free—never undervalue what is free—and some will require purchasing. Decide what knowledge you seek—and pursue it completely. The author spent more than twenty years interviewing people and studying success methods before writing this book.

Without specialized knowledge, your ideas remain mere wishes. Once you have acquired the knowledge you need, you can use your critical faculty of *imagination* to combine your IDEAS with this SPECIALIZED KNOWLEDGE, and make ORGANIZED PLANS to carry out your aims.

This is the formula for capability: *Using imagination to combine specialized knowledge with ideas and to form organized plans.*

The connecting ingredient is imagination, which we will now learn to cultivate.

Chapter Five
Imagination
The Fifth Step to Riches

The imagination is the workshop wherein are fashioned all plans created by man. The impulse, the DESIRE, is literally given shape, form, and ACTION through the aid of the imaginative faculty of the mind.

Through the medium of creative imagination, the finite mind of man has direct communication with Infinite Intelligence. Imagination is the faculty through which "hunches" and "inspirations" are reached. It is by this faculty that all basic or new ideas are handed over to man. It is through this faculty that thought vibrations from the minds of others are received. It is through this faculty that one individual may "tune in" or communicate with the subconscious minds of others.

The creative imagination works only when the conscious mind is stimulated through the emotion of a STRONG DESIRE. This is highly significant.

What's more, the creative faculty may have become weak through inaction. Your imagination becomes more alert and more receptive in proportion to its development through *use*.

After you have completed this book, return to this section and begin at once to put your imagination to work on the building of a plan, or plans, for the transmutation of *desire* into money, or your core aim. Reduce your plan to writing. The moment you complete this, you will have *definitely* given concrete form to the intangible *desire*.

This step is extremely important. When you reduce the statement of your desire, and a plan for its realization, into writing, you have actually *taken the first* of a series of steps that will enable you to covert your *thought* into its physical counterpart.

Chapter Six
Organized Planning
The Sixth Step to Riches

It is vital that you form a DEFINITE, practical plan, or plans, to carry out your aims. You will now learn how to build plans that are *practical*, as follows:

First

Ally yourself with a group of as many people as you may need for the creation and carrying out of your plan or plans for the accumulation of money—making use of the "Master Mind" principle described in a later chapter. (Compliance with this instruction is essential. Do not neglect it.)

Second

Before forming your "Master Mind" alliance, decide what advantages and benefits you may offer the individual members of your group in return for their cooperation. No one will work indefinitely without some form of compensation. No intelligent person will either request or expect another to work without adequate compensation, although this may not always be in the form of money.

Third

Arrange to meet with the members of your "Master Mind" group at least twice a week, and more often if possible, until you have jointly perfected the necessary plan or plans for the accumulation of money.

Fourth

Maintain *perfect harmony* between yourself and every member of your "Master Mind" group. If you fail to carry out this instruction to the letter, you may expect to meet with failure. The "Master Mind" principle *cannot* obtain where *perfect harmony* does not prevail.

Keep in mind these facts:

1. You are engaged in an undertaking of major importance to you. To be sure of success, you must have plans that are faultless.

2. You must have the advantage of the experience, education, native ability, and imagination of other minds. This is in harmony with the methods followed by every person who has accumulated a great fortune.

Now, if the first plan you devise does not work successfully, replace it with a new plan. If this new plan fails to work, replace it, in turn, with still another, and so on, until you find a plan that *does work*. Right here is the point where the majority of men meet with failure, because of their lack of *persistence* in creating new plans to take the place of those that fail.

Remember this when your plans fail: *Temporary defeat is not permanent failure*.

No follower of this philosophy can reasonably expect to accumulate a fortune without experiencing "temporary defeat." When defeat comes, accept it as a signal that your plans are not sound, rebuild those plans, and set sail once more toward your goal.

Finally, as you are devising your plans keep in mind these Major Attributes of Leadership—traits possessed by the greatest achievers:

1. Unwavering Courage
2. Self-Control
3. A Keen Sense of Justice
4. Definiteness of Decision
5. Definiteness of Plans
6. The Habit of Doing More Than Paid For
7. A Pleasing Personality
8. Sympathy and Understanding
9. Mastery of Detail
10. Willingness to Assume Full Responsibility
11. Cooperation With Others

CHAPTER SEVEN
Decision
The Seventh Step to Riches

Analysis of several hundred people who had accumulated fortunes disclosed that *every one of them* had the habit of *reaching decisions promptly*, and of changing these decisions slowly, if and when they were changed. People who fail to accumulate money, *without exception*, have the habit of reaching decisions, if at all, very *slowly*, and of *changing these decisions quickly and often.*

What's more, the majority of people who fail to accumulate money sufficient for their needs tend to be easily influenced by the "opinions" of others. "Opinions" are the cheapest commodities on earth. Everyone has a flock of opinions ready to be wished upon anyone who will accept them. If you are influenced by "opinions" when you reach *decisions*, you will not succeed in any undertaking, much less in that of transmuting *your own desire* into money.

If you are influenced by the opinions of others, you will have no DESIRE of your own.

Keep your own counsel when you begin to put into practice the principles described here by *reaching your own decisions* and following them. Take no one into your confidence *except* the members of your "Master Mind" group, and be very sure in your selection of this group that you choose ONLY those who will be in COMPLETE SYMPATHY AND HARMONY WITH YOUR PURPOSE.

Close friends and relatives, while not meaning to, often handicap one through "opinions" and sometimes through ridicule, which is meant to be humorous. Thousands of men and women carry inferiority complexes with them throughout life, because some well-meaning but ignorant person destroyed their confidence through "opinions" or ridicule.

You have a mind of your own. USE IT and reach your own decisions. If you need facts or information from others to enable you to reach decisions, as you probably will in many instances, acquire these facts or secure the information you need quietly, without disclosing your purpose.

Those who reach DECISIONS promptly and definitely know what they want and generally get it. Leaders in every walk of life DECIDE quickly and firmly. That is the major reason why they are leaders. The world has a habit of making room for the man whose words and actions show that he knows where he is going.

CHAPTER EIGHT
Persistence
The Eighth Step to Riches

PERSITENCE is an essential factor in transmuting DESIRE into its monetary equivalent. The basis of persistence is the POWER OF WILL.

Will power and desire, when properly combined, make an irresistible pair. Men who accumulate great fortunes are generally known as cold-blooded and sometimes ruthless. Often they are misunderstood. What they have is will power, which they mix with persistence, and place at the back of their desires to *ensure* the attainment of their objectives.

Lack of persistence is one of the major causes of failure. Experience with thousands of people has proved that lack of persistence is a weakness common to the majority of men. It is a weakness that may be overcome by effort. The ease with which lack of persistence may be conquered depends *entirely* upon the INTENSITY OF ONE'S DESIRE.

In short, THERE IS NO SUBSTITUTE FOR PERSISTENCE! It cannot be supplanted by any other quality! Remember this and it will hearten you in the beginning when the going may seem difficult and slow.

Those who have cultivated the HABIT of persistence seem to enjoy insurance against failure. No matter how many

Taking it All the Way

times they are defeated, they finally arrive toward the top of the ladder. Sometimes it appears that there is a hidden Guide whose duty is to test men through all sorts of discouraging experiences. Those who pick themselves up after defeat and keep on trying arrive at their destination. The hidden Guide lets no one enjoy great achievement without passing the PERSISTENCE TEST.

What we DO NOT SEE, what most of us never suspect of existing, is the silent but irresistible POWER that comes to the rescue of those who fight on in the face of discouragement. If we speak of this power at all, we call it PERSISTENCE.

There are four simple steps that lead to the habit of PERSISTENCE.

1. A definite purpose backed by burning desire for its fulfillment.
2. A definite plan, expressed in continuous action.
3. A mind closed tightly against all negative and discouraging influences, including negative suggestions of relatives, friends, and acquaintances.
4. A friendly alliance with one or more persons who will encourage you to follow through with both plan and purpose.

CHAPTER NINE
The Master Mind
The Ninth Step to Riches

The "Master Mind" may be defined as: "Coordination of knowledge and effort, in a spirit of harmony, between two or more people for the attainment of a definite purpose."

No individual may hold great power without availing himself of the "Master Mind." A previous chapter supplied instructions for the creation of PLANS for the purpose of translating DESIRE into its monetary equivalent. If you carry out these instructions with PERSISTENCE and intelligence, and use discrimination in selecting your "Master Mind" group, your objective will have been halfway reached, even before you begin to recognize it.

The Master Mind brings an obvious economic advantage, by allowing you to surround yourself with the advice, counsel, and personal cooperation of a group of people who are willing to lend you wholehearted aid in a spirit of PERFECT HARMONY. But there is also a more abstract phase; it may be called the PSYCHIC PHASE.

The psychic phase of the Master Mind is more difficult to comprehend because it has reference to the spiritual forces with which the human race, as a whole, is not well acquainted. You may catch a significant suggestion from this statement:

"No two minds ever come together without, thereby, creating a third invisible, intangible force which may be likened to a third mind."

The human mind is a form of energy, a part of it being spiritual in nature. When the minds of two people are coordinated in a SPIRIT OF HARMONY the spiritual units of energy of each mind form an affinity, which constitutes the "psychic" phase of the Master Mind.

Analyze the record of any man who has accumulated a great fortune, and many of those who have accumulated modest fortunes, and you will find that they have either consciously or unconsciously employed the "Master Mind."

Great power can be accumulated through no other principle!

CHAPTER TEN
Sex Transmutation
The Tenth Step to Riches

The meaning of the word "transmute" is, in simple language, "the changing or transferring of one element, or form of energy, into another." The emotion of sex brings into being a unique and powerful state of mind that can be used for extraordinary intellectual and material creative purposes.

This is accomplished through *sex transmutation*, which means the switching of the mind from thoughts of physical expression to thoughts of some other nature.

Sex is the most powerful of human desires. When driven by this desire, men develop keenness of imagination, courage, will power, persistence, and creative ability unknown to them at other times. So strong and impelling is the desire for sexual contact that men freely run the risk of life and reputation to indulge it.

When harnessed and redirected along other lines, this motivating force maintains all of its attributes of keenness of imagination, courage, etc., which may be used as powerful creative forces in literature, art, or in any other profession or calling, including, of course, the accumulation of riches.

The transmutation of sex energy calls for the exercise of will power, to be sure, but the reward is worth the effort.

Taking it All the Way

The desire for sexual expression is inborn and natural. The desire cannot, and should not, be submerged or eliminated. But it should be given an outlet through forms of expression that enrich the body, mind, and spirit. If not given this form of outlet, through transmutation, it will seek outlets through purely physical channels.

The emotion of sex is an "irresistible force." When driven by this emotion, men become gifted with a super power for action. Understand this truth, and you will catch the significance of the statement that sex transmutation will lift one into the status of a genius. The emotion of sex contains the secret of creative ability.

When harnessed and transmuted, this driving force is capable of lifting men to that higher sphere of thought which enables them to master the sources of worry and petty annoyance that beset their pathway on the lower plane.

The major reason why the majority of men who succeed do not begin to do so until after the ages of forty to fifty (or beyond), is their tendency to DISSIPATE their energies through over indulgence in physical expression of the emotion of sex. The majority of men *never* learn that the urge of sex has other possibilities, which far transcend in importance that of mere physical expression.

But remember, sexual energy must be *transmuted* from desire for physical contact into some *other* form of desire and action, in order to lift one to the status of a genius.

Chapter Eleven
The Subconscious Mind
The Eleventh Step to Riches

The subconscious mind is the connecting link between the finite mind of man and Infinite Intelligence. It is the intermediary through which one may draw upon the forces of Infinite Intelligence at will. It alone contains the secret process by which mental impulses are modified and changed into their spiritual equivalent. It alone is the medium through which prayer may be transmitted to the source capable of answering prayer.

I never approach the discussion of the subconscious mind without a feeling of littleness and inferiority due, perhaps, to the fact that man's entire stock of knowledge on the subject is so pitifully limited. The very fact that the subconscious mind is the medium of communication between the thinking mind of man and Infinite Intelligence is, of itself, a thought that almost paralyzes one's reason.

After you have accepted as a reality the existence of your subconscious mind, and understand its possibilities for transmuting your DESIRES into their physical or monetary equivalent, you will understand why you have been repeatedly urged to MAKE YOUR DESIRES CLEAR, AND TO REDUCE THEM TO WRITING. You will also understand the necessity of PERSISTENCE in carrying out instructions.

The thirteen principles in this book are the stimuli with which—through practice and persistence—you acquire the ability to reach and influence your subconscious mind.

Chapter Twelve
The Brain
The Twelfth Step to Riches

More than twenty years before writing this book, the author, working with the late Dr. Alexander Graham Bell and Dr. Elmer R. Gates, observed that every human brain is both a broadcasting and receiving station for the vibration of thought.

The Creative Imagination is the "receiving set" of the brain, which receives thoughts released by the brains of others. It is the agency of communication between one's conscious, or reasoning, mind, and the outer sources from which one may receive thought stimuli.

When stimulated, or "stepped up," to a high rate of vibration, the mind becomes more receptive to the vibration of thought from outside sources. This "stepping up" occurs through the positive emotions or the negative emotions. Through the emotions the vibrations of thought may be increased. This is why it is crucial that your goal have strong emotions at the back of it.

Vibrations of an exceedingly high rate are the only vibrations picked up and carried from one brain to another. Thought is energy travelling at an exceedingly high rate of vibration. Thought that has been modified or "stepped up" by any of the major emotions vibrates at a much higher rate than ordinary thought, and it is this type of thought that passes from one mind to another, through the broadcasting machinery of the human brain.

Thus, you will see that the broadcasting principle is the factor through which you mix feeling or emotion with your thoughts and pass them on to your subconscious mind, or to the minds of others.

Chapter Thirteen
The Sixth Sense
The Thirteenth Step to Riches

The thirteenth and final principle is known as the "sixth sense," through which Infinite Intelligence may and will communicate voluntarily, without any effort or demands by the individual.

After you have mastered the principles in this book, you will be prepared to accept as true a statement that may otherwise seem incredible, namely: Through the aid of the sixth sense you will be warned of impending dangers in time to avoid them, and notified of opportunities in time to embrace them.

With the development of the sixth sense, there comes to your aid, and to do your bidding, a kind of "guardian angel" who will open to you at all times the door to the Temple of Wisdom.

Whether this is a statement of truth, you will never know except by following the instructions described in this book, or some similar method.

The author is not a believer in, nor an advocate of, "miracles," for the reason that he has enough knowledge of Nature to understand that Nature *never deviates from her established laws.* Some of her laws are so incomprehensible that they produce what appear to be "miracles."

The sixth sense comes as near to being a miracle as anything I have ever experienced.

Epilogue
A Word About Fear

As you begin any new undertaking you are likely at one point or another to find yourself gripped by the emotion of fear.

Fear should never be bargained with or capitulated to. It takes the charm from one's personality, destroys the possibility of accurate thinking, diverts concentration of effort, masters persistence, turns the will power into nothingness, destroys ambition, beclouds the memory, and invites failure in every conceivable form. It kills love, assassinates the finer emotions of the heart, discourages friendship, and leads to sleeplessness, misery, and unhappiness.

So pernicious and destructive is the emotion of fear that it is, almost literally, worse than anything that can befall you.

If you suffer from a fear of poverty, reach a decision to get along with whatever wealth you can accumulate WITHOUT WORRY. If you fear the loss of love, reach a decision to get along without love, if that is necessary. If you experience a general sense of worry, reach a blanket decision that *nothing* life has to offer is *worth* the price of worry.

And remember: The greatest of all remedies for fear is a BURNING DESIRE FOR ACHIEVEMENT, backed by useful service to others.

Napoleon Hill's Secret

Epilogue by Mitch Horowitz

Napoleon Hill refers to a "secret" that runs throughout *Think and Grow Rich*. This secret, he writes, appears at least once in every chapter. But he does not specifically name the secret. Hill writes that it is more beneficial and penetrating for you to arrive at the secret yourself. Some readers, he says, grasp it almost immediately. For others it takes multiple readings. Sometimes, right in the midst of a chapter, the secret may flash into your mind. It often comes, Hill writes, when you are ready for it.

I had such an experience in assembling this volume. I found what I believe is the secret. In actuality, what I discovered is an expansion of something I've written about in an earlier book—but with a difference. I have previously written that the secret of *Think and Grow Rich* can be put this way: "Emotionalized thought directed toward one passionately held aim—aided by organized planning and the Master

Mind—is the root of all accomplishment." I stand by that. But a more basic conception of Hill's secret reached me as I was preparing the section on "applied faith." It is this:

The "secret" of *Think and Grow Rich* is to place yourself within the overall scheme of creation, obeying natural laws that inevitably and invariably beget growth, expansion, renewal, and generativity.

Each step in Hill's work is designed to bring you into *natural, cosmic alignment*. Once you are in alignment and work within its flow—toward continual growth and expansion—the laws of creation are at your back.

You become like the seedling that eventually bursts through the soil. All of nature operates to make this growth occur. Unlike the seedling, however, a sentient being must consciously and selectively labor. That is your role in creation. But when you are productively united, mentally, emotionally, and physically, in the direction of your aim, you naturally enlist these cosmic laws. These laws possess greater potential for a conscious being than they do on the seedling *because they not only aid your expansion but also allow for a dramatic re-creation of self.*

I want to share what I consider the most important passage in *Think and Grow Rich*. It appears in the chapter on "Imagination" and directly pertains to what I've been referencing:

> You are now engaged in the task of trying to profit by Nature's method. You are (sincerely and earnestly, we hope), trying to adapt yourself to Nature's laws, by

endeavoring to convert DESIRE into its physical or monetary equivalent. YOU CAN DO IT! IT HAS BEEN DONE BEFORE!

You can build a fortune through the aid of laws which are immutable. But, first, you must become familiar with these laws, and learn to USE them. Through repetition, and by approaching the description of these principles from every conceivable angle, the author hopes to reveal to you the secret through which every great fortune has been accumulated. Strange and paradoxical as it may seem, the "secret" is NOT A SECRET. Nature, herself, advertises it in the earth on which we live, the stars, the planets suspended within our view, in the elements above and around us, in every blade of grass, and every form of life within our vision.

Nature advertises this "secret" in the terms of biology, in the conversion of a tiny cell, so small that it may be lost on the point of a pin, into the HUMAN BEING now reading this line. The conversion of desire into its physical equivalent is, certainly, no more miraculous!

You can derive confidence, faith, a renewed sense of self, and authentic help by placing yourself within the cyclical scheme of creation. This is the secret into which Hill's work invites you. Now, go and build.

Napoleon Hill Timeline

1883
Oliver Napoleon Hill, known as "Napoleon," is born October 26 in Wise County, Virginia, to James and Sara Hill. Raised in a small cabin in a rural area, Hill experienced poverty firsthand as a child.

1893
Hill's mother dies.

1898
Hill begins his writing career, taking a job as a "mountain reporter" for several small rural newspapers.

1900
Hill graduates from high school, and leaves Wise County to attend a one-year business school in Tazewell, Virginia.

1901
Hill graduates from business school and seeks employment with prominent Virginia lawyer Rufus Ayres by composing a letter requesting to pay for the privilege of being Ayres's secretary. Impressed, Ayres hires Hill, with a salary.

1902
Hill is promoted to manager of a coalmine under Ayres's direction.

1903
Hill attends law school, but does not finish—he leaves to take a job as a sales manager at a lumberyard.

1908
Economic downturn closes Hill's lumberyard; he moves on, seeking work as a journalist.

1908
Hill, as part of his work for *Bob Taylor's Magazine*, reports interviewing industrialist Andrew Carnegie. (No such article appears.) Hill says that Carnegie, believing that success can be boiled down to simple principles available to anyone, advises the journalist to interview five hundred exceptional people in order to study their processes and discover a success formula.

1908–1928
Hill's project lasts about twenty years, during which time He interviews successful figures in every industry including Thomas Edison, Alexander Graham Bell, Henry Ford, Elmer Gates, Charles M. Schwab, Theodore Roosevelt, William Wrigley Jr., John Wannamaker, William Jennings Bryan, Woodrow Wilson, William H. Taft, John D. Rockefeller, E.W. Woolworth, Jennings Randolph, George Eastman, Luther Burbank, Clarence Darrow, Edward W. Bok, Julius Rosenwald, and Charles Allen Ward.

1910
Hill marries Florence Hornor.

1911
Son James is born.

1912
Son Napoleon Blair (called "Blair") is born.

1918
Son David is born.

1919–1920
Hill creates and works as editor and publisher of *Hill's Golden Rule* magazine.

1928
The Law of Success is published. Hill's study course outlines the "Philosophy of Achievement" and presents his fifteen principles for success.

1930
The Magic Ladder to Success, a condensation of Hill's earlier work, is published.

1931
Hill founds, edits, and publishes *Inspiration* magazine, which lasts just two issues.

1937
Think and Grow Rich, one of the most influential and bestselling self-help books ever, is published.

1941

Hill releases the first of sixteen planned volumes in the *Mental Dynamite* study course. Although the first volume sells out, wartime paper rationing prevents any further volumes from being printed.

1943

Hill marries Annie Lou Norman.

1945

The Master Key to Riches is published.

1952–1962

Hill partners with W. Clement Stone and his Combined Insurance Company of America. Stone makes Hill's success principles a cornerstone of his business philosophy. The businessman organizes seminars and publications based on Hill's work.

1970

Hill dies November 8 in South Carolina.

1971

Hill's final work, *You Can Work Your Own Miracles*, is published.

About the Authors

NAPOLEON HILL was born in 1883 in Wise County, Virginia. He was employed as a secretary, a reporter for a local newspaper, the manager of a coalmine and a lumberyard, and attended law school, before he began working as a journalist for *Bob Taylor's Magazine*, an inspirational and general-interest journal. In 1908, the job led to his interviewing steel magnate Andrew Carnegie. The encounter, Hill said, changed the course of his life. Carnegie believed success could be distilled into principles that anyone could follow, and urged Hill to interview the greatest industrialists, financiers, and inventors of the era to discover these principles. Hill accepted the challenge, which lasted more than twenty years and formed the building block for *Think and Grow Rich*. Hill dedicated the rest of his life to documenting and refining the principles of success. After a long career as an author, magazine publisher, lecturer, and consultant to business leaders, the motivational pioneer died in 1970 in South Carolina.

About the Authors

MITCH HOROWITZ is the PEN Award-winning author of books including *Occult America, One Simple Idea,* and *The Miracle Club*. A writer-in-residence at the New York Public Library and lecturer-in-residence at the University of Philosophical Research in Los Angeles, Mitch is the author of the Napoleon Hill Success Course series, including *The Miracle of a Definite Chief Aim*, *The Power of the Master Mind*, and *Secrets of Self-Mastery*. He is on Twitter @MitchHorowitz and Instagram @MitchHorowitz23.

www.ingramcontent.com/pod-product-compliance
Lightning Source LLC
Chambersburg PA
CBHW052007070526
44584CB00016B/1653